Agincourt

Agincourt

Myth and Reality
1415–2015

Stephen Cooper

PEN & SWORD
PRAETORIAN PRESS

First published in Great Britain in 2014 by
PRAETORIAN PRESS
an imprint of
Pen & Sword Books Ltd
47 Church Street
Barnsley
South Yorkshire
S70 2AS

ISBN 978-1-78159-462-9

A CIP catalogue record for this book is available from the British Library.

Typeset by Concept, Huddersfield, West Yorkshire.
Printed and bound in England by CPI Group (UK) Ltd, Croydon CR0 4YY.

Pen & Sword Books Ltd incorporates the imprints of Pen & Sword Archaeology, Atlas, Aviation, Battleground, Discovery, Family History, History, Maritime, Military, Naval, Politics, Railways, Select, Social History, Transport, True Crime, and Claymore Press, Frontline Books, Leo Cooper, Praetorian Press, Remember When, Seaforth Publishing and Wharncliffe.

For a complete list of Pen & Sword titles please contact
PEN & SWORD BOOKS LIMITED
47 Church Street, Barnsley, South Yorkshire, S70 2AS, England
E-mail: enquiries@pen-and-sword.co.uk
Website: www.pen-and-sword.co.uk

Contents

List of Illustrations

List of Plates

Henry V's chantry at Westminster Abbey.

Portchester Castle, the Palace of Richard II.

Titchfield Abbey.

Titchfield Abbey, the Tudor gatehouse.

Wolvesey Castle.

The Somme near Voyenne.

The battlefield, 2009.

The Calvary, *La Gacogne*.

Nicolas's map of area, 1827.

Nicolas's map of battlefield, 1827.

The Agincourt Museum, 2009.

Sir Lewis Robessart, Westminster Abbey.

The Jewel Tower, Westminster.

The Guildhall, London.

The Tower of London.

Henry V, York Minster.

Henry V in Cassell's *History*.

Owain Glyndwr, Pennal.

The Castle of Vincennes, Paris.

The Tower of Duke John the Fearless, Paris.

Thomas Chaucer, Ewelme.

Henry V's shield (Westminster Abbey).

Henry V's achievements (Westminster Abbey).

Gloucester's chantry, St Albans Cathedral.

Cardinal Beaufort, Winchester Cathedral.

Fotheringhay.

The 2nd Earl of Suffolk, Wingfield.

William ap Thomas, Abergavenny.

The Erpingham Gate, Norwich.

Sir Simon Felbrigg, Felbrigg.

Sir Roger Vaughan, Bredwardine.

Lord Bardolph, Dennington.

John de Roos, Bottesford.

The Albert Memorial Chapel, Windsor.

The Royal Window, All Souls College, Oxford.

Archbishop Chichele, All Souls College, Oxford.

Lyme Hall, Cheshire.

Groombridge.

An archer, Royal Armouries, Leeds.

Auchy-lès-Hesdin.

Henry V, Strawberry Hill.

Acknowledgements

First and foremost I am immensely grateful to Professor Anne Curry of Southampton University, who kindly read my text, made many comments and saved me from falling into serious error. I am also indebted to the numerous works with which she has changed the face of the subject, especially *Agincourt, Sources and Interpretation* (2000) and *Agincourt, A New History* (2005), but also the articles listed in the bibliography. Juliet Barker's *Agincourt, The King, The Campaign, The Battle* (2005) is full of ideas, problems and suggested solutions, as well as being a lively account. *The Reign of Henry V* by J. H. Wylie (published posthumously in 1919) has annoyed many people with its digressions and at times wearisome footnotes, but is a mine of information, as is René de Belleval's *Azincourt* of 1865. I also owe much to Richard Vaughan's biography of the second Valois Duke of Burgundy, *John the Fearless* (1973 and 2002); and to Emma Smith's *King Henry V* (2002), with its fascinating descriptions of the many performances of Shakespeare's play. Lastly, I should mention *The Great Warbow* by Matthew Strickland and Robert Hardy (2005), a truly comprehensive study of the subject.

The photographs of the tombs of Sir Lewis Robessart and of Henry V's chantry chapel in Westminster Abbey are reproduced with the permission of the Dean and Chapter of Westminster. Those of Henry V's shield and achievements were taken when these were on loan from the Abbey to the British Museum in 2012. The photograph of William ap Thomas is reproduced by permission of Jeremy Bolwell; that of Sir Simon Felbrigg's memorial brass by permission of Evelyn Simak; and that of John de Roos by permission of J. Hannan-Briggs. All three are copyrighted but licensed for re-use under the Creative Commons Licence. All other photographs are from my own collection.

Stephen Cooper,
Thorpe Hesley
1 June 2013

Foreword

The Battle of Agincourt has never ceased to fascinate, whether in its own time or in later centuries. It can indeed claim to be one of the most famous battles of all time, although how much of that is down to Shakespeare rather than Henry V is a moot point.

Stephen Cooper offers new perspectives on what Agincourt has meant over the years. He works outwards from the site itself, steering through key areas of interest and culminating on what the battle has come to signify over the century since its 500th anniversary in 1915. He offers a personal approach based on wide reading and deep reflection. He offers many intriguing details and real insights into the mind-set of different generations. He recalls the experiences of individuals and the development of family traditions about the battle. He ends with the thought that Bannockburn is 'easier' to commemorate than Agincourt since debates on Scottish independence have more current relevance than English ambitions in France. The kings of England did not surrender their pretensions to the throne of France until 1801 when they were kings of Great Britain and Ireland and France was no longer a monarchy. But perhaps there is some irony that, as I pen this preface, an Englishman helped to win the European rugby title for a French club. Maybe Robert and Thomas Wylkynson, archers on the Agincourt campaign, were his ancestors!

Anne Curry
Southampton
May 2013

For my father and mother,
born in August and November, 1915.

All the time of war during these forty years between England and France there were scarcely three or four men whom one could find to agree, in telling how a town or castle was won in France or how a battle was done there.

Bishop Reginald Pecock
(c. 1395–c. 1461).

Introduction

From Henry V to Winston Churchill

1415 was the year in which Pope Gregory XII resigned from the Papacy (the last time this happened before Benedict XVI resigned in 2013). It was also the year when the Hohenzollerns acquired the Electorate of Brandenburg, with momentous consequences for German history; and the year in which the Portuguese captured Ceuta in North Africa for Christendom; but in England the event which everyone heard about was the Battle of Agincourt, fought on St Crispin's Day, 25 October 1415. The defeat of a large French army by a smaller force led by Henry V was so crushing that the battle was regarded as a minor miracle. The victory restored the reputation of English arms and made Henry V's name.

Agincourt *was* celebrated in England on the anniversary of the battle in 1416; but the annual celebration began to lose its following within a few years, since the English invaders of France were turned back on the Loire in 1429, and driven out altogether in 1453 (except for Calais and the Channel Islands). Saints' days in general were dealt a heavy blow by the Protestant Reformation and by the middle of the eighteenth century 'Agincourt Day' passed by without much attention. Yet, amongst historians, Henry V's achievement continued to be praised, by Roman Catholics and Protestants alike, though Henry was an orthodox Catholic and an enthusiastic persecutor of the Lollards, at one time thought to be proto-Protestants.

The victor of Agincourt's reputation as warrior-hero was made secure, at least in English-speaking countries, by Shakespeare's play *Henry V*, written in the 1590s, though Spain rather than France was now the national enemy. Shakespeare turned the somewhat pedestrian accounts of the battle which he found in Tudor chronicles into wonderful poetry and drama; and he also turned an English victory into a British one, by including a Scotsman, a Welshman and an Irishman as officers in Henry V's army.

The Shakespearean myth proved very powerful. *Henry V* became a regular part of the repertoire of English theatre, especially after the Act of Union between England and Scotland in 1707. The play was popular each time the new British army went to war, and especially at the time of a centenary; and the spirit of Agincourt was repeatedly invoked in times of crisis. Shakespeare's St Crispin's Day speech was reproduced in the columns of *The Times* during the Battle of Loos in October 1915; and Winston Churchill undoubtedly had Agincourt in mind when he moved the nation with his speech about the achievement of 'the few' in 1940. As recently as 2009 the *Musée de la Bataille* at Azincourt in Picardy featured a montage linking Henry V with Nelson, Wellington and Churchill.

Yet the English view of Agincourt can seem distinctly Anglocentric and narrow when we look at events through French eyes. Agincourt never became famous in France, though it achieved a degree of notoriety. The French monarchy recovered quite quickly from the defeat and the French were soon able to recall Joan of Arc's victories over English armies at Orléans and Patay (1429) and Charles VII's at Formigny (1450) and Castillon (1453), the last battle of the Hundred Years War. Indeed King Charles became known there as 'the Victorious'. On the other hand, Shakespeare's *Henry V* has almost never been performed in France but hundreds of books have been written about Joan of Arc. Henry V cannot hope to compete in France with Joan and her story has long had international appeal, especially to women, in a way that Agincourt never could or can.

Even at the time, the French were more concerned with the civil war between Burgundians and Armagnacs, which wracked their kingdom between 1407 and 1435. Both sides in this regarded the English victory at Agincourt as a disaster for France, but ultimately, it was a side-show. The sub-title of the Burgundian Enguerrand de Monstrelet's chronicle is *An Account of the Cruel Civil Wars between the House of Orléans and Burgundy; of the Possession of Paris and Normandy by the English; their expulsion thence; and of other memorable events that happened in the Kingdom of France, as well as in other countries.*

French historians have never chosen to dwell on Agincourt. The view taken by the most famous of them, Jules Michelet (1798–1874), was that the French kingdom suffered along with its monarch, throughout the long reign of Charles VI (1380–1422). Just as Charles's life was blighted with insanity, so France fell prey to a kind of moral sickness, and it was this which brought calamity, more than the English army. In the early twentieth century French Marxists viewed the Hundred Years War as a struggle between rivals for the trades in wine, woollen cloth and salt. Later, the *Annales* school thought that it was the *longue durée* that mattered and that battles were mere transitory events. Even the leading French military historian, Philippe Contamine, devoted little time to Agincourt in his contribution to Corvisier's *Histoire Militaire de la France* (1992), and his own book on the subject (Juilliard, 1964) was brief and conventional. In her biography of Charles VI (1986) Françoise Autrand again devoted little space to Agincourt.

In recent times the traditional account of the battle has been radically revised. We have been told both that the English army was not so out-numbered as we used to think, and that archery did not play such an important a role as we once thought, while one archaeologist has even suggested that it was fought at nearby Ruisseauville, rather than at Azincourt. Some writers have concentrated on Henry V's cruelty and callousness, particularly in ordering the massacre of French prisoners. Others have portrayed him as an adventurer and a gambler; and Henry has even been condemned as a war criminal, both by literary critics in the UK and by lawyers in the United States. Novels about Agincourt – Herbert Strang's *Claud the Archer* (1928), Michael Cox's *Jenkin Lloyd* (2003) and Bernard Cornwell's *Azincourt* (2008) all focus on the experience of English, or Welsh, archers, while Henry V plays a comparatively minor role. In Anne O'Brien's *The Forbidden Queen* (2013) the narrator is Henry's wife and he is portrayed as a marital rapist with a soul encased in ice; but Shakespeare's play still plays to packed houses.

It is impossible to celebrate the victory at Agincourt now, in the same way as English people did in 1415. Britain and France were allies during the two World Wars of the twentieth century, and both have been members of NATO for more than half a century. Yet at the heart of the Shakespearean myth, there remains a remarkable true story. A small expeditionary force, making its way home through hostile territory in difficult circumstances, is trapped by the enemy's main field army, on ground of the enemy's choosing; yet it fights its way out, completely crushes the opposition, and emerges almost unscathed. This is the story of David and Goliath, or as Henry V might have said, the victory of Gideon over the Amalekites. The triumph of the human spirit can always be celebrated, as Shakespeare knew very well.

Chapter 1

Location

Until very recently, English and French historians alike thought they knew where the Battle of Agincourt was fought. After all, there were visitors to the battlefield, even in medieval times. One of these was the Breton prince, Arthur of Richmond (or *Richemont*). He must have remembered the battle because, according to Gruel's chronicle, he fought there, was left for dead underneath a pile of corpses, but was rescued, taken prisoner and brought back to England. He remained here five years before being released. Having served the French king in the glory days of Joan of Arc, he returned to the scene of the French defeat in 1436, twenty-one years after his ordeal.

> He came by Agincourt and explained to those who were with him how the battle had been fought and showed them where he and his banner had stood and where all the other great lords had been or where their banners stood and where the king of England had camped.

Likewise, Edward IV is known to have spent two nights at Agincourt in 1475, during an expedition designed to repeat the glorious achievement of 1415, though few details of the King's visit survive.

In 1833 the historian Sir Harris Nicolas noted that several officers and soldiers of the 12th Lancers who had fought at Waterloo were presented with their medals at Azincourt and 'those who travel to Paris via St Omer and Abbeville pass over the field of battle'. Charles Knight (1862) and Colonel Burne (1956) certainly visited the battlefield during the course of their researches, as did J. H. Wylie before the First World War. Wylie took the somewhat unusual view that the medieval *Gesta Henrici Quinti* (known as the Chaplain's account) was as good a guidebook for the tourist as it had been written 500 years earlier.[1] Dominique Paladilhe tells us that on the anniversary of the battle in 1914 a French group, which included the Marquis of Chabot-Tramecourt, erected a memorial stone containing Biblical quotations 'in memory of their ancestors who had perished' there. A year later, on the 500th anniversary, a ceremony of reconciliation was held at Azincourt, involving French and English soldiers now involved in their much more terrible struggle with Imperial Germany. Robert Hardy visited the area in 1961 when filming *The Picardy Affair*, though the family which owned the fields told him that 'it was a bad day for you as well as for us', claimed that they had 'defended [their] fields in 1415, 1915 and 1939 and looked ready to do so again'.

Things are very different today. A museum was opened in the village of Azincourt in 2001 which makes excellent use of modern techniques. Longbows and stakes are incorporated into the exterior design of the building and the centre is a triumph, though it is not the French war memorial that René de Belleval wished for in 1865. When I visited the Museum in 2009 the French were shown as proud bullies, heading for a fall. No wonder that most visitors to the museum are thought to be 'Anglo-Saxon', as are the majority who visit the eponymous Tapestry in Bayeux.

When we visit the site and the Museum today, there is nothing to cast doubt on the location; and, not so long ago, Professor Anne Curry wrote that historians had not hitherto disputed this.[2] Yet, when the Agincourt Battlefield Archaeology Project conducted investigations of the battlefield in 2002 and 2007, no artefacts or human remains were discovered; and, in two articles published in 2006 and 2009, Dr Tim Sutherland of the University of York urged that further archaeology was needed to solve this mystery, at the same time suggesting an alternative location. This is a startling development.

Traditionally the battle is supposed to have been fought around 45 miles South of Calais, in the fields to the south-east of the village of Azincourt (always known in England as 'Agincourt') and more specifically between the woods of Azincourt and Tramecourt. This is also where the French are supposed to have buried many of their dead, in gravepits near the hamlet of La Gacogne. In 1734 the Marquise of Tramecourt erected a chapel nearby and a memorial service was held there every twenty-five years, before the building was destroyed during the French Revolution. A Calvary was erected near La Gacogne in the 1860, which remains;[3] and in 1963 a monolith was erected to the South of the battlefield, next to the *Route de Blangy*, not far from Maisoncelle.

The traditional site is apparently confirmed by the chroniclers. The Burgundians Jean de Waurin (c. 1398–c. 1474) and Jean Le Fèvre (c. 1395–1468) both tell us that, on the night before the battle, the French 'lodged in the field between Azincourt and Tramecourt, where the battle was on the next day'. Most historians have adopted this location, which is shown in the maps reproduced in numerous articles and books on the subject, including those by Sir John Woodford (1818), René de Belleval (1865), Ramsay (1892), Oman (1898), Kingsford (1901), Lt-Colonel Burne (1956), Hibbert (1964), Keegan (1976), Contamine (1992), Strickland and Hardy (2005), Michael K. Jones (2005) and Christophe Gilliot (2007). Even J. H. Wylie (1919), who did not include maps because he thought them unreliable, still described the battle as taking place in the 'flat unbroken triangle' between the woods of Azincourt to the north-west, Tramecourt to the north-east and Maisoncelle to the south.

Historians have often included in their maps precise indications of how the English and French armies were drawn up, and even of their move-ments at various times during the day, though the battle was supposed to have been over in the space of three hours. This confidence has been reflected in modern times in films, videos, DVDs, websites and aerial photographs, in the French and English versions of *Wikipedia* and in-numerable battlefield tour guides. The museum at Agincourt has a web-site which shows the battle as taking place in a small part of the traditional location, between the *Rue d'Azincourt* (to the west) and the *Route de Blangy* or D 104 (to the east) and between the *Rue Henri V* (to the north) and the *Rue Principale* (to the south). This seems to be taking too literally the statement in the Chaplain's account, that the battle took place 'in a field named Agincourt', since a 'field' could vary tremendously in size and might consist of many smaller fields.[4]

Yet, when a team of archaeologists conducted a survey of the battlefield for Granada TV in 2002, using metal detectors on a sample of fields in the traditional location, they found only one medieval artefact, which might possibly (only possibly) be an arrowhead. This contrasts very sharply with the discovery of hundreds of medieval artefacts (including many arrow-heads) at Towton in West Yorkshire, where one of the largest battles of medieval times was fought in 1461, during the Wars of the Roses. Given the presence at Agincourt of some thousands of English archers, and several times that number of French troops, one would have expected to find some physical evidence there, even after 600 years – whether arrow-heads, horseshoes and nails, pieces of armour, or more personal items like rings and buckles.

The TV programme which resulted from these investigations was first broadcast on 23 November 2003, as part of the *Battlefield Detectives* series; and it had a strong storyline, as the title (*Agincourt's Dark Secrets*) indicates. It featured the archaeologists Tim Sutherland and Simon Richardson, the historians Anne Curry and Matthew Bennett and several types of scientist. Surprisingly, it did not cast doubt on the traditional location, and it confidently pronounced that the single find made with a metal detector was indeed an arrowhead. A reproduction was then used in a ballistic test, supposedly demonstrating the inability of such an arrowhead to penetrate steel plate-armour; and the assumption was made that many of the French knights, being noblemen, would indeed have been able to afford this type of armour. The programme-makers concluded that the heavy casualties suffered by the French could not have been due to English archery, and that the gravepits at La Gacogne may have been the burial place of prisoners killed in cold blood, on the orders of Henry V, rather than of men killed in a fair fight during the battle.

When Sutherland wrote about these investigations in 2006, he took a very different line, proposing an alternative location for the battle, near the village of Ruisseauville, to the North of Azincourt. He agreed that the gravepits at La Gacogne might contain the bodies of French prisoners and suggested that, over time, historians might have inadvertently moved the site of the battle nearer to the site of the graves than it actually was.[5] Moreover, Sutherland did not leave matters there. He pointed out that a magnetic and earth-resistance geophysical survey which had also been conducted in 2002 had detected large pits and the remains of a large rectangular structure at La Gacogne; and in 2007 he went back, surveyed this area again, and excavated.

Disappointingly, he again drew a complete blank, finding 'no evidence of either human bones or a grave-pit'. This again contrasts with the position at Towton, where a mass grave had been found in 1996, with skeletons which clearly belonged to archers and showed signs of violent death. Sutherland delivered a paper about his investigations to a conference in Germany in 2008, which was published the following year.[6] His controversial conclusion was that 'currently not only is there no physical evidence that there are, or ever have been, any human remains or large pits within the protected area of the enclosure at Agincourt, but there is currently no available evidence of the battle at Agincourt at all'(!).

The doubts arising from the archaeology caused Sutherland to re-examine the literary sources and maps used by historians during the last two centuries; and he duly found 'abundant contradictory evidence' and 'several potential locations' for the battle. His final conclusion was that there was a reasonable doubt about the traditional location, that further archaeological investigations of both possible sites should be undertaken; and that the alternative location to the traditional one had much to be said for it. In particular, this would have been a more logical place for the French to choose for the battle, because they would then have had the opportunity to deploy both their cavalry and their superior numbers of infantry to better effect.

Superficially these are attractive arguments; but in my view the doubts raised by the archaeology are not very serious; the evidence for the alternative location is not convincing, and the battle most probably did take place where the historians have always said that it did.

It is time to look at the historical evidence for ourselves. It is true that the mid-eighteenth century Cassini map of France shows the battle taking place to the north-west of Azincourt, and to the east of the road leading from Hesdin to Calais, nowadays the D 928: the site is indicated on this map by means of a symbol in the shape of a sword or banner. But, was this intended as an accurate representation of the precise location, or was it simply an approximation? Cassini produced his maps for practical purposes, and may have intended to do no more than indicate to the curious traveller that he was in the vicinity of the village of Azincourt, and of the famous battle associated with it; and, incidentally, his map does not show any road at all between the woods of Azincourt and Tramecourt.

Two maps are reproduced in Sir Harris Nicolas's book *The History of the Battle of Agincourt* (1827). One of these is a French map but looks to me like a copy of the Cassini map. The other looks like a sketch made by Nicolas himself, or under his direction, and is in any case ambivalent since it shows the two armies drawn up between two woods, but also shows both the woods and the armies lying to the west of Azincourt, near the D 928 (Anne Curry suggests that this is simply a mistake, on the part of Nicolas or his printer).[7]

The Chaplain's account states that 'the battle took place in a field named Agincourt, through which lay our road to Calais'. This seems to correspond to the location on the three maps just referred to; but the wording is highly ambiguous, because there was a second road which led in the direction of Calais, but which ran between the woods of Azincourt and Tramecourt. Nowadays, this is the D 104, the *Route de Blangy*. Of course, the modern road was not there in the early fifteenth century; but there was a way through, and it is not certain whether the Chaplain was referring here to a 'road', or merely to what we should call in England a 'route'.

Crucially, Sutherland argues that both the Chaplain and a Norman chronicle written around 1460 also say that the battle was fought 'in a *valley* near Agincourt'; and that the only place which could nowadays be described as a valley lies to the north of Azincourt, near Ruisseauville. Now it is true that, in Chapter 12 of his account, the Chaplain says that there was only a *vallem modicum* between the two armies; and the modern editors of the *Gesta Henrici Quinti*, Roskell and Taylor (1975) translate this phrase as 'only a valley and not so wide as that'. However, when the Chaplain used this phrase, he may conceivably have been referring to a mere interval or gap, rather than a valley – as for example the gap between two woods; and, if so, this would be consistent with the traditional location. It is worth noting that the Chaplain also refers in Chapter 13 to 'the woodlands which were on both sides of the armies' (*nemoribus que erant ad utrumque latus exercituum*).

Sutherland says that the Chaplain is generally regarded as the most reliable chronicler of Agincourt; but this is only true in a general sense. The Chaplain was after all a priest (or at any rate in holy orders) and he was chiefly interested in God's work and the favour He showed to the English, rather than in strategy, tactics and topography. There is therefore no reason to suppose that the Chaplain is accurate when it comes to the site of the battle. Indeed it would be surprising if he were, since he was English and had (presumably) never been in the neighbourhood of Azincourt before, when he arrived there on 24 October 1415.

The chronicler Jean de Waurin came from the local county of Artois (and was therefore 'Burgundian' since in 1415 the Duke of Burgundy's territories included the Counties of Artois and Flanders); and he was also a military man. Though he was only 15 at the time and did not write his memoirs until many years later, he was present at Agincourt, on the French side. He tells us that the battle was fought between Azincourt and Tramecourt and, more specifically, that it took place *entre deux petits bosquetz, lun serrant a Azincourt et lautre a Tramecourt* – 'between two small woods, one very close to Azincourt and the other to Tramecourt'.[8]

I believe that Sutherland makes too much of the fact that two French sources tell us that the battle was fought 'near Ruisseauville' or 'between Agincourt and Ruisseauville' and that another refers to 'the Battle of Ruisseauville'. At the time, the French gave the battle a whole variety of names: Rollencourt, Hesdin, Ruisseauville, Maisoncelle, Blangy, Thérouanne, and even 'the Picardy affair' and 'the Artois day'. Eventually 'Azincourt' prevailed in France, just as it did in England (though we find it spelt here as Egyne Court, Gincourt, Agyncoort and even Assyngcowrte); but none of this tells us anything about the precise location of the fighting: nor does the name given by the French to the road between Azincourt and La Gacogne – *Rue Henri V*. It is fair to say that when Thomas Johnes of Hafod near Aberystwyth published his translation of Monstrelet's chronicles in London in 1845, he included a plan, based on Barante's

Histoire des Ducs de Bourgogne, which showed the French army drawn up very close to Ruisseauville (and across the Hesdin–Calais road); but this was a highly inaccurate drawing, which also showed the English army between Azincourt and Maisoncelle and did not show Tramecourt, or the *Route de Blangy*, at all.

As to the archaeological evidence, Sutherland himself makes the point that his was not the first excavation of Agincourt, though it was the first one to use modern techniques. The French graves were excavated around 1818, albeit by an enthusiastic amateur. This was Sir John Woodford, a Quartermaster in the British Army which occupied the *Pas de Calais* after Waterloo, who found 'some remains of arms and arrowheads, four gold rings, some coins of the reigns of Kings Jean II, Charles V and Charles VI, three small elephants carved in ivory, three unusually large brass horns bearing inscriptions, and a large quantity of human teeth', all of which were taken back to England. Unfortunately, only one of these finds (a ring) was still in existence when Wylie made enquiries about the finds in 1902; but we should note there had been no doubt in his (or Woodford's) mind about the location of the battle.[9] Nowadays, there is also a good deal of information about Woodford's finds on *Facebook*, including the fact that the Victoria and Albert Museum in London has long possessed a medieval spur, supposedly found at Agincourt, but long believed to be a fake.

The remarkable finds at Towton do not prove anything about Agincourt. As to artefacts, it is possible that the battlefield at Agincourt was more thoroughly picked over than was the case at Towton. We know that the citizens of Amiens sent a team to recover arms and equipment, which succeeded in bringing back three large cannons, two smaller ones, some damaged *pavises* used by French crossbowmen, and pieces of tent (though the *Musée de Picardie* at Amiens holds none of these finds today). There are other stories in France that weapons were found in the past on the battlefield, though no trace of these remains either. We also know that the English, who nearly all survived Agincourt, were allowed to recover their own arms and arrows left behind, as well as take booty left by the enemy. They had every incentive to do so, since they still had over 40 miles of hostile territory to traverse, before they reached the safety of English Calais; but at the same time there is evidence that, as night fell, Henry ordered that no man should take more armour than he needed and that the surplus should be put into a house or barn and burned.[10]

The failure to discover any human remains in the area of the Calvary is harder to explain, because there are French witnesses who tell us that several thousand Frenchmen were buried there. Specifically we are told that around 5,800 French dead were buried in five large pits, the largest of them being – as de Belleval wrote – 'in a field still named La Gacogne'. It is of course possible that the ground was disturbed, perhaps by the building of the eighteenth-century chapel, or by Woodford's excavation. It is also possible that there is some feature of the local terrain or soil which caused the bones of the dead to decompose more rapidly than they evidently did at Towton. Towton, after all, was a moor at the time.[11]

There may be another explanation for the failure to find human remains at Agincourt. The *Chronique de Ruisseauville* and the researches undertaken by René de Belleval for his book tell us that the bodies of quite a number of noblemen were taken away by their retainers, for honourable burial on their own estates, that an unspecified number of anonymous local gentlemen were buried in churches or churchyards in the vicinity (even as far away as Amiens), and that other men had 'gone off to die of their wounds'. There are also stories that the suffragan Bishop of Therouanne took away the bodies of a dozen noblemen for burial in the cloisters of a local abbey (possibly at Auchy-lès-Hesdin?); and that much later, in 1950,

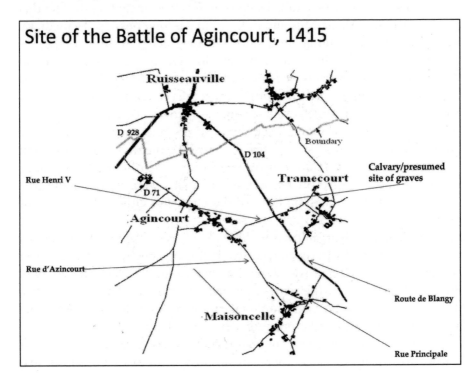

Site of the Battle of Agincourt, 1415

when an electricity pylon was put up, a dozen corpses were discovered in a nearby cellar.[12]

In conclusion it is worth noting that excavations at the traditional site of the Battle of Shrewsbury (1403) for the *Two Men in a Trench* TV programme failed to find any gravepits, while the graves at Towton were only found by accident, during modern building work on a house. More importantly, when the battlefield at Crécy was investigated with mine detectors in 1995, nothing was found that could be directly attributed to the battle, though it had been estimated that anything between 500,000 and 1 million artefacts were awaiting discovery. Yet Sir Philip Preston still considered that 'tradition's claim that this is where [the Battle of Crécy] took place deserves to remain intact'.[13] I think we would be justified in reaching the same conclusion about Agincourt, at least at present. It remains perfectly possible that further archaeology will produce astonishing results.

Chapter 2

English Victory or French Defeat?

Most people who write about Agincourt are English, since the battle is still regarded as a triumph here and a disaster in France. So while the English devote whole books to describing every aspect of it, French historians – even military historians – tend not to dwell on it. Yet it is worthwhile considering what they do have to say, because it was a battle which the French should have won.

Consider the following facts. Henry V invaded Normandy with an army which was relatively large by English standards but was nonetheless an expeditionary force, and could not hope to compete in size with the army which the French King could muster and put in the field, if given time; and Charles VI and his advisers were given that time, because Henry took longer than expected to reduce the port of Harfleur. The English King then set off for Calais, his force much reduced by death, sickness and the need to garrison Harfleur. His progress was obstructed on the Somme and he took much longer than expected to reach the approaches to Calais. The French had time to concentrate their forces and it was they who trapped Henry at Agincourt.

Whatever conclusions we reach about the exact size of the rival armies, the French outnumbered the English, and had a wider variety of forces at their disposal. They also had some of the best generals in Europe and they had devised a battle-plan, of sorts. Their commanders could afford to take their time, choose the ground and select the right moment to attack. Their men were fighting in defence of their homeland and were probably not so tired as their opponents. For their part the English had not won a major battle in France for several decades.

It is often said that the French had learned nothing from their mistakes at Crécy in Picardy (1346) and Poitiers in Central France (1356), where they had been soundly defeated. Yet they knew what to expect when they fought the English, and the French record on the battlefield was not as poor as we have been taught. The frequent references to Crécy and Poitiers, so well known in England, may lead us to overlook the crushing

French victory over the Flemings at Roosebeke (1382), and the Duke of Burgundy's defeat of the rebellious citizens of Liège at Othée (1408). By 1415 the great English victories in France were a matter of history (though the Duke of Berry, who had fought at Poitiers, was still able to give counsel in 1415). There was a living tradition of archery and of fighting on foot in England, but no-one who fought at Agincourt could possibly have remembered Crécy, though his grandfather may have told him about it.

French Defeat

In the circumstances, we may ask how the French could lose; but in fact this is easily answered. They were in the throes of a civil war, which had been going on, first in cold form then in hot, since Louis, Duke of Orléans, had been assassinated by the henchmen of his cousin the Duke of Burgundy in 1407. That murder had led to fighting between Orleanists (later known as Armagnacs) and Burgundians, and the conflict was not confined to the Duchy and County of Burgundy. Henry V has been criticised for invading France when the civil war was in progress, but the English were invited in, on more than one occasion. English expeditionary forces had been despatched to France in 1411 and again in 1412, on the first occasion in support of the Burgundians, on the second in alliance with the Armagnacs; and each side in France was prepared to offer generous terms in return for English support. As we shall see, the Duke of Burgundy stood aside in 1415 and instructed his vassals not to assist the King of France, though some of them disobeyed.

The French King Charles VI had been suffering from bouts of insanity since 1392. His illness had contributed much to the civil war, producing factions which struggled for power, at court and in the French provinces. It also meant that there was little chance that Charles would take the field at Agincourt; but in addition he was incapable of appointing an authoritative supreme commander, or of resolving the differences between aristocrats who claimed pride of place on grounds of birth, and professional soldiers, who should have been in charge but lacked influence.

Henry V's expedition crossed the Channel unopposed, since the French had no fleet to send against it. As recently as 1386, they had built a navy which was capable of invading England, but this had been allowed to run down during the long truce after 1389, while key alliances with the naval powers of the south, Castile and Genoa, had been allowed to lapse. The English also took the French by surprise when they landed near Harfleur, though they had been expected at Boulogne and in the Cotentin.

After the capture of Harfleur, the French authorities could not be sure what the English would do next, and they took precautions to defend places which were far removed from the line of march which was actually taken. This produced a curious incident near Saint-Quentin. On the night of 20 October the Mayor of Chauny thought that Henry V's army was only six or seven leagues (or 20 miles) away, when the distance was probably twice as far as that. He increased the state of alert, and went out at night to inspect the guard. Unfortunately, it rained, so he curtailed his inspection and returned home unexpectedly. When he arrived there, he found another man lurking in a passageway near his wife's bed. The man, Jean Mairel, was wearing only a shirt, and the wife was lying naked in bed. In his anger, the Mayor lashed out at Mairel, who died from the blow shortly afterwards.[1]

The defence mounted by the French authorities was not entirely ineffective. Marshal Boucicaut and the Constable Charles d'Albret were career soldiers and they used the time taken by the siege of Harfleur to raise an army. Men from the *Île de France*, Normandy and Picardy were assembled in Rouen, while men from the south and the centre of France gathered in Abbeville. They also arranged for the bridges and causeways across local rivers to be destroyed and they organised resistance to English victualling parties. David, Sire de Rambures, who was Grandmaster of the Crossbowmen, was sent to defend the area around the Pale of Calais (still in English hands) and managed to reinforce Boulogne and organise attacks on English stragglers. When a force of 300 Englishmen set out from Calais to provide support for King Henry's expeditionary force, it was ambushed and annihilated by the Picards.[2]

Henry V received the surrender of Harfleur on 22 September and set off for Calais on 8 October. Once the French discovered that the English were making their way along the coast towards Calais, the main body of their army advanced from Rouen to Amiens on the Somme. An advance guard shadowed the invaders at Honfleur and Arques in the Pays de Caux, and then made directly for Abbeville. Then they crossed to the north bank of the river, making it impossible for Henry to use the ford at Blanchetaque, where his great-grandfather Edward III had crossed in 1346. This manoeuvre forced Henry to prolong his march by several days and 100 miles, and could have spelt disaster for the English. As it was, the French continued to shadow their opponents, marching inland along the north bank of the Somme while Henry progressed along the opposite bank, past Piquigny, Boves and Corbie, and only managing to cross at Béthencourt and Voyennes.

The French prepared a battle-plan, re-discovered in 1984 by Christopher Philpotts in the Cotton Manuscripts in the British Library (quite a find, since the document had been damaged in the great Cottonian fire of 1731). This plan shows that the French were prepared to fight the English on the Somme, with fewer men than they eventually assembled at Agincourt. It appears from internal evidence that it was drawn up by Marshal Boucicaut, somewhere between Abbeville and Bapaume, between 13 and 21 October; but it was a 'Somme plan', not an Agincourt plan, and so, in the event, was not used.

French historians admit that their compatriots now made just about every mistake in 'the book'. In the first place, it would probably have been better if they had not sought to bring Henry to battle at all, but let him pass to Calais, as Boucicaut and d'Albret both advised; and it is likely that the old Duke of Berry would have given the same advice, based on his experience at Poitiers; but the cooler heads were overruled by the leading Armagnac princes. It is perhaps significant that the latter were younger men – Charles of Orléans was 24, Jean de Bourbon was 33 and Jean d'Alençon was 30.

The French got ahead of the English and decided to give battle, but they put themselves at a disadvantage by forming up between the woods of Azincourt and Tramecourt, which prevented them from outflanking the enemy. Moreover, their tactical dispositions were poor. The Somme plan had provided for a cavalry force to fall upon the English archers and break them, and for crossbowmen to be placed in front of the infantry; but the French cavalry charge was ineffective – only a few hundred horsemen were committed to it – and, as Jean le Fèvre noted, 'the French had plenty of archers and crossbowmen but nobody wanted to let them shoot. The reason for this was that the site was so narrow that there was only enough room for the men-at-arms.'[3]

When the French sent in their cavalry, they could only charge head-on, because of the woods on either side; and many writers have stressed the deleterious effect of the charge and the subsequent retreat on sodden ground, which was churned into mud. According to Philippe Contamine, writing in Corvisier's *Histoire Militaire de la France* (1992) the French should have made a more determined attack, with a larger detachment of men than actually took part, if they were to stand any chance of achieving the objective set by the Somme plan. The Marshal and the Constable had recommended that around 1,000 mounted troops should charge the English archers, but, according to Le Fèvre, only 160 men took part.

This is hardly credible. Juliet Barker cites evidence that only 420 cavalry-men were involved, 120 from one side of the vanguard and 300 from the other; but if those figures are more accurate, the numbers were still too few.[4]

The Constable now led an infantry attack. Some accounts describe the vanguard alone as containing about 5,000 men-at-arms, which would have equalled some estimates of the entire English army; but, before these men could engage in hand-to-hand fighting they again had to cross muddy ground under a constant hail of arrows. It now appeared that the French generals had chosen an unfortunate place and time to fight, since it had been raining heavily and the battlefield had been newly ploughed and sown. The French were more heavily armed than the English, and conditions underfoot were very difficult for them. Le Fèvre, Waurin and Walsingham all mention a sea of mud and the Monk of St Denis wrote of men sinking up to their knees. At the least, the infantrymen were probably overcome with fatigue before they reached the enemy lines. The English TV programme *Agincourt's Dark Secrets* conducted tests and found a type of soil at Azincourt which was very retentive of moisture: a knight in full armour would have found walking through the mud like walking with 15 bags of sugar on each leg. Pierre Naudin's historical novel about the battle (2006) is entitled, *Le Bourbier d'Azincourt* ('The Quagmire').

The confined nature of the battleground was also a problem for the French. The effects of 'the press' are described by the Chaplain.

> For when some of them, killed when battle was first joined, fell at the front, so great was the undisciplined violence and pressure of the mass of men behind that the living fell on top of the dead, and others falling on top of the living were killed as well.

The Monk of St Denis confirms that 'the [French] vanguard, composed of about 5,000 men, found itself at first so tightly packed that those who were in the third rank could scarcely use their swords'.

In later years the Italian humanist Tito Livio wrote a *Life of Henry V* for Humphrey Duke of Gloucester (who fought at Agincourt). He tells how the French were boxed in between the woods, while the English writer John Hardyng also stressed the disastrous effects of the crush.

> *And then the press of enemies did surprise*
> *Their own people, that more were dead through press*
> *Than our men might have slain in time no less.*

In *Le Jouvencel* (c. 1470) Jean de Bueil blamed the French defeat on fatigue, which is ironic, since several writers say that it was the English who had most reason to be exhausted.

> During the night [the French] slept in a field where they had been in mud up to their knees, and the following day they marched across a large stretch of fallow land, before meeting with the enemy, when there was still a considerable distance between them, so it came about that when it came to the fighting they were able to assemble very few of their people, and one man after another became short of breath and they were defeated. And it is no good, in these circumstances, having to fight on foot.[5]

As for morale, the French were defending their homeland and they expected to win. Yet, even at the time, there were French commentators who accused their own men of cowardice. They pointed to the failure of the third French line to join battle at all, and the relatively slight casualties suffered by their cavalry. Gilles le Bouvier wrote of Frenchmen who had 'failed to do their duty ... and never struck a blow'; and the normally patriotic Thomas Basin wrote that one Englishman chased off ten terrified Frenchmen at the end of the battle. In the nineteenth century, during a period of Anglo-French reconciliation, there was a tendency on both sides of the Channel to emphasise heroism on both sides; but older attitudes remained entrenched, despite the signing of the *Entente Cordiale* in 1904. As late as 1974, the popular historian Charles Kightly could still write that 'It is also at least partly true that the English won the battle because most of them were brave men; and that the French lost it because many of them were cowards'.[6]

This is very hard to believe. It may have been true that some French troops were reluctant to fight, but large numbers of them, including the cavalrymen and infantrymen who were ordered to charge the archers, displayed courage worthy of the Light Brigade during the Crimean War. They paid the penalty for the internal divisions in the French high command and the numerous mistakes made by their leaders.

The French may have made some use of cannon at Agincourt. There is a record in the Exchequer accounts of at least one English archer – Roger Hunt, who was in the retinue of the Lancashire knight Sir James Harington – who was killed 'with a gun';[7] and Le Fèvre tells us that the French had 'serpentines' and 'culverins'. However, if artillery was used, it must have been deployed incompetently. Even without it, Agincourt has the reputation of being one of the bloodiest of medieval battles. The arrow storm led to disproportionate loss of life, especially amongst the French nobility; and the use by the English archers of longbows and heavy warhammers (rather than swords and spears) during the *mêlée* added an extra dimension of horror in the minds of contemporaries who were used to writing for the gentry.

The fighting lasted about three hours, though the chroniclers differ as to whether it finished around midday or sunset;[8] but there was also at least one French attack or counterattack which had some success. Various accounts tell us that some French knights made a rush at Henry, that a piece of his crown was hacked off, and that his helmet was dented. To this day, the visitor can even see a large helmet in Westminster Abbey, which has a large dent in it; but, for reasons explained below, its preservation tells us more about the importance of the Abbey as a tourist attraction, even in medieval times, than it does about Agincourt.[9]

In France it is said that it was the Duke of Alençon who led an heroic attack on the English king, and that he managed to strike off part of Henry's crown and kill the Duke of York, before being hewn down himself. René de Belleval described Alençon as 'the true hero of the day', and there are fanciful Victorian illustrations of Henry V which show him under attack. (Dominique Paladilhe even suggests that part of Henry's motive for invading the Duchy of Alençon, during the conquest of Normandy between 1417 and 1419, was to revenge himself for this attack). However, according to both Waurin and Le Fèvre, the charge took place at an earlier stage of the *mêlée* and was led by two men who fought under the banner of the Lord of Croy (near Amiens).[10]

Why did the French launch this desperate, almost suicidal, attack? Thomas Walsingham has a revealing passage about a similar episode during the Battle of Shrewsbury, when the enemy decided to attack Henry IV. 'Thinking that [Henry IV] was worth ten thousand of his men, they looked for him, mowing down those who stood in their way and searching for him with death-dealing spears and swords ...'. Clearly if a king were present on a medieval battlefield, one would expect at least one determined attempt to kill or capture him: the English had, after all, managed to capture Jean II at Poitiers in 1356; but the only truly successful attack made at Agincourt was against the lightly-protected English baggage train. This was led by Ysembart d'Azincourt, and it managed to seize some of Henry's personal treasures, including a crown. In some accounts this attack took place towards the end of the battle, and led the English to think they were being attacked from the rear. In Shakespeare's

Henry V, based on Tudor chroniclers, this is presented as a cowardly attack on defenceless 'boys', though we should remember that boy-soldiers were commonly employed to look after horses. French chroniclers, anxious to find scapegoats for the disgrace occasioned by the defeat, tend to criticise this raid as ill-advised and unauthorised, but in his reminiscences Gilbert de Lannoy describes it as linked to the late arrival on the field of the Duke of Brabant, younger brother of the Duke of Burgundy.[11]

The truth about this incident may have been more complex. In Françoise Autrand's view, it was more than just a raid mounted by cowardly pillagers. It may be that, rather than a mere raid on the baggage train, it was actually a badly-executed attempt to attack the English positions as a whole from the rear, and thereby encircle the smaller force. Tactics like this had been part of the secret of the Anglo-Gascon success at Poitiers in 1356.[12]

As a result of French counterattacks, or the threat of them, the English became alarmed that the French, who were still very numerous, might be regrouping, and in particular that the French third line might at last join the fray. The Chaplain relates that the weary English saw that the French rearguard was still present 'in incomparable number, and fresh'. Le Fèvre and Waurin confirm that it was the sight of the French rearguard, regrouping and 'marching forward in battle order', which made the English think they were still endangered. At this point, Henry ordered that the French prisoners who had already been taken should be put to the sword.

The massacre which followed is one of the most controversial events in medieval history; but it is fair to point out that there is argument about the most basic of facts – including the numbers who were actually done to death. Monstrelet suggested that there was a great deal of reluctance on the part of the English to carry out Henry's orders, and that he had to depute 200 archers, a kind of death squad, to carry out the foul deed. The French writer Pilham de Pilham (1697) thought that Henry countermanded his order before it was implemented. John Keegan (1976) and Christopher Allmand (1997)[13] doubted that it would have been possible to kill a large number of prisoners in the short space of time available, and suggested that Henry's motive in giving the order was to intimidate, rather than exterminate. In *Shaping the Nation* (2005) Gerald Harriss also suggests that the order may have been given to 'to cow rather than despatch the prisoners'. It seems, at any rate, that around 1,000 of them were eventually brought back to England. The Monk says there were 1,400, Waurin, Le Fèvre and Monstrelet say 1,600.[14]

However, great men attract the attention of historians more than little men; and amongst the prisoners who were killed on the King's orders were many French noblemen. Curiously, the Duke of Brabant, of the Burgundian ducal house, may have been amongst them. All the main French sources – Monstrelet, Waurin, Le Fevre, Fenin, des Ursins and Gruel – tell us that he ignored his brother's orders to stay away from the battle, though he arrived late and, in his haste, wore improvised armour and a surcoat made from a trumpeter's flag. He fought valiantly but was captured and killed, presumably by Englishmen or Welshmen unaware of his high status and value. His murder would have done nothing for Anglo-Burgundian relations, always of critical importance.[15]

English Victory

Meanwhile what of the English? In the summer of 1415, Henry V stayed at Portchester Castle and Titchfield Abbey near the Solent, and Wolvesey Castle in Winchester, while he mustered a force of around 12,000 combatants at Southampton. Professor Curry calculated that there were either 11,248 or 11,791 (according to which figures are used) and these included either 2,266 or 2,316 men at arms, and some 9,000 archers. This contrasts starkly with the 4,000 men whom the Duke of Clarence had taken to France only three years earlier.[16] It was a very large force, by English standards.

In addition, the army of 1415 was well equipped, and the Chaplain wrote of 1,500 vessels, 'not including those which stayed behind, of which there were about 100', which is also the figure mentioned by the poet John Lydgate, of Bury St Edmunds (c. 1370–c. 1451) and historians have tended to accept the figure uncritically. On this basis it is often said that the English invasion fleet was several times larger than the Spanish Armada of 1588, whose numbers are known more precisely. A more sober estimate for the English fleet in 1415 would be around 500 ships. Nevertheless, the assembling of this 'English Armada' was a tribute to the organisational abilities of Henry V and his advisers.

Henry's spectacular victory on land in October has obscured his achievement at sea in August 1415. He would not have been able to transport such a large force of men across the Channel and lay siege to Harfleur, without being sure that he could defend them, land them and re-supply them. He was confident of his ability to do so because, from the moment he became King, he had been spending unprecedented sums on building up a 'Royal Navy'. This expenditure is also good evidence that William Catton is the unsung hero of the Agincourt expedition. Paid only a shilling a day, he was Keeper of the King's Ships between 1413 and 1420, and responsible for creating a new dockyard as well as new ships. Henry was the first English King (after Alfred the Great) to realise the importance of sea-power but Catton was his instrument.[17] When the fleet carrying the troops of the Agincourt expedition left Southampton in August 1415, it was accompanied by no less than fifteen royal ships, including Henry's flagship the *Trinity Royal*. This may not seem many, compared to the size of the British fleet in later centuries; but the presence of these mighty armed escorts was something new. They were more than a match for the galleys which the French had once sent against the south coasts of England. Henry V was already 'master of the narrow sea'.

Returning to Southampton, we have been taught that the English were a nation united in arms, but military activity on such a large scale was bound to present some problems for the civilian population living in and around the port; and on 28 July the King felt compelled to order the Sheriff of Wiltshire

> To command divers hired soldiers, English and Welsh, on their march to the King's presence through Warminster and elsewhere in that county, who have taken divers victuals from his lieges there and will not pay for the same ... to pay the lieges as lawful is ...[18]

It was also predictable that there would be some fighting between the locals and soldiers drawn from many different parts of the country. The Salisbury General Entry Book records an affray at Fisherton, involving some of the archers who had arrived from the territories of the Duchy of Lancaster.

> On 4 August, the Sunday after St Peter in Chains, a crowd of the Duke of Lancaster's men (as it was said), lodged at Fisherton by Salisbury, whose leader was James Harington, and engaged to set out with the King overseas, attacked many of the city's men on Fisherton bridge, driving them off with arrows and swords and killing four of them with arrows ...

The clerk who recorded this made a note 'to consider what to do about the deaths and the terrible affray, with bells rung all around'. Later, Mayor Evesham recorded the following payments

> To an official from Wales for bread and oats when taking measurements in the city's defence at the time of the attack at Fisherton bridge by the Earl [*sic*] of Lancaster's men, 1s 6d; in drink given to

another official ... 8d; for having a watch at St Edmund's Gate against hostile strangers at the time of the great watch, (1s 1d?); for expenses in burying John Tanner, killed by those attacking the city at Fisherton bridge 11d.

The local historian Oswald Barron, who studied the original entries in the City records noted that the Mayor also paid

A certain Welsh minstrel for repairs to his clothing [and] remaking his hood, because he had lost it in the defence of the town when he was attacked upon the bridge at Fisherton by men from the Lancashire company 18d.[19]

The expedition of 1415 benefited from the fact that Henry V was still relatively new to the throne. There was a flush of enthusiasm for the young monarch, which resulted in generous parliamentary grants of taxation. Nevertheless, it would be an exaggeration to say that the enthusiasm was universal. On the eve of the King's departure for France, a serious plot was discovered, to kill the King and replace him with Edmund Mortimer, the Earl of March. The conspiracy involved the Earl of Cambridge, Baron Scrape of Masham and Sir Thomas Gray. These were influential men, who had been very close to the King, but all three were swiftly tried and beheaded.

Having crossed the Channel, the English fleet rounded the chalk cliff known as the *Chef de Caux* – which the English called 'Kidcaus' or 'Kidcocks'[20] – and landed unopposed near the village of Frileuse, at the mouth of the Seine, on 14 August 1415. The chroniclers tell us that a small scouting party including John Holland, Gilbert Umfraville, John Cornwall, John Grey and William Porter, went ashore and selected a suitable spot for an advance guard of around 1,000 men to land; but almost twenty years later Sir John Fastolf claimed that 'he was the first to disembark and jump into the sea up to his sword-belt, and the King gave him the first house he saw in France'.[21]

Harfleur had strong walls and no less than twenty-four towers; but Henry had taken a powerful artillery train with him. Cannon and gunstones feature large in John Lydgate's poem about the siege. He refers to Henry's ships as having 'waists decked with serpentines strong' and tells us the names of some of the guns used at Harfleur, including 'London' and 'The King's Daughter'. However, despite a sustained bombardment the town did not surrender immediately. Its citizens flooded the land around the walls. While this allowed the King to use boats to communicate with his brother Clarence's camp, it also produced dysentery, which wreaked havoc amongst the English. Lydgate wrote

> *Great sickness amongst our host was, in good fay,*
> *Which killed many of our Englishmen*
> *There died beyond seven score upon a day;*
> *Alive there was left but thousands ten.*

Medieval writers were ignorant of microbes. The Monk of St Denis thought that the epidemic was caused by an *excès du besoin et des privations* (need and privation). Others have attributed it to the propensity of the English to eat too much shellfish and rotten fruit whilst in France.

Henry was very severe with his own men – he did not allow anyone to leave the siege until Harfleur was taken. He was utterly ruthless towards anyone he regarded as a rebel (including the 'rebellious' French, who had not known English rule for generations); and he relied on Biblical authority to justify his actions. The Law of Deuteronomy was relevant here, since this required that peace be offered to an enemy town before an attack was made; but it also provided that, if such an offer were rejected, the town could sacked, and its inhabitants put to the sword. The people of Harfleur knew the rules and they duly surrendered, after a siege lasting four weeks, on 22 September 1415. It was only then that Henry arranged for his sick and the injured – at least 1,400 men – to be invalided home.[22] The King then installed a garrison of 300 men at arms and 900 archers in Harfleur and set about introducing English settlers.

The month spent in reducing Harfleur meant that Henry had little time left for a prolonged expedition; but he decided to reject the unanimous advice he received to return home immediately. It is important to realise what this meant, in terms of the normal campaigning season. Crécy had been fought in August 1346, while Verneuil was to be fought in August 1424 and Edward IV's expedition to Picardy undertaken in the summer of 1475; but in 1415 the march to Agincourt was undertaken in October. This inevitably meant that conditions would be far from ideal for a pitched battle, at the end of the journey, however short it was. On any reckoning, Henry was taking a huge risk.

Why did Henry decide to make for Calais nonetheless, when he had no need to do so? It was important that a medieval monarch should show himself to his subjects. According to Monstrelet, Henry IV had announced several times that he intended to 'visit his possessions' in France; but Wylie also thought that Henry V's march was 'a deliberate provocation aimed at the Dauphin Louis, who had failed to respond to Henry's personal challenge to combat at Harfleur'. The makers of the TV programme *Agincourt's Dark Secrets* argued that it was a 'victory march' – but if that was so, it could only have been a march celebrating the capture of Harfleur, not the victory at Agincourt.

Henry's journey is usually described, and shown on film, as a 'march', but does this mean that all the men marched, or did some of them ride? The Chaplain says that supplies were reduced to a minimum; but horses were an essential part of the equipment of every knight and man at arms (even if the English habitually fought on foot); and even the archers were of two kinds – mounted and foot. Moreover, an army needs mounted foragers and scouts, if it is to know where it is going and where to cross the rivers. Nicolas cited evidence that, when it left England, the army consisted of 2,500 men at arms, 4,000 mounted archers and 4,000 foot archers but Oman wrote that the whole army, including archers, were provided with mounts. On the other hand, Michael K. Jones tells us that the troops were travelling light and were therefore on foot, and there are also stories of men marching with their trousers or leggings 'rolled down for the possible easement of troubled bowels', so it is difficult to be certain. The weight of the evidence supports the idea that this was a mounted expedition, rather than a march 'up country', in the manner of Xenophon's Greeks; but at the same time, the speed with which the expedition travelled must have been determined by any soldiers who did make the journey on foot, and by the baggage-train, reduced as it was.[23]

Some French historians have described Henry V's march from Harfleur to Calais as a *chevauchée* – an armed raid of the kind made famous by Edward III and the Black Prince in the previous century; but, if Henry had wanted to organise that kind of raid, he might have chosen Calais as his starting point, as his predecessors had done in 1373 and 1380. As it was, the Agincourt campaign proved to be the first stage of a war of conquest, rather than a resumption of any fourteenth-century strategy. Yet the idea of a *chevauchée* in 1415 has taken hold, even in England.

In fact, Henry V proclaimed that France was now his own country and his men must therefore refrain from harming his new subjects. In addition, he probably issued Ordinances, designed to keep his troops under strict control, and did his best to enforce them. The scene in Shakespeare's *Henry V*, where the king orders that his old friend Bardolph be hanged for stealing a pyx, is based on a real incident. The Ruisseauville chronicler wrote that 'the English robbed neither men nor churches, nor did they start a single fire in France; and the king did all he could to see that we had justice'.[24]

But there is no truth in the idea, now popular with some English ex-patriates, that the English were made welcome in Normandy because of a residual kinship between the two peoples, dating from 1066. Henry V may have claimed that he was returning to an ancient inheritance but the link between Normandy and the English Crown had been broken in 1204; and the bonds of blood and feudalism had dissolved. While many of the nobility in England still spoke French, the average English soldier did not. Even when an Englishman and a Frenchman could make themselves understood, there was no basis for trust. Monstrelet tells us of an English-man, Sir James de Harcourt, who paid a call on a Frenchman of the same name in 1418, greeting him as a long-lost cousin, but he did so only to lull him into a false sense of security, so that he could take him prisoner; and the story that Sir Gilbert Umfraville was greeted by some citizens of Rouen in 1419 as sharing 'that old blood of that country of Normandy' does not prove any real affinity. The city of Rouen was at the mercy of the English at the time.[25]

The route across Northern France to Calais lay through territory which was entirely hostile. In her TV series *Chivalry and Betrayal*, first broadcast in February 2013, Dr Janina Ramirez used a map of France which showed Ponthieu, including Abbeville and Amiens, in English hands in 1415; but Ponthieu had been re-conquered in 1369 and it was still in French hands when the English arrived there forty-five years later. There was no welcome for Henry on the Somme in 1415 – even from Burgundian garrisons – and he had to travel a long way inland, before he could cross the river.

As we have seen, the French caught up with him in Picardy. On 24 October, the English camped at Maisoncelle, and scouts reported that a very large French force was camped on the road to Calais, barring the route to the Channel and home. The English had marched 260 miles in seventeen days – instead of the 160 miles they would have completed if they had been able to take the most direct route – and they were not in the best of form or health. Henry apparently ordered total silence in the camp, so that everybody to get some sleep. His men were so quiet that some of the French thought that they had slipped away in the night.

The following day, 25 October 1415, the battle lines were drawn up in the early morning, and battle commenced around nine o'clock. It was all over by what we would call lunch-time. What was left of Henry's army inflicted one of the worst defeats which the French had ever suffered in the field. There is now much dispute about the numbers involved; but there is no doubt about the result. In the words of one modern French historian, the French army was 'annihilated'. English casualties were light, the French catastrophic. Thousands were killed, and hundreds were captured: a list was made by Monstrelet in the fifteenth century and augmented by de Belleval in the nineteenth. The result came as a surprise to both sides. France was a much more powerful and populous country than England and had hitherto been accounted the first nation of chivalry.

English poets tended to emphasise the 'blood and guts' – the tremendous carnage wrought amongst men and horses

> *Steeds there stumbled in that stand*
> *That stood there stuffed under steel*
> *With groaning great they fell to ground*
> *Their sides sundered when they go to feel.*
> *But when an arrow hath pieced through his side*
> *To ground he goeth and cast his master down*

The English poets also emphasise the personal role played by the King in the fighting

> *Our gracious King men might know*
> *He fought that day with his own hand*
> *He spared neither high nor low*
> *There was no man his dint might stand*
> *The Earls was discomfited upon a row*
> *That he had slain I understand.*[26]

For all we have said about the latent weaknesses of the French kingdom, its internal divisions and the many failures of leadership, the victory remains a remarkable triumph of English arms. Even if the language employed by the Victorian editors of Bishop Thomas Percy's *Reliques of Ancient English Poetry* (1868) seems a little old-fashioned, the average English reader will still want to recognise 'the splendid pluck with which the little English army, wasted by dysentery, ill-fed, and harassed by long marches and hostile skirmishers, nevertheless went at its enemies, facing the terrible odds ... and put to ignominious rout the vaunting knights of France'.

Chapter 3

The General and the Army

The General

Henry V was one of the most famous soldier-kings of the late Middle Ages. Like William the Conqueror, Richard I and Edwards I and III, he led his men into battle; and this contrasts starkly with Charles VI, who was intermittently insane and stayed well away while Agincourt was fought. Yet we do not even know the year in which Henry was born. It may have been 1386 or 1387. All we really know is that he was born in Monmouth Castle.

We also think that we know what the King looked like, because we have all seen Laurence Olivier or Kenneth Branagh in the role, or else pictures of the 'real' king in biographies or history books; but these are idealised portraits, based on early Tudor paintings now in the Royal Collection, the National Portrait Gallery or Queen's College Oxford; but how realistic was even the earliest of these portraits? It is painted in profile and shows the left side of the sitter's face, which is unblemished. Yet we know that this side of Henry V's face must have been scarred, because he was badly wounded by an arrow at the Battle of Shrewsbury in 1403, when he was around 16 years old. The incident is recorded by Thomas Morstede in his treatise on surgery, written between 1420 and 1450. This tells us that Prince Harry was 'smitten in the face beside the nose on the left side with an arrow'; that the arrow entered 'overwharte' (sideways); that the shaft was taken out, but this left 'the head of a bodstyll [bodkin] in the hindpart of a bone of the head'; and that the wound was six inches deep.

Henry was taken from Shrewsbury to the Lancastrian castle of Kenilworth in Leicestershire, some 65 miles away, and was healed by the surgeon John Bradmore, after several other quacks (whom Morstede called 'lewd chattering leeches') failed to help. Bradmore, who was consulted 'at the last', was able to remove the arrowhead from deep within the Prince's cheekbone, using a specially-made instrument, which Morstede drew for the benefit of his readers.

Morstede describes this as an 'instrument ... made in the manner of a tongs ... round and hollowish, by the means thereof entered a little wise

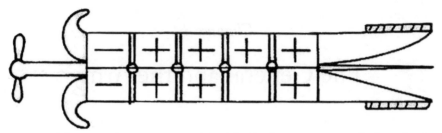

Drawing of the surgical instrument used by John Bradmore to extract the arrowhead.

with the which instrument, was pulled out the arrowhead'. He also tells us that

> Afterward the wound was washed with wine and cleansed with mun-
> dificatype [cleansing] ointment of 4 parts of populion [poplar leaves
> or buds] and the 4th part of honey so containing the space of 7 days
> and afterward the place was healed with *unguentum fuscum cirurgicum*
> [a dark surgical ointment].

It is inconceivable that Henry would have been left unscathed by this wound, and by the operation on the left side of his face which saved his life. It may also have had some effect on his personality.[1]

The earliest surviving portrait also shows the King as clean-shaven and with a kind of 'short back and sides' haircut, which corresponds with the verbal description in Tito Livio's biography, yet there is a statue of Henry on the Kings' Screen in York Minster, thought to have been carved in or around 1421, when he visited the northern city, and this shows him with a small beard and a moustache, as well as an extraordinary 'Afro' hairstyle.

The truth is that it is impossible to be sure what Henry looked like, or for that matter what sort of man he was. Each age has re-cast him and his character to suit its own tastes and prejudices. In the eighteenth century the citizens of Monmouth, who admired him greatly, had a statue erected in Agincourt Square, seven feet tall, which shows him with a crown and medieval armour, but also with a field-marshal's baton and Georgian knee-breeches.

Henry's contribution to the Agincourt campaign was in a class of its own. In his late twenties, he was young and dynamic. He led the army in person and he was also supreme commander. There was clearly a unity of command and purpose on the English side which was totally lacking on the French. Moreover, he was a remarkable all-rounder. K. B. McFarlane thought him the ablest man ever to sit on the English throne.

Henry had built up a strong retinue as Prince of Wales and employed many of his father's most experienced soldiers, including Lord Camoys, the German knight Hartung von Klux and John Robessart (an Englishman, despite his French name). Several knights who had served with him against Owain Glyndwr were awarded the Order of the Garter: these included John Blount, William Harrington, John Grey and Lewis Robessart. As King, Henry also had the resources of the Duchy of Lancaster at his disposal and was therefore able to contribute a large personal following to the expedition of 1415. The precise number of men is difficult to gauge but it was certainly far larger than the 960 whom his brother Clarence indented for, and the 860 whom his youngest brother Gloucester agreed to put in the field. Furthermore, there is evidence that Henry re-invigorated the administration of Duchy estates to produce record sums for the royal Exchequer.[2]

The King also enrolled almost his entire household, and there were several hundred specialist troops: gunners; armourers, marshals and heralds, even men in charge of the tents (the yeomen of the pavilion). In addition there were grooms and saddlers, purveyors, smiths, messengers, cooks, bakers, 'clerks of the spicery', carpenters, cordwainers (shoemakers), fletchers, bowyers, wheelwrights, colliers, almoners, clerks, chaplains and fifteen minstrels, including several men with the surname Trumper, several called Pyper, and a certain Snayth Fidler. The chief surgeon Thomas Morstede brought twelve other medical men with him, while William Bradwardine brought nine.[3]

What was Henry's previous experience as a soldier? The Chaplain wrote that he was 'young in years but old in experience' but was this anything more than a conventional compliment? Apart from Shrewsbury, Agincourt was the first large pitched battle he was ever involved in (and it proved to be the last). During the years between Agincourt and his death in 1422 he was exclusively involved in siege warfare. Though Henry was one of the founders of the Royal Navy, he took no part in the Battle of the Seine in 1416, when his brother Bedford relieved Harfleur. As for Shrewsbury, this battle had been fought when Henry was still very young and we know virtually nothing about his part in it. It has sometimes been assumed that the Prince 'distinguished' himself there but this seems to be based on nothing more than the severity of his wound.

Henry V went on Richard II's Irish expedition of 1399, but he was only some 13 years' old at the time, and not much older when he was given nominal command in Scotland the following year. He was Captain of

Calais from 1410, but there was no fighting there at the time and he did not participate in the French expeditions of 1411 and 1412. More relevant is his experience in Wales, against Owain Glyndwr's rebels. Mowat (1919) regarded this as his 'school of war', while Hutchison (1967) and Christopher Allmand (1992) both argued that his presence contributed to the success of the royal campaign, and that this was the foundation of his later success. In 1987 Desmond Seward wrote that 'Henry V's Welsh wars prepared him for the conquest of France. He learnt siegecraft and gunnery ... also how to control large areas of conquered territory by carefully sited small garrisons – using systematic famine and calculated conciliation to hold down the hostile population ...'.[4]

However, much of the fighting in Wales consisted of raids and siege warfare and the evidence for Henry's involvement, even in this kind of fighting, is circumstantial. T. B. Pugh (1988) thought that Henry's part in fighting the Welsh rebels had been exaggerated. He found no evidence that Henry was in Wales every summer between 1401 and 1408, as Harriss had stated in *The Practice of Kingship* (1985).[5] Likewise, Anne Curry (2005) tells us that Prince Henry's career in Wales was 'not partic- ularly successful'. She concedes that the Welsh were more formidable adversaries than anyone had expected but thinks that Henry's military experience was limited to 'small-scale inconclusive campaigns against guerrillas' and regards his failure to take Aberystwyth, at the end of the first siege in 1407, as sheer incompetence.

Perhaps we should not make too much of Henry's relative lack of expe- rience on the battlefield, prior to 1415. Historians now tell us constantly that, contrary to legend, major battles were few and far between in the Middle Ages; but, in any event, Henry would have been trained to fight as a knight when he was a boy and he had occupied important posts, in Wales, as Constable of Dover, Lord Warden of the Cinque Ports and Captain of Calais, though these may have been little more than nominal commands.

Henry was certainly popular, as were his three brothers, who became the Dukes of Clarence, Bedford and Glouecster, all of whom were closely associated with him in government and war. When he became King, the Carmelite friar Thomas Netter, wrote to his fellows suggesting that they should pray for him because

> He is ours in a very special way. He is now our king and he was in the past our own prince and our own little child – even ours from childhood. And beyond this he was ours from his grandfather and

great-grandfather; indeed he is ours by prescriptive right, always ours to the present day.[6]

This may have been royal propaganda; but, when Henry died prematurely in 1422, he was widely mourned and his death was commemorated annually in the City of London, throughout Henry VI's long reign. The Grocers' Company hired a barge each year to take them to Westminster to attend 'the late king's annual dirge and requiem'. This was an honour which Londoners had accorded to none of his predecessors.[7]

Henry V is chiefly remembered for his conquests; but when he came to the throne, the House of Commons reminded him of the need to defend the kingdom. They requested that he

> maintain good governance: in particular in the Scottish marches, and for the safeguard of the sea, and for the town and march of Calais, and for the land of Guyenne, and for the land of Ireland, and in resisting the Welsh rebels, and ending the riots and fighting in the Welsh marches, bearing in mind particularly the riot which recently took place in Cirencester.

The medieval attitude to war was different from our own. It was accepted that the first duty of the Sovereign was to defend his people and lead them into battle; and it was also accepted that there was little difference between the interests of a dynasty and those of the country at large. It was their performance as war leaders which made Edward III and Henry V the two most successful kings of the late Middle Ages; and it was partly because of their perceived desire to appease the French that Richard II and Henry VI lost their thrones.

The English did not much like foreigners, particularly the French, who were widely regarded as duplicitous, arrogant, aggressive and untrustworthy. They were thought to have broken all the treaties they had ever signed. Henry knew how his countrymen thought, and he played to the gallery. He promoted the use of English by the letters he wrote in that language. His father, grandfather and great-grandfather had all fought in France (though Henry IV's fighting had been confined to the tournament-field). These men were all warriors and they were renowned and respected as such.

Yet historians who have written about Henry V during the last hundred years have been divided in their view of him. Many have clung to the heroic tradition, including Charles Kingsford, J. H. Wylie, K. B. McFarlane, Colonel Burne and A. L. Rowse. On the other hand, Édouard Perroy considered that Henry was an unscrupulous empire-builder and 'a Prince worthy of Machiavelli's praise', while A. J. P. Taylor regarded him as 'a mere *condottiere*'. T. B. Pugh alleged that Henry behaved cruelly towards vulnerable women. Desmond Seward thought that he had 'more than a little in common with Napoleon and even Hitler'. When a group of Oxford scholars combined to produce *Henry V and The Practice of Kingship*, they showed that the King was an exceptionally able man, that he studied his brief, was an able diplomat and negotiator, worked hard at the job, cared about the routine of government, and wrote a good letter; but they declined to take sides when it came to making the value judgment.

It must be wrong to judge Henry V by modern standards. In articles in *History Today* and the *BBC History* magazine, published at the same time as his *1415, Henry V's Year of Glory*, Ian Mortimer argued that historians were 'intoxicated with the great man view of Henry V', whereas – in his view – the King was a callous and hypocritical warmonger, an autocrat and a prude. Likewise, in *BBC History* in January 2012, Tom Holland proposed Henry V as 'the most overrated character in history':

> Agincourt, a victory won by a combination of incompetence and English technological prowess, was a triumph snatched from the jaws of the disaster into which Henry had almost led his army ... For a century and a half after his death, the mirage of winning a second Agincourt continued to tantalise a succession of English kings – with unfailingly disastrous consequences ...

But was Henry unusually cruel and callous, or Machiavellian? A comparison with his contemporary, Duke John the Fearless of Burgundy, would suggest not. The main thing the Duke is famous for is his part in the assassination of his cousin Louis of Orléans in 1407, which he then sought to justify in law (though he was guilty of numerous other examples of calculated cruelty). Despite the plea of justifiable homicide, the Duke was widely condemned for the murder at the time – indeed, it helped to provoke the civil war in France.

The main act of cruelty which is laid at Henry's door is the deliberate killing of French prisoners at Agincourt; but, at the time, there was remarkably little criticism of this in either France or England, despite the obvious breach of the rules of chivalry.[8] The Chaplain expressed pity for the dead but had no doubts as to the legality of the killing: the threat posed by the prisoners had to be eliminated 'lest they should involve us in utter disaster in the fighting that would ensue' – *ne nobis in ruinam essent in venienti proelio*. In his chronicle Peter Basset explained that a French commander had rallied the enemy, to the number of 20,000(!) and was about to mount a fresh attack 'and this was the cause why so many nobles were killed'.[9]

On the other hand, there was at least one French account which aimed to aggravate the crime rather than to excuse it. Although Guillebert de Lannoy has little or nothing to tell us about the fighting at Agincourt (which he called the battle of 'Ruisseauville'), he is very eloquent when it comes to the massacre. His story is that he was wounded in the knee and head and lay with the dead until he was found by the English, then taken prisoner and held under guard, before being taken to a nearby house with ten or twelve others. Then

> When the Duke of Brabant made his attack, there was a cry that each [English]man should kill his prisoners. To do this more quickly they set the house on fire, but I was able to drag myself out and away from the flames on all fours.[10]

Historians are by no means unanimous in describing what happened as a massacre. Nicolas noted that 'this fearful measure has scarcely a parallel in modern warfare and nothing but the most urgent motives of self-preservation can prevent its being deemed an act of barbarous atrocity'; but added that 'the cause (an expected counterattack) was not questioned, even by French writers'.[11] Even Jules Michelet did not condemn Henry's conduct. He related that the fateful order was given in response to twin alarms – the attack on the English baggage train (by disloyal Burgundian brigands) and the fear that some part of the French army (Bretons and Gascons) might even now mount a counterattack. Yet in *Azincourt* (1865) René de Belleval described the killing of the prisoners as 'barbarous' and an 'indelible stain' on the King's reputation. He wrote that the English knights 'wept when they thought of the dishonour which this horrible execution deed would bring on their heads'; and he compared Henry with the Turkish Sultan Bajazet, who had deliberately beheaded a large number of French crusaders at Nicopolis. In 1892 Sir James Ramsay used the phrase 'cruel butchery'. In 1925 Hanotaux described the killing as *un incident atroce*.

The key question may be whether the French would have acted any differently, if the boot had been on the other foot. In 1919 Wylie, who thought there could be no excuse for 'cold-blooded wholesale murder' was still in no doubt that 'the French would have done the same themselves' and he is not alone in so thinking.[12] However, one piece of evidence used in support of this thesis is of dubious relevance. It is widely believed that the French unfurled the *Oriflamme* at Agincourt – the blood-red battle standard which was a sign that they would give no quarter; but, although the French standard bearer, Guillaume Martel, took the *Oriflamme* from Paris to Rouen, and was present at the battle, this does not prove that the flag was ever unfurled. Normally, this was only done when the French king was present in person, and we know that Charles VI was not at Agincourt.[13]

In March 2010, Henry V was tried for war crimes in a mock trial staged in the United States. A *Supreme Court of the Amalgamated Kingdom of England and France* ruled unanimously that the massacre was legally unjustified. Essentially they held that there was insufficient evidence of an imminent counterattack to justify the summary execution of prisoners who had become non-combatant. Essentially, their verdict was the same as Winston Churchill's, in his *History of the English-Speaking Peoples* (1956) – the killing was not a 'necessary' course of action. This is yet another case where Henry was judged according to modern notions of law and morality. The 'Supreme Court' of England and France purported to try the case according to its own understanding of the medieval laws of war; but of course it couldn't, and didn't.

We should remember the verdicts of contemporaries. The English, almost unanimously, thought that Henry V was a paragon of kingship; but even the Burgundian George de Chastellain, writing after the alliance between England and Burgundy had been terminated and after the English had been expelled from France, called him 'the prince of justice, both in himself, for the sake of example, and towards others, according to equity and right; he upheld no one through favour, nor did he allow any wrong to go unpunished out of kinship'.[14]

The Army

The English army was assembled and deployed for a specific purpose. It was held together by a series of interlocking loyalties – lordship cemented by contract, knighthood, comradeship and kinship. Several ranks of society were present, from the king down to the archers and the boys who looked after the horses. Henry's was an army where the bulk of the troops entered into written contracts (or 'indentures'), most of them signed in April 1415 and intended to last for a year.[15] In another sense, it was 'feudal', not in the strict legal sense of its being related to the system of landholding, but because most men formed part of the retinue of a lord or knight who was their social superior. The largest retinue was Henry's own. As head of the House of Lancaster, he could rely on his household and his retainers, to whom he gave livery and emblems, as well as financial reward. As monarch, he could call on the loyalty of all his subjects, but in particular on the select group constituted by the Order of the Garter, of which he was also the head. His three brothers were all Knights of this Order, as were the Earl of Arundel, the Earl of Oxford, the Earl of Warwick, Lord Camoys, Sir Thomas Beaufort, Sir Thomas Rempston, Sir Thomas Erpingham and Sir John Cornwall. Membership of the Garter 'anticipated the award of medals and decorations in later time'.[16]

In his *Wealth of Nations*, Adam Smith wrote that 'the history of all ages, it will be found, bears testimony to the irresistible superiority which a well-regulated standing army has over a militia', but noted that 'a militia of any kind ... which has served for several successive campaigns in the field, becomes in every respect a standing army'. The army of Henry V was not a standing army but it may perhaps be likened to Smith's militia.[17] Many of the knights and men at arms went from one contract to another and were virtually professional soldiers. Some of them had probably participated in the French expeditions of 1411 and 1412. In addition, the majority of the English at Agincourt had been through the siege of Harfleur and the 'march' through Normandy and Picardy. They were to that extent hardened and used to working together, whereas the French army which confronted them was a motley force, assembled late in the day.

As for the English captains, Shakespeare included parts in his play *Henry V* for Gloucester, Bedford, Exeter, Erpingham, Salisbury and Westmoreland. Henry mentions some of these in his great 'St Crispin's day speech':

> *Then shall our names,*
> *Familiar in his mouth as household words,*
> *Harry the king, Bedford and Exeter,*
> *Warwick and Talbot, Salisbury and Gloucester,*
> *Be in their flowing cups freshly remember'd.*

But, although Henry, Gloucester and Salisbury did fight at Agincourt, the others did not. The Duke of Bedford was left behind as Guardian of England; Exeter was left in charge of Harfleur when the army moved on; and the Earl of Warwick did not even indent for the Agincourt campaign, since he was in charge of Calais. As for the Talbot referred to, there was more than one man of that name whose services Henry V could call on: indeed one historian has referred to a whole 'fighting family' of Talbots. The record shows that it was Gilbert, Lord Talbot who indented for the

Agincourt expedition (with thirty men at arms and ninety mounted archers); but it is unlikely that Shakespeare intended to refer to him – and much more likely that he intended to refer to Gilbert's younger brother, Sir John Talbot, 1st Earl of Shrewsbury. This man became the most famous English general of his day, founded a dynasty which wielded enormous power in the late sixteenth century and features prominently in Shakespeare's *Henry VI*. A copy of his effigy may still be seen in the Victoria and Albert Museum and his portrait appears in a stained-glass Window of the Six Worthies in Sheffield Cathedral. Yet the inconvenient truth is that John Talbot did not participate in the Agincourt campaign at all, because he was Lord Lieutenant of Ireland between 1414 and 1419, and was kept very busy there.[18]

Shakespeare errs in other respects. According to him it is the Earl of Westmoreland who wishes that the English were more numerous at Agincourt (and thereby provokes Henry's famous speech about 'the few'):

> *O that we now had here*
> *But one ten thousand of those men in England*
> *That do no work today.*

But, in fact, Westmoreland was not at Agincourt either: he had been left in charge of the Scottish Marches. If anyone told the King to his face that the English were hopelessly outnumbered, it was Sir Walter Hungerford – at least this is what the Chaplain tells us.[19]

The reality is that the English army was divided into three parts on the 'march' from Harfleur to Agincourt: the vanguard under Sir John Cornwall and Sir Gilbert Umfraville (both experienced soldiers), the main battle group under the King and his brother Gloucester and the rearguard under the Duke of York and the Earl of Oxford. For the battle itself, the Chaplain tells us that Henry put York in command of the right wing and Camoys in charge of the left, retaining the centre for himself.

Edward, Duke of York was of royal blood, being a grandson of Edward III. Although he conspired against Henry IV after the revolution of 1399, he survived and succeeded his father as Duke in 1402. Henry V aimed to heal the divisions which his father's usurpation had created and York's title was confirmed in the Parliament held in April 1414, when he was declared 'purged and free of all suspicions'. Nevertheless it was an honour to be given the command of the right wing at Agincourt, and a sign of the lengths Henry was prepared to go to, in pursuit of his policy of reconciling the nobility to the House of Lancaster.

After the king's three brothers, York was the most senior member of the royal family at Agincourt. In addition he had previous experience as a soldier, having participated in the Duke of Clarence's French expedition of 1412, when he had indented for 1,060 men. He was one of a number of councillors who advised the king about the defence of the kingdom in 1415, when he joined Dorset, Lord Scrope and Sir Thomas Erpingham in urging the importance of defending the sea-lanes, the frontiers and the port of Calais. York had also contributed a substantial retinue to the expedition – 100 men at arms and 300 archers. In *Henry V as Warlord* (1987) Desmond Seward denigrated him by using the epithet 'the fat Duke of York' each time he mentioned him. T. B. Pugh did much the same in *Henry V and the Southampton Plot* (1988) – indeed, he painted a pathetic picture. York was now both fat and childless; but these statements are probably based on nothing more than Leland's statement in the 1540s that York led 'the vanguard of the battle ... where being much heated and thronged, being a fat man, he was smouldered to death ...'. Being child-less is hardly a disqualification for high command; and if York was fat, we do not how that his corpulence impeded his ability to fight and command. In any event, there was another tradition that the Duke was killed by a blow to the head. All we really know for certain is that he was killed at Agincourt.[20]

Lord Camoys commanded the left wing. He had previous military experience too. Born in 1350, he had served with his kinsman William, Lord Latimer when the Earl of Buckingham led the last of the great *chevauchées* in France in 1380. He was a knight banneret by 1383 and took part in Richard II's Scottish expedition of 1385, but transferred his allegiance to the Lancastrians in 1399. He served in Wales from 1400 or 1401 and with Henry (later Cardinal) Beaufort as an envoy to France in 1406. He established a connection with Prince Henry and was elected a Knight of the Garter in September 1414, on the death of Lord Roos.[21] When the Agincourt expedition was proposed in 1415, Camoys (like York) helped to plan the campaign; and he indented for around 100 men in all: one knight (Thomas Hoo), thirty men at arms or 'lances' (of whom six died or were taken ill at Harfleur) and sixty-nine archers, of whom all but ten certainly fought at Agincourt.

Camoys was probably chosen for his age and experience: he was 65 at the time of Agincourt, one of the oldest men in the field. His brass at Trotton, in West Sussex, shows him wearing a coat of mail with a skirt of steel bands (*lamelles*), his neck protected by a *gorget* or *bevor*; and there are round pieces (*rondels*) to protect the gaps between the plates at his armpits and elbow joints. Although a peer of the realm and a very experienced soldier, his armour was not old-fashioned.

Erpingham was a seasoned veteran, though he was a knight, not a duke as some French authors say. Born in 1357, he had served both the king's grandfather John of Gaunt and his father Bolingbroke (later Henry IV). He had been a soldier in France and Spain, journeyed to Prussia and the Holy Land with Bolingbroke and fought the Scots.[22] He was elected Knight of the Garter in 1401, was Constable of Dover Castle and Warden of the Cinque Ports between 1399 and 1409 and Marshal of England in 1404–05, and was a member of the Privy Council. Henry re-appointed him Steward of the Household in 1413. At Agincourt, he was in charge of the archers – perhaps the most critical position of all.[23]

The men who mustered at Southampton were overwhelmingly English. The point is worth making because the army which marched with the Black Prince in 1355 and 1356 had been an Anglo-Gascon force, but there were no Gascons with Henry in 1415. Nor is it true that the English relied on foreign 'mercenaries', Irish or otherwise, though Pierre Cochon, author of the *Chronique Normande*, written in the early 1430s, tells us that Henry was a man who

> Never slept but continually looked to his interests and made alliances and provision, as he saw fit, of young men from various lands, some Irish, all with bare feet and no shoes, dressed in scruffy doublets made out of old bedding, a poor skullcap of iron on their heads, a bow and a quiver of arrows in their hand and a sword hanging at their side ... There was also a large quantity of scum from several lands.

Dominique Paladilhe (2002) claimed that Henry had Portuguese mercenaries with him, while Christophe Gilliot (2007) refers to 200 German mercenaries whom Henry hired to look after his artillery train; but there is no evidence that foreigners were present in any significant numbers in the English army.

In Shakespeare's *Henry V*, Captains Jamy, MacMorris and 'Fluellen' – a Scotsman, an Irishman and a Welshman – have starring roles; but this was done for dramatic effect. The supposed Irish involvement was non-existent. Ireland had been slipping from the English grasp for decades and Henry V did little to reverse this. As we have seen, he appointed Sir John Talbot for a full six-year term as lieutenant there, prior to his departure for France, but he kept him short of cash. The Irish writer who compiled the Gaelic *Annals of Loch Cé* did not even mention Agincourt, though he recorded a local battle when Talbot defeated some local Gaelic chiefs, noting that the Englishman took the opportunity to 'plunder many of the poets of Erinn'.

Scotland presented a different kind of threat. The Scots were a fiercely independent kingdom, allied with the French by means of the 'Auld Alliance' and disposed to invade the North of England whenever the opportunity arose. Henry therefore had to leave forces in the Scottish marches to ensure that the Scots did not cause trouble for him at home. The main Scottish chronicler of the day Walter Bower (1385–1449) was very hostile to Henry and all his achievements.

Accordingly, there were no Irish contingents in Henry's army, and no Scots either. By contrast, the Welsh did have a hand in the English success at Agincourt; but there is a lively controversy as to how numerous they were. There is a fashion for writing about the battle as if it was a Welsh victory – see for example the late Michael Cox's children's novel *Jenkin Lloyd* (2007). But, although some Welshmen certainly distinguished themselves at Agincourt – and Daffyd ap Llewelyn, nicknamed Davy Gam, and Roger Vaughan, his son-in-law, were both killed in the fighting – the idea that the Welsh played a dominant role seems to be something of a myth.[24] Records show that the counties of Carmarthen and Cardigan provided ten men at arms, thirteen mounted archers and 327 foot archers, with the lordship of Brecon providing a further ten men at arms, thirteen mounted archers and 146 foot archers;[25] but Anne Curry (who has received hate mail for saying this) has pointed out that, if one examines the financial records, 'only as many archers were recruited in South Wales as in Lancashire', and that none were recruited in North Wales, whose loyalty was still in doubt in 1415.

In Shakespeare's version of events Fluellen claims the King as his countryman; but Henry V was scarcely Welsh, though he was born in Monmouth and Owain Tudor was one of his squires. It is a strange kind of Welsh hero who crushes the only significant Welsh rebellion of the later Middle Ages; and Henry V was personally responsible for putting Owain Glyndwr's estates at Sycarth and Glyndyfrdwy in North Wales to the torch. There is an entry in the Calendar of Patent Rolls for 20 February 1416 which is puzzling if we are inclined to think that Shakespeare's 'Fluellen' was at all representative of Welsh attitudes to the Lancastrian monarchy.

Grant to the king's brother Humphrey, Duke of Gloucester, and the heirs of his body of the castle and lordship of Llanstephan in Wales in the king's hands, on account of the rebellion and forfeiture of William Gwyn, Welshman, and the forfeiture of Henry Gwyn his son, who was killed at Agincourt in the company of the king's adversaries of France, with rents, services, fines, amercements and other profits and commodities.[26]

This shows that there was at least one Welshman who fought on the *French* side at Agincourt. How many others may there have been?

Surprisingly, there was also at least one rebel *Englishman* who fought on the wrong side! There is a fascinating passage in Tito Livio's book, concerning a man known only as Olandyne, who travelled to France to fight for the French, taking twenty other fighters with him; and in *The First English Life of Henry V* (1513) we are told

> At Southampton, [Henry] found a certain gentleman, whose name was Olandyne, in whose company were twenty men well apparelled for the war. This Olandyne of time past had given all his substance and goods to poor people for Christ's sake, and in great devotion entered a monastery of the Charterhouse, and was professed in the same; whose wife was also a professed in a house of religious women, and there continued devoutly during her life. But this Olandyne, at the instigation of the devil, enemy to all virtue, after a little time repented his profession and made suit and labour that he obtained from the Pope a dispensation to leave his religion and to reprise his former temporal estate; and in the estate of a temporal man, offered to do the King service in his war. But when the most virtuous King was informed of his life and conversation as the child of God, he refused the company of this gentleman, as an inconstant man, and a contemner of the religion of Christ; at whose refuse this Olandyne, having indignation as a man replete with pride, departed from the King and went [in]to the aid of his adversaries in France; whereafter he was slain at Agincourt, right sore fighting against the Englishmen.[27]

So far as we know, Olandyne and his retinue were wholly unrepresentative of English views, and they have been very little mentioned by English writers. They do however feature in Pierre Naudin's novel *Le Bourbier d'Azincourt*. This is an entertaining read; but it exaggerates Olandyne's importance out of all proportion. Indeed, reading Tito Livio and *The First English Life*, we may think that the whole story was fiction, designed to show how the noble Henry put religion before everything, including his own need for men.

How many Englishmen fought at Agincourt, and how many French? According to the records compiled by Thomas Rymer in *Foedera* (1704–13) Henry V's army numbered around 10,500 men when it assembled at Southampton: 2,536 men at arms, 4,128 mounted archers and 3,772 foot archers; and Anne Curry has shown that these numbers were large, in comparison with other expeditions in the fifteenth century, which rarely exceeded 2,000 men. Only the expedition of 1417 had more men – at 10,809 – and 10,500 is more than a 'happy few'. Yet, even if all the men who crossed into France had fought at Agincourt, they would scarcely have amounted to one 'division' in modern terms.

As it was, the English numbers had been much reduced by the time they reached Agincourt, especially by disease at Harfleur; and there were several deaths affecting the royal entourage. These included the Earl of Suffolk, the Bishop of Norwich, the Earl of Arundel and Sir John Phelip (described on his tomb in Kidderminster as a 'friend' of the King), while Henry's brother Thomas of Clarence fell sick and had to be sent home. It seems very likely that Sir John Fastolf of Caister in Norfolk suffered the same fate, although there is a persistent myth that he fought at Agincourt.[28]

We must also deduct a number for casualties and another for the men left in garrison at Harfleur, and add any reinforcements sent out from England in time for the battle. These figures are difficult to estimate and in the past historians often chose to follow the Chaplain's account (because he was an eye-witness) and concluded that there were around 5,000 archers and 900 knights and men at arms present at Agincourt and 60,000 French. Walsingham has 8,000 and 140,000; Basset around 9,000 and 150,000; Monstrelet, Le Fèvre and Waurin 2,000 men at arms, 13,000 archers and 50,000 French, while the Monk of St Denis wrote of 12,000 English archers (ranged in a circle around Henry V!) and 14,000 French troops. A contemporary English ballad states the number of French as 60,000. On the other hand, it is interesting that medieval French writers did not all agree. Des Ursins's history states that there were 38,000 English and only 8,000 French; Berry Herald has 1,500 knights and 15,000–16,000 archers on the English side and 10,000 men at arms on the French. Arthur of Richemont thought there were 11,000–12,000 English and 10,000 French.[29]

At the time, the English certainly thought they were outnumbered and the tradition has persisted in this country. It was set in stone by

Shakespeare, who numbered the English at 12,000 and the French at 60,000 (*Henry V*, Act IV, Scene 3). But there were foreign historians who queried the traditional picture of a vastly outnumbered English army. Before the First World War, the German historian Hans Delbrück proposed that the English numbered 9,000 men, while the French had between 4,000 and 6,000. Wylie described this hypothesis as 'purely fanciful' but it was briefly revived after the Second World War by Ferdinand Lot. Modern French historians do not agree with him. Philippe Contamine proposed 9,000 men at arms and 4,000–5,000 *gens de trait* (crossbowmen and archers) on the French side but was content with 1,000 men at arms and 5,000 archers on the English.[30] The French version of *Wikipedia* tells us that a last-minute pact agreed upon by the Orléanists and Burgundians to meet the emergency broke down, and that as a result the French could 'only' field 20,000 men!

Professor Curry has changed our way of looking at the numbers. Her study of archival sources on both sides of the Channel, including indentures, payrolls, muster rolls, ships' logs, rosters, tax records, letters of protection and post-campaign accounts, led her to conclude in *Agincourt: A New History* (2005) that the English numbered around 8,000 when they reached the battlefield. Despite the losses incurred at Harfleur, she thinks that Henry had been able to bring over substantial numbers of reinforcements. As for the French, fewer records have survived, but she concluded that there may have been only some 12,000.

Not all historians accept these figures. Clifford J. Rogers has argued that the archives are too incomplete to substantially change the traditional narrative.[31] Michael K. Jones thinks she has got the timing wrong: the French may have been unable to assemble their full strength in Rouen but there was a last-minute influx of recruits, as French enthusiasm for the war, lacking during the siege of Harfleur, grew. Many Burgundian retinues rallied to the national cause late in the day, despite the fact that the Duke of Burgundy stayed away. Indeed the French army was still mobilising on 25 October. In particular, the Duke of Brittany was still on his way, and never got closer than Amiens.

One source of confusion is the number of non-combatants who marched with each army. We are used to the idea that in a modern, mechanised army, there need to be several of these to support every fighting man; and we perhaps assume that this was not so in medieval army, but we would be wrong. Neither the English nor the French records included non-combatants, who may have included boys and servants, tradesmen of all kinds and a variety of camp followers;[32] and these may have been very numerous, especially amongst the French host, which was on home ground. This could account for the impression of very large numbers to be found, for example, in the Chaplain's account. He tells us that, just after the English had passed by the town of Péronne, they came across the tracks made by the enemy. 'We found, about a mile away, the roads quite remarkably churned up by the French army as it had crossed ahead of us many thousands strong.'

When the Chaplain first saw the French army itself, as opposed to its tracks, near the 'River of Swords', he wrote of 'the grim-looking ranks of the French ... in compact masses, battles and columns, their numbers being so great as not to be even comparable with ours ... filling a very broad field like a countless swarm of locusts'.

Likewise, John Lydgate described how Henry

went upon a hill high
And looked down to the valleys low:
He saw where the Frenchmen came hastily
As thick as ever did hail or snow.

And Pseudo-Elmham wrote of the French army as a 'huge host that could not be numbered'.

Yet the English may not have met the full strength of the French royal army. When John the Fearless, Duke of Burgundy, was asked by the Dauphin to contribute 500 men at arms and 300 archers, he sought to impose conditions, and pretended to take offence. Although he wavered, he took no personal part in the defence of the homeland and he never ordered his vassals to take up arms against the English, though he may have provided some armaments. Moreover, he ensured that his son Philip took no part.

Why would a Duke of France and a member of the royal family behave in this way? It may not indicate sympathy with the English, but it certainly demonstrated deep hostility towards the Armagnac lords who were marshalling the French army. In 1949 the French historian Joseph Calmette wrote that Duke John 'played the English card' in 1415 and left the task of confronting the English to his political opponents. In 1961 Colin McEvedy wrote that the Duke was a 'separatist' whose alliance provided Henry with 'a solid base on which Henry's military skill could build'. There is a degree of exaggeration here, since Burgundy in 1415 was at most a state in the making, and Duke John certainly did not wish to separate his Duchy from France altogether; but there is also an element of truth.[33]

The Dauphin's response to Burgundy's refusal to co-operate was to go over the Duke's head and issue a summons directly to the Burgundian vassals; and an unknown number of them did rally to the cause and fight at Agincourt. These included Duke John's younger brothers, Antoine, Duke of Brabant and Philip, Count of Nevers. The former recruited men in Brussels, Louvain and Antwerp, though only thirty-seven men who fought under Brabant can be identified by name. We also know the names of several other prominent Burgundians who fought on the French side – the Count of Vaudémont; Jacques de Créquy, Sire de Heilly; Guillebert de Lannoy; the three brothers Saveuses; Jean, Sire de Croy and his eighteen squires. Anne Curry thinks that there were 'many' who did the same, and cites at least twenty-two Burgundian captains among the dead. Yet, whatever the numbers of Burgundians who were there, the French army which went down to defeat at Agincourt was largely Armagnac, certainly in terms of its leaders, probably in terms of their followers.[34]

The French would undoubtedly have been stronger still in numbers, if Duke John had fully participated, for he could certainly have raised far more men than he was asked to do. He had on occasion raised 1,000 men as a personal bodyguard. When he entered Paris in 1405 for his mother's funeral, he arrived with 5,000. For the campaign in Picardy in 1406 he had raised 3,800 knights and squires, 1,800 crossbowmen, about 1,000 pikemen and 3,500 pioneers. For the Battle of Othée near Liège in 1408, he had mustered 1,411 from the Burgundies and 2,334 from Flanders and Artois, including 1,117 archers and arbalestriers. In 1411 he may have raised as many as 10,000 men; and in 1417 another Burgundian army was stated to number 3,600 men at arms and 2,000 bowmen.[35]

More importantly, the outcome at Agincourt could have been different if the Duke had been in command, because John the Fearless was the natural leader of the French army. He was an experienced general. He had fought the Turks at Nicopolis in 1396, where he had acquired his nickname, and demonstrated considerable skill in the civil wars in France. For that matter the French high command might have made better use of the considerable store of armaments, stored in the Duke's special arsenal in Dijon. As it was, the French high command remained divided and incompetent.[36]

Whatever the exact numbers, there is no dispute that the English had more archers, both relatively and absolutely; and the possession of this missile arm made them a formidable fighting force, given the expertise and rapidity with which the archers could pour down a hail of arrows.

The French needed some kind of answer to the longbow, if they were to prevail, and this they had failed to find.

It is worth saying too, that superior numbers were not always an advantage on a medieval battlefield. This tends to be overlooked, because the Chaplain tells us clearly that the English were intimidated by the size of the French army; and Voltaire was not alone in thinking that 'God is on the side of the big battalions'. Bernard Shaw put the same phrase in the mouth of the Count of Dunois in his play *St Joan* (1923); but none of these men was ever a fighting soldier. Vegetius and Frontinus, Roman theorists held in high esteem by late medieval writers who did know about warfare, thought that discipline and training were more important than sheer numbers. This was what had enabled civilisation to prevail over barbarism throughout the long centuries of the Roman Empire. Christine de Pisan (1365–c.1434), wrote that 'a small force which is highly trained in the conflicts of war is more apt to victory: a raw and untrained horde is always exposed to slaughter'. When he dedicated a translation of Frontinus's *Stratagems* to Charles VII, the Dean of the Faculty of Theology in the University of Paris wrote that 'He who would search through all the histories would find more battles to have been won by ruses and subtleties ... than by greater numbers ....'

Shakespeare's Henry V rejected the suggestion that he needed more men; and the Old Testament had several examples where a 'happy few' had triumphed over a numerically-superior adversary, for example in the stories of Joshua, David and Goliath, Gideon and the Amalekites and Judas Maccabeus. The Chaplain mentions the last of these stories in his account of the exchange between Henry and Walter Hungerford. He has Henry say

> Do you not believe, that the Almighty, with these His humble few, is able to overcome the opposing arrogance of the French, who boast of their great numbers and their own strength? As if to say He can if he wishes. And, as I myself believe, it was not possible, because of the true righteousness of God, for misfortune to befall a son of His with so sublime a faith, any more than befell Judas Maccabeus ...

The Chaplain's heart sank when he saw the massed ranks of the French, but this was because he had little idea of the strength which several thousand archers lent to his own side. The rapidity and accuracy of their shooting seems to have taken him by surprise as did the ability of the archers to join the *mêlée* when the time came; but these things would not have surprised Henry and his generals. Likewise, the Chaplain gives us a dismal impression generally of the state of English morale. He constantly reminds us that the English were far from home, nervous, short of supplies, hungry, tired, vastly outnumbered and afraid, but he was not a warlike man – despite fooling himself that he was part of the 'clerical militia'. There is no reason to think that either the men at arms or the archers were so timorous.

Chapter 4

Casualties and Survivors

Casualties

The French suffered far more casualties during the war between Burgundians and Armagnacs than ever they did at Agincourt. Michelet tells us that the Duke of Burgundy boasted of killing between 80,000 and 120,000 men, for the loss of between sixty and eighty knights and squires, when he crushed the city of Liège in 1408; and the harrowing of Liège was merely one episode in a civil war which lasted for over twenty years.

Yet Agincourt was still a very bloody encounter. Clifford Rogers has argued that one reason for this is the relatively lowly social status of the English archers: commoners did not command large enough ransoms to make their capture worthwhile, and they were disinclined to take prisoners themselves. Nor did they share the fellowship of arms which had become a hallmark of chivalry in preceding centuries.[1]

Historians may doubt the exact numbers of casualties (particularly on the English side) but no one has ever has ever disputed the disparity, for the French lost far larger numbers than the English. In an age when no-one argued that democracy was desirable, it was indisputable that the best of society had perished, along with the aristocracy. The names of the French dead, and of the prisoners taken by the English, occupy many pages in French chronicles. The Constable, three dukes, five counts and ninety barons all died. Among the prisoners were the Duke of Orléans (head of the Armagnacs) and Marshal Boucicaut, the most famous soldier in France. French sources give the number of the French dead as 4,000–10,000, the English as 1,500–11,000. Around 1,000 prisoners are supposed to have been killed on Henry V's orders, and between 1,500 and 1,600 taken to Calais. We know very little about the wounded, though it is said that Arthur, Count of Richemont was disfigured by facial wounds received in the battle. Interestingly, Jean Le Fèvre, who later became a King of Arms in the Duke of Burgundy's service, tells us that it was the heralds' job to count the dead and that French and English co-operated with each other in the task.

For, during the battle, all officers of arms, as much on the one side as the other, kept together; and after the battle, the French heralds went their way and the English heralds stayed with their masters, who had won the battle. As for me, I stayed with the English.[2]

John Keegan (1976) thought that some of the more lurid sights, of heaps of dead men 'higher than a man', must have been invented; but the butcher's bill was horrifying enough and the Chaplain reported that even some of the English wept at the sight. Orléans and Boucicaut were found buried under heaps of dead. Monstrelet has a story of what was found on the battlefield when the English had departed.

> Many of the French returned to the field of battle, where the bodies had been turned over more than once, some to seek for their lords and carry them to their own countries for burial, others to pillage what the English had left. King Henry's army had only taken gold, silver, rich dresses, helmets and what was of value, for which reason the greater part of the armour was untouched and on the dead bodies; but it did not long remain thus, for it was very soon stripped off, and even the shirts and all other part of their dress were carried away by the peasants of the adjoining villages. The bodies were left exposed, as naked as when they came into the world.

Writers on this side of the Channel have downplayed the number of English casualties, and French writers have exaggerated them. In a contemporary manual designed to help the English learn French, there is a dialogue where English losses are stated to have been sixteen. In Act IV, Scene 8 of Shakespeare's *Henry V* the number of the French dead is stated to be 10,000; but when Henry asks *where is the number of our English dead?*, the herald shows him another paper and announces

> *Edward the Duke of York, the Earl of Suffolk,*
> *Sir Richard Ketly, Davy Gam, esquire;*
> *None else of name; and of all other men*
> *But five and twenty*

Laurence Olivier's film version of the play increased this to 'five and twenty score' – which is 500 dead, not twenty-five. Pilham de Pilham wrote that '2,000 Englishmen met the same fate as the Duke of York' and Michelet's figure, evidently based on Monstrelet's, was 1,600. Régine Pernoud's estimate is between 400 and 500.[3] Using the lowest French estimate of their own dead would imply a ratio of nearly 9–1 in favour of the English, or over 10–1 if the prisoners are included; but on the other hand, the leading French medievalist Françoise Autrand states, without naming her authority, that the English lost 'a good 1,500 combatants'. She concludes that, although Agincourt was a clear victory for Henry, it was a costly one in terms of men and resources – not a point that has ever been made by an English historian.[4]

The fact that there were so few English casualties accounts for the small number of monuments in England which relate to the heroes of the Agincourt campaign. Apart from those of Henry V (in Westminster Abbey) and the Dukes of York and Gloucester (Fotheringhay and St Alban's), there seem to be only around a dozen. These are the tombs of Sir Lewis Robessart (Westminster Abbey), Sir John Holland (St Peter ad Vincula in the Tower of London), Michael de la Pole, Earl of Suffolk (St Andrew's, Wingfield), Sir William Phelip (St Mary's, Dennington), Richard de Vere, Earl of Oxford (St Stephen's Chapel, Bures), Sir Thomas Erpingham (Norwich Cathedral), Sir Roger Vaughan (St Andrew's, Bredwardine, William ap Thomas (St Mary's, Abergavenny) and John de Roos (St Mary's, Bottesford); and the brasses of Lord Camoys (Trotton), Sir John Bernard (St Andrew's, Isleham) and Sir Simon Felbrigg (St Margaret's, Felbrigg). Interestingly Felbrigg's brass shows him carrying a standard, which raises a controversy about the identity of the English standard bearer, just as there is about the French. In England, there are several contenders for the title: Felbrigg, Thomas Strickland, William Harrington and Lewis Robessart.[5]

It is sometimes possible to check the chronicles against medieval records; and the post-campaign account of Edward Duke of York shows that no less than ninety-three of his men were killed at the battle, along with their lord. This was a quarter of the retinue which had left Harfleur.[6] If this casualty rate was suffered by the English army as a whole, it would clearly make nonsense of the idea of an almost bloodless victory, though it is conceivable that York's retinue suffered disproportionately.

York's death was noted by all contemporary English writers, while Shakespeare also recorded the death of Michael de la Pole, 3rd Earl of Suffolk (son of the second Earl, who had died at Harfleur) in a moving scene where Suffolk and York lie wounded together on the battlefield

Suffolk first died, and York all haggled o'er
cries aloud, tarry, dear cousin Suffolk!
My soul shall keep thee company to heaven.
Tarry, sweet soul, for mine, then fly abreast

As in this glorious and well foughten field
We kept together in our chivalry.

York's bones were brought back to England and were buried in the church at Fotheringhay, where he had founded a college. The church retains its medieval splendour; but unfortunately, the tomb was wrecked during the Reformation (though a replacement was constructed in 1572). Michael de la Pole, 3rd Earl of Suffolk, was buried on the north side of the rood screen in St Mary's Church, Ewelme, in Oxfordshire, where a plain marble slab marks his grave.[7]

We know about the death of William Lovell, of Titchmarsh in Norfolk, because of a complex legal dispute which took place in later years. This is referred to in the correspondence of Sir John Fastolf with his servants Howes, Shipdam and Spirling, concerning a land-deal in East Anglia in the 1440s. On 12 January 1449 they replied to a query their master had raised about the year in which Lovell had died: 'As to the 6th article of your said letter ... we cannot say without more clear search, saving, as we understand, he was slain at the Battle of Agincourt, which was in the 3rd year of Harry V.'[8]

A more famous casualty was the Welshman David Gam, thought to be a prototype for Shakespeare's 'Fluellen'. He had remained loyal to the Crown during Glyndwr's rebellion, fighting vigorously against the rebels; but he fell at Agincourt, along with Sir Roger Vaughan of Bredwardine in Herefordshire and Sir Watkin Llwyd of Brecknock. Sir Harris Nicolas tells us that 'several' squires were made knights at Agincourt and relates a tradition that these three were dubbed *as they lay expiring on the field*.[9] It is also said that the alabaster effigy on the south side of the chancel in St Andrew's church, Bredwardine, is Vaughan's;[10] and there is another Herefordshire tradition that Sir Rowland Lenthall of Hampton Court Castle was knighted at Agincourt, though he survived the battle. But, in all cases, contemporary evidence for these tales seems to be lacking.

What of the English commoners who died? The Chaplain gives the total of English casualties as thirteen while Hardyng has ten commoners. Walsingham has twenty-eight. Tito Livio gives 100, the Pseudo-Elmham 102. It is reasonable to suppose that some English pages or boys were killed when the French raided the baggage train.[11]

Death is said to be the great leveller but, when it came to burying the French dead, the nobility were treated differently from the common herd. The Constable was buried at Hesdin. The bodies of the Dukes of Brabant, Bar, Alençon, of the Counts of Nevers, Blamont, Vaudemont and Fauquembergues, and of the Admiral of Dampierre were taken up, washed and delivered to their servants who took them back to their familial domains for burial. De Belleval also discovered the fate of some eight other prominent individuals who were buried in churches in the locality; but the commoners were treated quite differently.[12] According to Monstrelet the local graveyards were overwhelmed and it was Philippe Count of Charolais who then took responsibility, setting gravediggers to work near Tramecourt wood.

> They measured out a square of twenty-five yards, wherein were dug three trenches twelve feet wide, in which were buried, by an account kept, 5,800 men. It was not known how many had been carried away by their friends, nor what number of the wounded had died in hospitals, town, villages. And even in the adjacent woods; but ... it must have been very great.

Survivors

Henry V wanted to reward those who had served him at Agincourt. The highest honour which could be bestowed on a knight was election to the Order of the Garter, of which the King was *ex officio* President. The Dukes of York and Gloucester, Sir Thomas Erpingham and Sir John Cornwall were already Knights of the Order; but the following were elected for service in France, from 1415 onwards: the Earl of Oxford and the Earl of Huntingdon (1415), Lord Willoughby de Eresby (1416), John Blount (1417), Sir William Phelip and Hugh Stafford, Lord Bourchier (1418), John Grey (1419), Sir Walter Hungerford (1420), Lord Clifford, Sir Hartung von Clux, John Mowbray (Earl Marshal) and William de la Pole (later Duke of Suffolk) (1421). The Agincourt Roll confirms that many of these men fought at Agincourt, though Eresby, Stafford, Clifford, von Clux, Mowbray and de la Pole did not – Mowbray being amongst those who were invalided home from Harfleur. Sir Lewis Robessart, who was amongst those made a Knight of the Garter in 1421, also obtained the ultimate honour of a burial in Westminster Abbey, after he was killed in action in 1431.[13]

Other honours were bestowed. Sir John Holland, who distinguished himself on the battlefield, was not only made a Knight of the Garter, but also had his father's title of Earl of Huntingdon restored to him in 1416. Sir John Popham, who was the son of the Constable of Southampton and a man-at-arms with the Duke of York, was knighted as a result of services during the campaign, and went on to hold high office in England and

France, becoming lord of Torigny in Normandy. Sir Thomas Rempston acquired land in the *bailliages* of Caen, Cotentin and Alençon. Sir John de Assheton held the offices of Seneschal of Bayeux in 1417 and *bailli* of the Cotentin in 1418.[14] Sir John Grey, who was made a Knight of the Garter, was later made Captain of Mortagne and created Count of Tancarville, as well as being given property in England. Sir John Fastolf, who was invalided home from Harfleur but returned to defend the town against the French attempt to re-take it in the winter of 1415–16, became Baron of Sillé-le-Guillaume, in Maine.[15]

It is also known that the Duke of Gloucester obtained a grant of the manor of Lanstephan in Wales; Sir William Phelip (who fought at Agincourt though his brother John had died at Harfleur) went on to become a powerful courtier and a man of influence throughout East Anglia; Sir William Porter received the manors of Wadele and Wickingham in Berkshire; Sir William Bourchier, a beneficiary under the will which Henry V made in July 1415 (when he was promised one of the King's best horses) was made Constable of the Tower, with special responsibility for keeping French captives, and eventually Count of Eu in Normandy. In some cases, it is difficult to know whether a man's wealth derived from his being at Agincourt, or the service he subsequently rendered. For example, Ralph Cromwell, 3rd Baron Cromwell, was undoubtedly at Agincourt, when he was only 22. He went on to become Treasurer of England between 1433 and 1443, and to build Wingfield Manor in Derbyshire and the magnificent Tattershall Castle in Lincolnshire, so memorably restored by Lord Curzon between 1911 and 1914.[16]

Nicolas has a list of seven relatively humble men who were knighted at Agincourt: John Feries, Ranolde Graystoke, Peter Tempest, Xroter (Christopher?) Morisby, Thomas Pekeringe, William Hodelston and John Hosbalton; and indeed it was once thought that every man who fought at Agincourt was allowed to bear a coat of arms thereafter. Nicolas pointed out long ago that this was a 'common error', possibly deriving from some words which Shakespeare put in the mouth of Henry V:

For he today that sheds his blood with me,
Shall be my brother: be he ne'er so vile
This day shall gentle his condition.

The 'common error' was also based on a misunderstanding of the terms of the order issued by Henry prior to his second expedition to Normandy, when he tried to restrict the number of men bearing a coat of arms, to those who could show a right to do so by ancestry or express grant, but exempted 'those who bore arms with us at the Battle of Agincourt' from the effects of this new rule. However, this was surely intended to mean that anyone who had borne a *coat of arms* in 1415 should not have to prove their right to do so again, in 1417. It cannot have been intended to confer the right to wear a coat of arms on the mere basis that a man had taken part *in the fighting*. That would have conferred an honour on every 'common' archer, something which was scarcely within the contemplation of any Plantagenet king.[17]

Agincourt did not lead immediately to a major re-distribution of land in France. The only territorial gain from the campaign of 1415 was the port of Harfleur (since Calais was already in English hands); but on the other hand, there is evidence that some soldiers who fought at Agincourt did eventually settle in Normandy. Two of the settlers in Rouen had certainly been at Agincourt. The name Thomas Halliday appears twice in the records in 1415 – once in the service of Sir William Cromwell and once as a minstrel attached to the royal household. Then in 1434 he appears as a *bourgeois* of Rouen, when he buys a tenement in the parish of Saint-Vincent for 50 *saluts d'or* from the *bailli* Sir John Salvain, while in the early 1440s he is *vicomte* of Pont-Authou and Pont-Audemer.[18] It would be surprising if there were not also cases of Englishmen who fought at Agincourt and stayed on as settlers in Caen, the 'second capital' of Normandy.

Another little-known survivor of Agincourt was Sir Bertram Entwistle, a knight from Lancashire, born in 1396 and therefore 19 at the time of the battle. He was knighted in Agincourt year. His master was William de la Pole, Earl and later Duke of Suffolk. When Suffolk was captured at Jargeaux in 1429 Entwistle acted for him in relation to the ransom and bought the lordship of Briquebec in the Cotentin; and he is said to have become both Viscount of Briquebec and Lord of Hambye. In 1437 he married the daughter of another English settler, who was then *bailli* of the Cotentin and subsequently became *bailli* himself. He was expelled along with the rest of the English in 1450 and killed at the Battle of St Albans in 1455, the first skirmish in the so-called 'Wars of the Roses'.[19]

As for wages, in March 1416 the King ordered that the first 'quarter' (of financial year 1415) should be reckoned from 8 July, and payment be made in respect of those who had died at Harfleur, as well as to those who had been permitted to return to England after the siege of the port. In addition, those killed at Agincourt – or rather their next of kin – should be paid at the same rate as those who had survived. In the Acts of the Privy Council for 1417, there is the following order:

> And with regard to the second quarter [of the financial year] the King wishes that those who died at the battle of Agincourt, as with those who came with him to Calais, should be allowed their wages and the regard mentioned, from the beginning of the said second quarter until eight days after the arrival of the King in the port of Dover.[20]

The 'regard' was a customary supplementary payment but there might be other types of 'bonus' payable. In Tudor times, Holinshed wrote that John Bromley, who had recovered the battle standard of Guienne after it had been captured during a French raid, made on the English army at Corbie on the Somme in 1415, was given an annuity of £40 per annum for life two years later, as well as being allowed to bear the standard as a crest on his coat of arms. However, Curry points out that there is no evidence in the relevant pay records that Bromley even took part in the Agincourt campaign, and the story may have been invented to enhance his descendants' claim to fame.[21]

Not everyone who served at Agincourt was able to capitalise on the experience. Sir Thomas Chaworth, who was already an M.P. for Nottinghamshire, had thrown in his lot with his fellow M.P., Sir John Oldcastle's Lollard rising in 1414, and been imprisoned in the Tower. He was lucky to escape with his life, and doubtless hoped that he would redeem himself in the King's eyes by indenting to serve with a retinue of eight men at arms and twenty-four archers; but it seems that he never quite recovered the position of trust he had once enjoyed. Similarly, some men had to wait many years for their wages: Thomas Strickland remained unpaid until 1424. Henry Inglose charged John Tiptoft in the Court of Chivalry with refusing to pay arrears of wages.[22]

There is also a petition to Henry V's successor from an old soldier named Thomas Hostell, who tells the king that at the siege of Harfleur he was

> smitten with a springbolt through the head, losing his one eye, and his cheek bone broken. Also at the Battle of Agincourt and after the taking of the carracks on the sea[23] there with a gad of iron his plates smitten asunder and sore hurt, maimed and wounded, by means whereof he being sore feebled and debruised, now fallen to great age and poverty, greatly indebted, and may not help himself.

It is not recorded whether Hostell received the arrears he claimed.[24]

The most important profit of war was a ransom, especially if it related to a member of the nobility. There are English indentures of war, relating to the Agincourt expedition, which provide for the division of ransoms to be taken and refer to the possibility that the French king himself, 'the Adversary of France' might be taken – clearly not an unforeseeable event, in view of the Black Prince's capture of Jean II at Poitiers in 1356, and one which is provided for in other indentures. Moreover, despite all the tales of massacre, large numbers of Frenchmen did survive to be taken prisoner. Indeed Michelet wrote that 'a whole French colony was transported to England ... one might have advised a man wanting to see France, to go to London'. Yet simple economics must have dictated that only the more important men were brought back to England. In the main these were the noblemen, though it has been said that some more ordinary Frenchmen also 'found their way as menials into the service of the great houses and abbeys of England'.[25]

Nicolas printed a list of those Englishmen who became entitled to the ransoms of French prisoners, and whose names appear in the Norman Rolls between 1415 and 1430. Sir Walter Hungerford is listed as being entitled to the ransoms of five men.[26] De Belleval's work contains a list of dozens of prisoners. Sir John Cornwall was given the ransom of Peter de Reux, Marshal of France and eventually acquired the ransom of Louis de Bourbon, Count of Vendôme. Indeed, the *Oxford Dictionary of National Biography* credits him with being a leading exponent of 'ransom brokerage'. Sir Gilbert Umfraville was granted a valuable wardship and subsequently became captain of Caen, Pontoise, Eu and Melun; and Sir Roland Lenthall was rewarded with the wardship of the son and heir of Sir John Mortimer.

Yet there were clearly some cases where the English gained little or no financial advantage. Marshal Boucicaut (who had been captured by the Turks in 1396 and captured again at Agincourt) died in captivity in England. The Count of Richemont was released in 1420 when he helped to persuade his brother to sign the Treaty of Troyes. The Count of Eu was released in 1438 when he was exchanged for the Earl of Somerset. The most famous prisoner of all, Charles, Duke of Orléans, was released unconditionally in 1440.

Where ransoms were collected, the amounts varied greatly. Geoffrey du Puy paid a mere 2,120 *écus* for his release. Aléaume de Boufflers's ransom was fixed at 5,000 *livres*: he was allowed to return to France to raise the money, leaving his English host with a sacred relic as security. The *Sire* of Ligne en Hainaut was given a safe-conduct, so that he could go to France to arrange his ransom of 14,400 *écus*: we presume that was done. Guy Quiéret obtained his release upon payment of a sum which we are only told was 'large' (*forte*). The same thing happened in the case of the *Seigneur* of Roye. Pierre de Boylesve raised his ransom and was released in 1431, but again we are not told the amount. Before his death in 1430, the Duke of Bourbon's ransom had been fixed at 60,000 gold *écus*, and two instalments were paid in 1421 and 1423, but Henry V had subsequently tried to raise the ransom to 80,000.

There was litigation in England about the ransoms of French prisoners taken at Agincourt. At some date between 1415 and 1417 two common soldiers (John Craven and Simon Irby) brought proceedings in the Chancery Court at Westminster. They alleged that they had taken prisoners (at a place which the clerk recorded as 'Achyngcourt'); but that a third man, a squire named William Buckden, had somehow or other taken these and released them, thereby depriving them of their profit, and the King of his rightful share of it. They further alleged that part of that money, amounting to about 200 marks, was now in the hands of the wife of the Treasurer of Calais, Maude Salvayn.

This case may mark a stage in the development of the law, because at this point the claimants asked for an unusual remedy, which could not have been granted at common law, but could be granted by the Lord Chancellor's new 'Equity'.[27] They asked for an interim injunction, restraining Maude Salvayn from parting with the money in her hands, until the rightful ownership of the disputed ransoms should be properly determined. They also asked that the defendant Buckden be required to state the names of the prisoners he had released. Although the outcome is unknown, these proceedings are very revealing. The reference to Calais seems to confirm Wylie's view that many of the prisoners were sold and released there, before the army of Agincourt came home to England. It is also interesting that the third party in the case was a woman. Indeed we know that Roger Salvayn, Treasurer of Calais between 1415 and 1419, made a practice of delegating routine business to his wife, and that it was she who presented his accounts for audit after his death.[28]

Some French prisoners remained in the hands of private individuals, but some passed into the hands of the King; and Henry V aimed to win diplomatic advantage from this, as Edward III had done from the capture of Jean II. According to Michelet, Henry V often spoke to the prisoners when he was in England, particularly Orléans and Bourbon, and attempted to put pressure on them; and it was Henry's dying wish that Orléans should not be released, at least until Henry VI came of age. However, no diplomatic advantage was ever obtained. In January 1417, an agreement was reached at Pontefract that the Duke of Bourbon and the Lord of Gaucourt (taken prisoner at Harfleur but imprisoned in the Tower of London in 1417) should be released on parole and sent to France in connection with the peace negotiations then current; Orléans and Boucicaut were privy to this agreement and agreed to stand as sureties for their fellow prisoners; but these negotiations likewise came to nothing. In 1418, when Henry seriously contemplated making peace with the Dauphin, he again referred to the possibility of ransoming Orléans and the other prisoners, but the item was placed well down the agenda.[29] Orléans was used again on two separate occasions in the 1430s, but again the negotiations bore no fruit.[30]

Writing almost 400 years after the event, Pilham de Pilham wrote that his hero, Marshal Boucicaut, had suffered much.

> There was much to be endured, whether from the wounds he received, from the long duration of his imprisonment, and finally from the ill-treatment which he received at the hands of a nation which was a natural enemy of France, and which showed almost no pity to the prisoners it held.

More recently (2002) Dominique Paladilhe wrote of the 'long and harsh captivity' endured by French prisoners. Yet the royal houses of England and France were closely related: the Duke of Orléans's first wife was Isabella of Valois, former queen of Richard II. It was hardly likely that aristocrats like these would treat other harshly during their so-called 'imprisonment'; and in the view of his biographer Pierre Champion, Orléans *knew neither chains, nor straw nor dungeon, but rather the respect due to a prince of the blood.*

When the French prisoners were first brought to England, many were initially accommodated in and around London and there is a writ (first printed in Rymer's *Foedera*) for the provision of

> beds, curtains, blankets, coverlets, mattresses, and other 'necessaries' against the arrival of the Dukes of Orléans and Bourbon and the lords knights and esquires of France, being prisoners of the King, at Eltham, the Tower of London, Westminster, Windsor and other places.

No sign here of rough treatment. On the contrary, the places mentioned were royal palaces. Eltham was a moated manor-house, much frequented by the medieval English kings, and literally fit for a king. Henry V himself stayed there, on the night before he entered London to celebrate his victory.

Eventually, the noble prisoners were 'farmed out' around the country. Security was a concern, but so was comfort.[31] The French Rolls printed in 1883 are replete with references to safe conducts, granted to the servants of the prisoners and giving them leave to leave England, travel to France and come back again, as well as to bring a whole variety of items with them. The Duke of Orléans was able to continue to manage his library throughout his long captivity. The English reputation for hospitality does not seem to have suffered: indeed the opposite is the case. There is a story about some French merchants who were unfortunate enough to be captured three times in 1417, by the English, the Burgundians and the Armagnacs. They reported that the Burgundians – who were after all their own countrymen – treated them worse than the English, while the Armagnacs treated them worse than the Saracens would have done.[32]

There were stories about 'escapes', but the word is something of a misnomer, since the noble prisoners taken at Agincourt were not usually confined in anything which resembled a prison. The understanding was that the prisoner was spared his life when originally captured, on condition that he remained in the custody of his captor, unless and until a ransom was arranged. In a chivalric society 'jailer' and 'prisoner' operated on the basis of trust, in a way which is inconceivable now. All a 'prisoner' had to do to 'escape' was break his word of honour and decamp (as Prince Louis of France had done in the early 1360s, much to his father's disgust).

However, an escape makes for a good story. So, it is said that Jacques de Créquy, Sire de Heilly, was captured twice and escaped twice. The first occasion was in 1402, when he was captured by the Percys while in command of a French force in Scotland. The second was in 1413 when he was captured by Thomas Beaufort, Earl of Dorset, in Aquitaine. He was then imprisoned in Wisbech Castle but escaped again, when he heard of the fall of Harfleur in 1415. Evidently he did this just in time to make his way home and re-appear as one of the French heralds who approached Henry V for a parlay before the battle at Azincourt.[33]

The story is also told in France that the Count of Vendôme, captured at Agincourt by Sir John Cornwall, 'escaped' from the Tower of London in the 1420s. On his return home to Vendôme on the River Loir, he is said to have founded a procession to commemorate his deliverance; and supposedly the ceremony was observed as late as the eighteenth century, when local people celebrated their lord's escape every year, by releasing a common criminal who had been condemned to death. Can the legend be verified? Certainly, de Belleval stated that Vendôme escaped, that the ransom demanded for him was excessively large and that the Count 'miraculously' decamped to France when he had only paid 54,000.[34]

This is an attractive story but, unfortunately for those who tell it, detailed records survive. These show that in 1417 the King assigned (or re-assigned) the Count to Sir John Cornwall. His ransom was fixed at 46,665 gold crowns (valued at 11,665 English marks, or £7,776 13s 4d). However, the Count then became entitled to the ransom of John Holland, Earl of Huntingdon, when the latter was captured at Baugé in 1421. At this point Vendôme suggested that he should be released in exchange for Huntingdon; and a deal was done, whereby Sir John Cornwall agreed to abate the Count's ransom, and two other French prisoners were also released. All of which makes an escape improbable.[35]

'Abscond' would be a better word than 'escape', to describe the circumstances in which the Count of Richemont returned to his home in Brittany when he learned in 1422 that Henry V had died. It is said that he considered that the King's death released him from the obligation to remain in England, though this was certainly not the law; but, once more, the records (kept in this case at the Tower of London) contain no reference to any such escape.[36]

There is a tradition that the Duke of Bourbon was held for nineteen years (between 1415 and 1434) in Melbourne Castle in Derbyshire, one of the castles which belonged to the Duchy of Lancaster.[37] Barker tells us he was released on parole but, unable to negotiate an acceptable ransom he returned to England, and died at Bolingbroke in Lincolnshire in 1434, after fathering an illegitimate daughter. He was buried in the Greyfriars church in London. In 1451 the king's squire, and usher of the chamber, Robert Whittington was given permission to exhume the body and return it to 'such places of France or Normandy as shall be desired by the Duke's son and heir, by such persons, English or French, as seem good to him'. This was a year after the loss of English Normandy, when anti-French feeling might have been expected to be at its height. Yet the Duke of Bourbon is not the only French nobleman whose body was returned to France. Harrison's records of the Tower of London contain the information that when Marshal Boucicaut died in captivity in 1421, his remains were conveyed to France for burial in the church of St Martin of Tours.[38]

The French archives contain some stories about enemy survivors. In 1417 Charles VI pardoned a squire called Colin de Sales, who was imprisoned in the *Châtelet* in Paris. He was now 18 and the son of a knight from the Beaujolais region. He had been arrested as a 'cutpurse' and convicted of stealing a silver necklace, purses, pendants and belts. The pardon explained why he had turned to a life of crime:

> This Colin had served us, with one of his brothers, under the command of our very dear and well-beloved Duke of Bourbon, at the battle fought in Picardy, when we encountered our enemies and adversaries of England, in which battle, the brother of the aforesaid petitioner had been killed, though the petitioner escaped unhurt. And, being returned to Paris, with his brother's belongings, which were worth perhaps £600, he lived on some part of this, but had been robbed of the other part. And after this, seeing that he was young but that he had no means of support, it was through inexperience and the temptation of the Devil [*ennemi*] that he stole.[39]

It comes as a shock to realise that a medieval government was prepared to treat involvement in a battle as a mitigating circumstance for crime; and likewise to find the authorities providing financial support to the relatives of those killed in battle; but, in the accounts of the French Receiver General, there are two such payments. The second was to

> Perrette, widow of Georges de Saint-Sariol, who was *échanson*[40] to the king, for his military service at the voyage of Blangis,[41] in which he lost his life, leaving his wife with four little children, one of whom bears the name of the King, and for the sake of God and as alms, so that she may be better able to deal with her late husband's creditors.

Perhaps the government had mixed motives here? These payments were made in 1418, when the Duke of Burgundy had regained control of Paris. It may have been a question of rewarding the Burgundian faction, rather than loyal Frenchmen and women as a whole. The family in question had been evicted from their home by the Armagnacs, and one member had subsequently been taken prisoner and ransomed by them.[42]

Amongst the pardons granted by Charles VI was another addressed to a servant named Jean Chevreau, who was 28 and originally came from Gien on the Loire. Jean had served a squire named Pierre des Essars, who lived (with his wife) in the region near Chartres; and both men had fought at Agincourt. The squire was captured and taken to England, but the servant escaped. The pardon tells of a crime committed by Jean Chevreau after he had returned home, and became incensed by the activities of a fraudster. The villain was going around, taking advantage of the relatives of the prisoners taken at Agincourt, by selling them what purported to be news of their nearest and dearest. When Chevreau learned what was going on, he decided to take the law into his own hands.

> Whereas a battle was lately fought in our territory of Picardy by our relatives and vassals, when they met with our adversary of England, at which battle Jean Chevreau was present with Pierre des Essars, esquire (whose servant the said Jean Chevreau was and is);[43] and whereas the said Pierre was taken prisoner there by our adversary of England or his people. And this Jean Chevreau, who had been with him as his valet and had looked after his horses, returned to the placed called Séchereville, near the town of Gallardon, where Pierre and his wife have their home; and the said Chevreau has been their servant for the space of three or four years. And whereas this Jean Chevreau had occasion to go into the town of Gué-de-Longroi, to have one of his master's horses shod; and there came upon a common fellow, who was passing through that country, sometimes claiming to be a priest, at other times a knight and, at other times again, to belong to some other class of men; and Chevreau had seen him before in the town of Gallardon. Wherever he went, he took with him a young woman, who was in the habit of frolicking with the other fellows who travelled with him. This fellow claimed to have a roll containing the names of all the French prisoners, and he claimed that he had information about them. At the time, the man was staying in a tavern in the town of Gué-de-Longroi, keeping company with Jean Legendre, Simon Berbion, Jean Plessis and two other young women.

Chevreau was suspicious; and he decided to expose and punish the villain.

> Jean Chevreau spoke to this fellow and asked him if he had any news of Pierre des Essars, his master; but the fellow had no true information about him. For this reason, Chevreau and certain other men from the same region, seeing that the fellow was simply a charlatan, who put on an act to part people from their money, as he had in fact already done with several poor gentlewomen and other folk in the area, whose husbands and relatives had been at the battle; which was a great pity and shame, in view of the widespread loss and grief this had caused. And so, they all became very angry and indignant about what had happened on the day of the battle; and especially Jean Chevreau, about the capture of the said Pierre des Essarts, his master, so much so that, soon after midnight, he and some of the other local men, made their way to a place called Viée, about a league and a half from

Gallardon, with the intention of waylaying the villain. This was where the fellow was staying, in lodgings which belonged to some poor man who lived there. The place was also the home of the poor man's wife, who had slept with some of the gang, of her own free will.

Jean and his makeshift posse found Viée and entered the right house in the middle of the night:

When the fellow came down the stairs from his room, which was above, he was accompanied by two young men in holy orders; but Jean Chevreau came up behind him. He drew his sword and put it against the fellow's chest, telling him that if he made one false move, he would kill him. Then he and the others led the fellow into a small wood, where they stripped him of the coat of mail he was wearing and made him promise that he would not inform on them; but otherwise they did not harm him in any way. At this point they left him, taking the coat of mail with them. This was probably worth around 10 francs, though Jean Chevreau only received an advance of 10 *sous* of Paris for his share.

The 'victim' of this robbery must have broken his promise to keep quiet, since Jean Chevreau was arrested and thrown into jail at Chartres for his part in the affair; but his relatives and friends interceded for him; and he was pardoned in August 1416. The authorities were clearly sympathetic towards Jean, although he had taken the law into his own hands, because he had after all punished someone who was 'cashing in' on a great tragedy which had befallen the French nation.[44]

The chroniclers did not record that any Englishmen were taken prisoner at Agincourt; but there may have been some. Pierre Champion has an intriguing footnote about an English prisoner who was kept chained up in the prison at Beauvais, and knew only five words of French, which meant *God and our Lady help me*! Wylie also wrote of seven Lancashire archers captured on the march to Azincourt. These men were in the retinue of Sir Richard Kyghley and were captured on the day before the battle, as they crossed the river at Blangy. When Raoul de Gaucourt attempted to negotiate his release with Henry, the King referred to the need to secure the release of 'seven or eight score' of his servants and subjects who 'were being very harshly treated as prisoners in France' (though it is not certain that these men were taken at Agincourt).[45]

that he was on our side – notably at Crécy (1346), Poitiers (1356), Agincourt (1415) and Verneuil (1424). The defeats more recently suffered are the work of the Devil, or else of incompetency and treachery. It may seem now, in the late fifteenth century, as if God has deserted us, but the setbacks in Normandy and Aquitaine are merely temporary and the day can still be saved, if only the English are true to themselves. The French will always be our enemies, so there is no point in negotiating with them. The foolish policy of appeasement, eagerly pursued in the 1440s, has inevitably and utterly failed. The only answer left is to launch a further strike.[2]

If these attitudes seem insular and xenophobic today, they were the conventional wisdom at the time, actively supported by the Church in England. Henry V was a devout and orthodox Christian, equally famous for prosecuting and persecuting heresy as he was for foreign conquests. In one letter of 28 July 1415 he refers to Lot and Abraham, beseeches his enemy to do him justice 'in the merciful bowels of Jesus Christ' and cites the Law of Deuteronomy, which prevents a king from waging aggressive war unless he offers peace first. When Henry founded two religious houses in 1414, the second of them was named 'Syon' because it was a vision of peace chosen by 'a true son of the God of peace, who gave peace and taught peace and chose St Bridget as a lover of peace and tranquillity'.[3]

Henry may not have realised the size of the task he was taking on. Jean Froissart, who died in 1400, wrote of a conversation he had with the Count of St Pol, who had once been a hostage in England. The Count said

> that England was only a little country by comparison with France, for he had ridden the length and breadth of it several times and had given much thought to its resources. Of the four or five regions into which one could divide the kingdom of France the poorest would offer more revenue, more towns and cities, more knights and squires than the whole of England. He was amazed at how they had ever mustered the strength to achieve the conquests they had.

The Count clearly knew his geography but not every Englishman did. In 1417 Thomas Polton, who headed the English delegation at the Council of Constance, made some startlingly inaccurate remarks.

> From the North to the South of England, she extends over 800 miles, or forty days' journey. By common report France is not so big. The English nation comprises eight kingdoms, that is to say England,

Chapter 5

Who Started It?

Inherited Rights

The English started to apologise for the Hundred Years War at an early date. In 1830 an English lady who happened to find herself in Boulogne approached the Abbé Haffreingnes, saying that she wanted to do what she could to expiate the sins of her ancestors, and gave him 25 francs towards a new cathedral. In 1996 Desmond Seward concluded that 'England did France a great wrong'; but it is curious that we (or some of us) have come to feel guilty about Henry V, when the French still feel proud of Napoleon, the Greeks of Alexander the Great and the Mongols of Genghis Khan.

Who started it? At first sight the answer is obvious: it was Henry V, when he invaded Normandy. However, there was no peace treaty in place in 1415, only an uneasy truce which had repeatedly broken down during his father's reign. The Scots had invaded England in 1402, the French had invaded Gascony in 1406 and there had been incessant seizures, raids and reprisals in the English Channel, the result of piracy and privateering. When Henry V came to the throne in 1413 both sides thought there was unfinished business.

Henry's determination to pursue his ancestral rights, if necessary by force of arms, was entirely typical of the English nobility's attitude to property in general. The King's view of the situation was put to the Sheriff of Southampton in an order of May 27 1415, when he required the inhabitants to make ready for his arrival: 'The sheriff is aware that the king is shortly sailing to foreign parts in order to recover the heritage and rights of the Crown, long wrongfully withheld.'[1]

In William Worcester's *Boke of Noblesse*, first written in the 1450s and re-written for Edward IV in the 1470s, the author blames the French for starting the Long War, in Edward III's time, when they confiscated the English King's Duchy of Aquitaine; and, in his view, they were also responsible for prolonging it, by refusing to accept God's verdicts in battle. They repeatedly went back on promises made in solemn treaties, particularly in 1360 and 1420. Fortunately, God has repeatedly shown

Scotland, Wales, Ireland and four others, and the Orkneys, where there are sixty islands, whose size surpasses that of the kingdom of France. England has 32 counties and 52,000 parish churches, without counting cathedrals, collegiate foundations, priories and hospitals, whereas in the whole of France there are no more than 6,000 parish churches and only four or five counties.[4]

It is not easy to know what Henry's objectives were in 1415. Was he interested in conquering Normandy only, in setting up a claim to a greater Aquitaine, or in laying claim to the French throne? Did he even see these as alternatives? Between 1415, when he invaded the Duchy and 1420 when he was recognised as heir to the French kingdom, Henry promoted the idea that he had come to re-claim Normandy;[5] but equally important was his claim to the Duchy of Aquitaine, known in England as 'Guienne' or 'Gascony', though the two were originally distinct. While he was at Titchfield Abbey in 1415, Henry asked to see copies of the treaties made by his father Henry IV with the French, relating to Aquitaine. At Winchester in June Henry told the French embassy that, if he was not given the hand of Princess Katherine, the Duchies of Aquitaine, Normandy, Anjou and Touraine, together with the counties of Poitou, Maine and Ponthieu 'and all other places which once belonged to his predecessors by right of inheritance', he would make war, with all his power. This was more than Edward III had won at Brétigny in 1360, or even demanded. In fact, as Lydgate realised, Henry was asserting his right to all that Edward I (1272–1307) had laid claim to.

Our king sent into France full wrath,
His Herald that was good and sure.
He desired his heritage for to have:
That is Gascony and Guienne and Normandy.
He bade the Dolphin [Dauphin] deliver. It should be his:
All that belonged to the first EDWARD
'And if he say me, Nay! iwis
I will get it with dint of sword!'

Shakespeare's audience would have rapidly concluded that the most important point in dispute was the claim to the French throne; and there is some evidence of this – notably in the strong language used by Henry in his letters to Charles VI of 7 and 15 April 1415. Henry refers there to 'rights belonging to us and our Crown for so long a time that we could say it is entire ages since we have been deprived of them'. At the same time he asks for something new – the hand of the Princess Katherine in marriage; and he talks of bringing about the union of the two kingdoms in his own person.

In the early fifteenth century, France posed a potentially lethal threat, not only to the English possessions in France but to England itself. Whatever the English thought, she was a much larger and potentially more powerful country, in terms of area, population and wealth. Successive French kings had done their best to extinguish English rule in France altogether. Philip IV, Charles IV and Philip VI had all exploited their position as overlord of Gascony, legally and militarily. They allowed legal appeals from the Duchy of Aquitaine to be heard in the *Parlement* of Paris; and in 1293, 1324 and 1337 they summoned the English king to appear before them. When he refused, they confiscated his Duchy and enforced this by military action. It is also important to recall that, although English successes on the battlefields of the Hundred Years War are often remembered, the French were extremely successful in the late 1360s and early 1370s, when the armies of Charles V (1364–80) re-conquered most of English Aquitaine, and did so very rapidly. Looking at the medieval period as a whole, the French can easily be portrayed, not merely as the dominant power in Western Europe, but as the most aggressive nation. It is for this reason that at least one historian has argued that 'in certain respects the English could be regarded as fighting a defensive war' in 1415.[6]

In the early fifteenth century the French presented a threat to England itself. They refused to recognise Henry IV as a legitimate sovereign and they were more than ready to fish in the troubled waters of his reign. They habitually allied with the Scots. They launched an undeclared and covert naval war against English shipping in the Channel in 1402, following this up with attacks on the Channel Islands, Plymouth and the Isle of Wight.[7] In 1405 they allied with Glyndwr in Wales and the Castilians in Spain and a Franco-Welsh army advanced as far as Worcester, while the Spaniards used galleys to raid and burn all the way from Cornwall to Southampton, before taking refuge in Harfleur for the winter. Don Pero Nino's standard-bearer tells us that Spanish galleys sailed into the North Sea in 1406, making an (unsuccessful) attempt to raid East Anglia, engaging in battle with an English fleet in the Channel and using a fire-ship to destroy English shipping.[8]

By 1413 the English Crown was labouring under an enormous burden of debt, by reason of the expenditure required to maintain hundreds of castles in England, the marches of Scotland, Wales and Ireland, and especially in the Pale of Calais. This alone absorbed a third of ordinary revenue. When Henry V came to the throne, his first Parliament reminded him of the need to defend the kingdom, though he scarcely needing reminding. It may well be that he concluded, as Edward III had done, that the best means of defence was attack.[9]

The Domestic Agenda

In Shakespeare's *Henry IV Part II* the King – who knows that his life is drawing to a close – advises Prince Hal on how to govern the English kingdom. He tells his son that his own reign has been a troubled one and predicts that his son's will be more tranquil, but thinks there is a price to pay.

> *How troublesome it [the Crown] sat upon my head*
> *To thee it shall descend with bitter quiet.*

Henry advises Hal to involve the English nobility in a foreign war (any will do, evidently) in order to prevent their causing trouble at home.

> *Therefore, my Harry*
> *Be it thy course to busy giddy minds*
> *With foreign quarrels, that action, hence borne out,*
> *May waste the memory of the former days.*

Some historians have considered that Shakespeare was fundamentally right here, and that one of Henry V's motives for launching the invasion of France in 1415 was to promote domestic harmony, particularly amongst the nobility. This is a view which has also commended itself to some scholars of English literature, who draw conclusions from a deep study of Shakespeare and a superficial study of history. Cedric Watts (2000), basing himself on Labarge's study of Henry V, concluded that 'Henry V did not have a legitimate claim to the throne of England, let alone to that of France'.[10] As the son of a usurper, his claim to the throne was weak, when compared with that of Edmund Mortimer; but this is an entirely opposite view to that taken, for example, by the historian T. B. Pugh in *Henry V and the Southampton Plot* (1988).

In *Henry V as Warlord* (1987) Desmond Seward repeats the Shakespearean thesis.

> Henry's ambition was inspired by something more complicated than mere desire for conquest. It was a need to prove that he really was the King of England. His father had usurped the throne and, as the

Yorkists would demonstrate during the Wars of the Roses, there were others with a better right to it in law. If he could make good his great-grandfather Edward III's claim to France he would show in trial by battle that God confirmed his right to the English crown.[11]

Seward goes so far as to say that 'few people' felt 'a natural loyalty' to the House of Lancaster in 1413. He includes the story of Richard Burton who was prosecuted in 1415 for saying that for Henry V was not the real King of England; and he rehearses Adam of Usk's stories about the fierce storms and floods which supposedly attended the new king's coronation, and were seen as portents. Seward also states that the Southampton Plot in the summer of 1415 'very nearly succeeded'; but this is directly in conflict with the unanimous and authoritative view of the Oxford historians who co-authored *The Practice of Kingship* (1985). They concluded that Henry V had the kingdom well under control before ever he set off for France.[12]

It is anachronistic to think that Henry V's belief in his claim to the French throne was insincere, or less serious than Edward III's had been, simply because his father Henry IV had seized power and pushed Richard II to one side in 1399. All the signs are that, from his earliest days, Henry V had no doubts. He was a true believer in the divine right of kings, long before the Stuarts turned this into an unpopular theory. He invaded France for the reasons he gave himself – to pursue his legal rights there, if necessary on the battlefield. War was not an end in itself, but a way of pursuing the same objectives as his great-grandfather Edward III. He regarded himself as Edward's rightful descendant, and in his mind he had inherited a legitimate and righteous claim to both kingdoms. He was accepted as the legitimate sovereign when he came to the throne, even in Aquitaine, where men might have entertained the greatest doubt. Agincourt was merely divine confirmation.[13]

The Revenge for Soissons?

Soissons is said to be the place where the cobbler saints, Crispin and Crispinian, lived and were martyred in late Roman Times (though Faversham in Kent also lays claim to them);[14] and there is a tradition in England that Agincourt was the English revenge for what was done to our archers there. G. A. Henty's novel *At Agincourt, A Tale of the White Hoods of Paris* (1897) tells the story of Guy Aylmer, a youth of around 16, of relatively humble origins, who wins fame and fortune by his sword. Along the way, we are told how Agincourt came to be fought and why the French lost the battle. In Henty's tale Henry V makes a rousing speech, in which he reminds of the terrible fate of their comrades. 'When the Orléanists had taken Soissons, a few months before, they had hung up like dogs 300 English archers belonging to the garrison. He told them they could expect no mercy.'

Bernard Cornwell's entertaining novel *Azincourt* (2008) also makes much of the action at Soissons. The hero, Nicholas Hook, is an Englishman of peasant stock, who is outlawed. He takes service as an archer and finds himself in Soissons in 1414, in the service of the Burgundians, when the town is attacked by the French. When they enter the town and round up their enemies, Hook hides in a house, where he finds a traitor attempting to rape a nun, and kills him. He rescues the girl, Mélisande, and they hide together in the roof. From here, they witness the sickening massacre of the Soissonnais, and the butchery of those English archers unwise enough to hide in the church, where they might have expected to enjoy the right of sanctuary.

The sack of Soissons became a byword for all that was worst about medieval warfare; but is there any historical basis for these stories? Jean Juvenal des Ursins did record that, when Henry addressed the French prisoners taken at Agincourt, he contrasted the behaviour of his own troops with the way in which the French had behaved: 'He had not come as mortal enemy, for he had not consented to burning, ravaging, violating nor raping girls or women, as they had done at Soissons.'

Des Ursins also tells us that 'very many of the townsmen, English archers and soldiers of the garrison were hung on a gibbet without Soissons'. Thomas Basin mentioned that the sack took place on the feast of Crispin and Crispinian; but, if Monstrelet is right, the capture of Soissons was a good deal more complicated than simple myth would lead us to believe. In his account, English soldiers fought on *both sides* of the action, and their role was not entirely honourable.

> During the storm, the commander of the English forces within the town, having held a parley with some of his countrymen in the [French] king's [Armagnac] army, caused a gate leading to the river to be cut down, through which the Count of Armagnac's men rushed, and hoisted, on the highest tower, the banner of their count; and the greater part of the English suddenly turned against the townspeople.

The Monk of St Denis mentions the presence of foreigners in Soissons – *une soldatesque étrangère* – but these were Bretons, Gascons and Germans, and they fought for the Armagnacs, not for the Burgundians. He also mentions a gibbet, set up near the King's lodgings, from which twenty members of the garrison were hanged; but he does not say that the hanged men were English. For that matter, he mentions that Soissons was a town which had a number of magnificent churches, and was home to an especially valuable collection of relics, but he makes no mention of Saints Crispin and Crispinian. Nor do the English feature in Françoise Autrand's brief account of the affair.[15]

On the other hand Juliet Barker relates that:

Contingents of English mercenaries, said to be archers, were present in the Burgundian garrisons of both Soissons and Arras when they were besieged by the Armagnacs in 1414. With typical medieval xenophobia, the English archers at Soissons were accused of betraying the town to the Armagnacs by opening one of the gates, and forty of them were later hanged, though this was more likely to be because they were English and mercenaries, rather than for any betrayal, real or imagined.

Much the same account is given by Richard Vaughan and Michael K. Jones.[16]

If there were English archers in Soissons in 1414, they were not part of an official force, because the English and the Burgundians had no treaty at the time. Any English troops present would have been mercenaries, hired by the Burgundians and attached to the garrison. It is therefore unlikely that their fate was of any concern to Henry V, and inconceivable that the massacre of a contingent of archers would have influenced his decision to invade in 1415. It is much more likely that these stories about Soissons began to circulate *after* the Battle of Agincourt.

'War is Always About Money'

In the nineteenth century Michelet wrote that the English people *needed* war in 1415, to gain money and power, or to counteract the effects of primogeniture; but this is all a little far-fetched. In fact the English Parliament was initially reluctant to go along with the king's designs; and on several occasion between 1413 and 1415, M.P.s acted as a brake on royal ambition, insisting that the King engage in further negotiations, and only granting him the necessary taxation when he had persuaded them that there was no alternative.

The idea of a belligerent English nobility finds some support in a letter written to Henry V in 1415, which indicated the willingness of the peerage to accompany their sovereign. The peers declare that they recognise in full that Henry is entitled to invade in pursuit of 'the old rights of your

Crown, as well as for your rightwise heritage'; and they blame the French for their obstinacy in refusing to recognise his legitimate demands; but the peers did not offer unconditional support. They wanted Henry to seek a peaceful settlement first. Great as his power was, the King of England was not an absolute monarch, and the peers were not his slaves. This goes a long way to explaining why Henry tried so hard to obtain a diplomatic settlement, or at least gave the appearance of doing so.[17]

Gilbert de Lannoy (1386–1462) wrote a treatise in which he made it clear that war was one of the ways in which a brave and virtuous man could win riches, and do so honourably. He emphasised the wealth which could be derived from the taking of prisoners. One such captive could make a knight's fortune for the rest of his life, as well as making it easier to contract a profitable marriage.[18] But this was only one view. There must have been many a soldier, setting off for the wars, who feared that the outcome might not be favourable; but fear is not the stuff of which treatises are made.

In France, some still take the crude Marxist view that the Hundred Years War was a struggle for the control of the wine, textiles and salt produced in Aquitaine, Flanders and Brittany, a 'confrontation between two different economic, social and religious systems'; and that the Burgundians were in favour of the English 'model' while the Armagnacs defended the French.[19] In his explicitly Marxist *People's History of England* (1938), A. L. Morton argued that late medieval England was a feudal society, displaying 'growing internal conflicts among the leading noble families' and violent premature attempts at social revolution. He did not think that Henry V renewed the war with France for narrow pecuniary reasons; but he did think that there were 'clear economic motives' for the Hundred Years War as a whole; and that the English nobility looked on the renewal of war as an opportunity for 'unlimited plunder'. The invasion of 1415 was also the sign of a 'dying class following a policy blindly for no better reason than that it had been tried before'. Morton wrote before the Second World War, and likened the situation in Agincourt year to that which he saw around him in 1938. This was 'characteristic of an age on the edge of a great social transformation and can be paralleled by the equally blind and suicidal impulse driving the bourgeoisie today towards war and Fascism'. Nowadays this sounds very old-fashioned to all but the most committed Marxist, but as late as the 1950s there was a school of thought in England which believed that Henry V waged an 'imperialist' war, which was against the country's true interests – a view which did not look altogether strange until the collapse of the Soviet Union in the early

1990s. Desmond Seward, who took a very dim view of the Hundred Years War in general, wrote that Henry's conquests were 'as much about loot as dynastic succession, accompanied by mass slaughter, arson and rape'.[20]

These ideas utterly fail to convince, if only because real power in France, England and Burgundy lay with the nobility, and the nobles had little or no interest in trade and commerce. They were much more interested in preserving and expanding their landed inheritances and Henry V was cast in the same mould. There is no sign at all that the fate of the Gascon wine trade or for that matter of the English woollen industry (let alone the Breton salt industry) played any part in his deliberations as to whether to take the 'way of peace' or the 'way of action'. Likewise, the Duke of Burgundy was careful to keep the peace, if he could, between Flanders and England, but this did not stop him from pursuing his wider ambitions in France. In fact he pursued two sets of negotiations at the same time, one for his possessions in the Low Countries and one for those in Continental France.[21]

Between the 1940s and the 1960s there was a lively debate between K. B. McFarlane and M. M. Postan, in the *Economic History Review*, the *Transactions of the Royal Historical Society* and *Past and Present*, as to whether the English as a whole could be said to have profited from the Hundred Years War. According to his friend A. L. Rowse, McFarlane liked to wound, whereas Postan was a brilliant theorist who made elementary mistakes of fact; but Postan thought he had morality as well as economics on his side. He was clearly affronted by the idea that an honourable nation could ever make a profit out of war; and for various reasons he simply 'refused to believe that the profits of war could have been sufficiently high to match the English outlay, both public and private'. For his part, McFarlane wrote that some of what Postan wrote was 'the purest moonshine'.[22] Whichever of these titans was right, their researches and conclusions are not of much help when it comes to explaining the profit and loss account of the Agincourt campaign. This did not yield any territorial gains apart from Harfleur, while the battle produced only booty and prisoners. Even McFarlane thought that the greatest profits of war in the fifteenth century were derived from the occupation of Normandy and Maine which followed Henry V's second invasion of Normandy in 1417.

John Leland was an antiquarian who toured England for Henry VIII in the 1530s and 1540s. He wrote that everywhere he went 'from Ampthill in Bedfordshire to Hampton Court near the Welsh border, from Streatlam in County Durham to Farleigh Hungerford in Somerset', he had been told of castles raised in brick and stone, built 'from the spoils of noble prisoners taken in the French war' – *ex spoliis nobiliium bello gallico captorum*. One question is whether this building activity can be linked to Agincourt.[23]

To start with the penultimate of Leland's castles, we can dismiss the idea that Streatlam, which was near Barnard Castle and belonged to the Bowes-Lyon family derived from money made in 1415. Leland wrote about its builder, Sir William Bowes (c. 1389–1465), but the oral tradition he recorded concerns Sir William's service under John Duke of Bedford in the 1420s. There is no evidence that he was even in France at the time of Agincourt.[24]

The Hampton Court referred to should not be confused with Henry VIII's great palace on the Thames. Instead, it is situated near Leominster in Herefordshire and Leland wrote this about its owner: 'This Lenthall [Sir Rowland Lenthall] was victorious at the battle of Agincourt, and took many prisoners there, by the which prey he began the new building and manor place at Hampton ...'[25] We can confirm that Sir Rowland Lenthall built this Hampton Court, because there is an abstract of a document relating to it in the Patent Rolls for 6 November 1434:

> Licence, by advice of the council, for Rowland Lenthall, knight, and Lucy his wife, to crenellate, turrellate and embattle their manor of Hampton Richard [*sic*], co. Hereford, and to make a fortalice there; also to impark 1,000 acres of land.[26]

We can also say that Sir Rowland was present at Agincourt: he served in the king's retinue with twelve men at arms and thirty-six foot archers; and he was among those who received pledges of 'plate and jewels, tablets, images, crucifixes, notre-dames and tabernacles' against the wages which were due to them. However, it is not certain that Lenthall built Hampton Court with ransom money earned on the battlefield. As Leland himself noted, Lenthall's estate in Herefordshire derived from his first marriage

> This place was erected sumptuously by one Sir Lenthall knight, that thus rose up by service: he was yeoman of the robes with King Henry IV and being a gallant fellow, either a daughter or very near kinswoman of Henry IV fell in love with him, and in continuance was wedded onto him. Whereupon after he [rose] in estimation, and had given him £1,000 lands by the year for the maintenance of him and his wife, and to their heirs ...

Agincourt ransom money may have been used to finance the building work, rather than the purchase of the site, at Hampton; but Lenthall's marriage may have brought in more money than the wars; and when

Lenthall drew up his own accounts in the early 1420s, he did not include any profits of war.[27]

As we have seen Sir John Cornwall, later Lord Fanhope (c. 1364–1443), undoubtedly fought at Agincourt and captured the Count of Vendôme there; and Leland recorded that

> The castle and town of Ampthill [Bedfordshire] with diverse fair lordships thereabout belonged to the Lord Fanhope, a man of great renown in the reigns of Henry V and Henry VI. This Lord Fanhope built this castle as it is now standing stately on an hill, with 4 or 5 fair towers of stone in the inner ward, beside the base-court of such spoils as it is said that he won in France.

Yet, even here, Leland himself records that there were other foundations of Fanhope's wealth – not least that he married a sister of Henry IV

> It appeareth by the East window in the chapel within the castle of Ampthill that he married in a noble blood; as I remember she was the Duchess of Exeter; it may chance that the marriage of her was a great cause of the sumptuous building there.[28]

Lastly, when he came into Somerset, Leland noted the tombs of the Hungerford family, at 'Castle-Farleigh' (and gave a description of those members of the family who were buried and commemorated in the Hungerford Chapel in Salisbury Cathedral). He noted the building works at the castle, and in particular that 'the hall and three chambers within the second court be stately' and recorded: 'There is a common saying that one of the Hungerfords built this part of the castle by the prey of the Duke of Orléans, whom he had taken prisoner.'[29]

What truth is there in this tradition? Sir Walter Hungerford, 1st Baron Hungerford of Farleigh Hungerford in Somerset (1378–1449), was certainly at Agincourt with sixteen lances, according to the Agincourt Roll; but the *Oxford Dictionary of National Biography*, noting that he took several prisoners at Agincourt, nevertheless concludes that his wealth was 'largely the reward of a long and adventurous career'. This is also the opinion of the learned editors of *The History of Parliament*.[30]

The conclusion is that Leland has little to tell us about the precise origin of the castles and seats he describes. However, he does show that the English victory at Agincourt was already legendary by 1530, having given rise to several popular myths concerning the origin of the wealth of the English gentry.[31] And there are other stories, similar to Leland's, told about Sudeley Castle, Gloucestershire, built by Sir Ralph Boteler (c. 1394–1473) and Caister Castle, Norfolk, built by Sir John Fastolf (1380–1459), though it is unlikely that either fought at Agincourt. On the other hand, there may be some substance to the stories linking the building of Herstmonceaux Castle in Sussex with the battle, since the Agincourt Roll lists James Fenes or Fiennes, 1st Baron Saye and Sele, as a member of the Duke of Gloucester's retinue, and the castle was built around 1441. In this case, the connection with the battle has been elaborated by the ubiquitous English ghost story, which tells of a drummer from Agincourt, nine feet tall, who walks the battlements from time to time.[32]

But the truth is that war is seldom about money alone, and in the Middle Ages economics might be involved at some level but so were service, loyalty and religion. Medieval people thought a great deal more about all of these things than we do, and especially about the last. So far from being an adventure driven by the pursuit of money, M. R. Powicke thought that the campaign of 1415 was undertaken with an 'almost crusading fervour'.

Chapter 6

Kingdom and Capital

England

England was much smaller than France but it had strengths which the French kingdom lacked. The English kings presided over a unitary state, rather than several loosely-bound provinces. This unity had been achieved by King Alfred but was greatly reinforced by the Norman Conquest, when a French-speaking aristocracy took over the widely-scattered estates of their Anglo-Saxon forebears; and the dominance of the Crown made it difficult for even the mightiest of subjects to compete. Civil wars in England were fought for the control of the centre, and rebels aimed to gain influence at the royal court, not undermine it. At the same time, the royal power grew, and the King's judges developed a common law which applied throughout England, with some exceptions in the counties palatine. By contrast, the French kingdom remained divided between several jurisdictions as late as 1789.

Edward III had made his eldest son the Prince of Wales, and the others Dukes of Clarence, Lancaster, York and Gloucester; and, when he did so, he endowed them with what the French called *appannages*, or landed estates, which they held in their own right; but in Henry V's time the Duke of York was a child, while the King controlled the vast revenues of the Duchy of Lancaster, as well as the Duchy of Cornwall, the Principality of Wales and the Palatinate of Cheshire, and the Crown lands themselves.[1]

The men who fought with Henry V at Agincourt mostly came from central and southern England; but all regions made a contribution; and there are strong traditions regarding the archers of Cheshire and Lancashire, as well as Kent. Wylie mentions a legend that, when the Kentish bowmen returned home after the battle they feasted at an inn in Speldhurst, near Tunbridge Wells;[2] but the contribution of archers from the County Palatine of Chester and the Duchy and County Palatine of Lancaster is apparent in the archives. Thus, the Chamberlain of Cheshire, William Troutbeck, agreed to bring 650 archers, and 500 archers were raised in Lancashire. These were grouped into companies of fifty, though the Agincourt Roll shows only 180 Cheshire archers present at the battle, 209 of whom were from Lancashire.

Some of these men have been remembered by name. In the case of Cheshire, there is Sir Peter de Legh of Lyme Hall; Sir William Stanley of Cheadle; the second Sir John Savage of Runcorn; Sir Ralph Bostock of Bostock, between Northwich and Middlewich; and Sir John Bromley of Baddington near Nantwich, a groom of the King's Chamber who heroically recovered a battle standard at Corbie, during the march from Harfleur to Agincourt.[3] We learn of ten Lancashire captains who agreed to contribute 500 men to the Agincourt expedition, the indentures being signed at Wilnwick near Newton-le-Willows on 27 June 1415. One of these ten was Sir Richard Kyghley from Inskip in the Fylde, who led fifty archers, including a personal retinue of six men at arms and eighteen archers (Kyghley was killed at Agincourt, together with four of his archers William de Holland, John Greenbogh, Robert de Bradshaw and Gilbert Howson). Likewise, we find John Southworth of Wilnwick, with two men at arms and six foot archers (four of whom were killed and two more wounded); Robert Laurence of Ashton Hall, with two men at arms and six foot archers; Sir William Harrington of Farleton-with-Hornby and Hornby Castle, who brought ten men at arms and thirty foot archers; and the Sheriff of Lancashire, Robert Urswick, who led no less than 500 foot archers.[4]

The contribution made by Lancashire may be distorted by confusion between the County and Duchy. The County was a unit of government, the Duchy was feudal and more far-flung. There were 'Lancastrian' castles at Tutbury in Staffordshire, Kenilworth in Warwickshire, Dunstanburgh in Northumberland and the 'Three Castles' of Monmouthshire. There were also men who held office in the Duchy but who came from various parts of the country: for example Sir Walter Hungerford, who owned Farleigh Hungerford in Somerset and held office in that county as well as in Wiltshire and Dorset; Sir Robert Babthorpe, who was from Yorkshire; and Sir Roger Leche (Keeper of the King's Wardrobe) who was from Derbyshire.[5]

There was a North–South divide in England, even in the fifteenth century; and foreign observers all noted the relative prosperity of the South. By 1400 there were areas, particularly in East Anglia and the Cotswolds, which had long ceased to be dependent on farming alone, having developed a vigorous wool and textile industry, whose exports to the markets of Flanders and Italy paid for imports of every kind. In times of war the Crown was able to draw on the wealth of the whole kingdom, but especially on that of the South, by means of direct and indirect taxes. Direct taxation was possible because of the existence of a central Parliament, with a House of Commons which represented every county and every borough. Whatever difficulties there may have been, from time to time, in managing it, the Crown benefited from the ability to bargain with a single body, rather than having to haggle with many different communities in turn, as was the case in France. The Crown had experienced near-bankruptcy during the reign of Henry IV but, by exploiting traditional revenues and asking Parliament for assistance, Henry V was able to amass a war-chest of £130,000 for the Agincourt campaign. In addition, he borrowed large sums.[6]

The English Church played an extremely important role in providing moral support for the monarchy, but also in royal finance. Whereas Henry VIII dissolved the monasteries to pay for his wars, Henry V harnessed the wealth of the Church in quite a different way. The Convocations of Canterbury and York granted the King as much clerical taxation in the nine years of his reign as it had to Henry IV in the thirteen years of his and, in the same period, well over 100 religious houses and corporations lent money to the Crown. Lenders included the Archbishop of Canterbury, the Bishop of Lincoln and numerous abbots, priors and deans, while the most important financier of all was the King's uncle Henry Beaufort, Bishop (and later Cardinal) of Winchester. Beaufort advanced a total of £35,630 during the early years of his nephew's reign and £200,000 between 1417 and his retirement from active politics in 1443.[7]

It is also possible that the Church assisted Henry in a less obvious way, by providing him, not only with civil servants, but with a secret service. The bishops and 'mitred abbots' who sat in the House of Lords and served him as diplomats were mostly University men, more than able to compete with their French counterparts diplomatically, and it may be the case that Richard Courtenay, Bishop of Norwich from 1413, Keeper of the Royal Jewels and a long-time friend of Henry's who accompanied him to Harfleur, also acted as his spymaster. It is known that Courtenay had been on diplomatic errands to France, and at least tried to recruit Jean de Fusoris (a doctor of Lombard origin, a canon of Notre-Dame and an astronomer) as a spy, when the latter visited England early in 1415. During the siege of Harfleur, the English took a number of French prisoners and Courtenay interviewed one of them, Raoul le Gay, and 'persuaded' him to take a message to Fusoris in Paris. This message was designed to spread disinformation, in that Le Gay was supposed to tell

Fusoris that Henry had landed with 50,000 men and sufficient material to last for a siege of six months; but Le Gay was also meant to enquire what the French had been doing to oppose Henry, whether the French King, the Dauphin and the Duke of Burgundy were in the field, and how many lords and other men had been mobilised to meet the English invasion.[8]

Françoise Autrand pointed out the importance of spies in her biography of Charles VI. She tells how they accompanied the embassies which all sides used in diplomatic embassies; but gives particular emphasis to the English 'Intelligence Service' established by Bishop Courtenay. She claims that he recruited several 'notable Parisians', including Fusoris. She also thinks that the English made good use of spies based in France before they attacked Harfleur and again prior to the battle itself, when they captured prisoners along the line of march, tortured them, discovered the French battle plan and suggested to Henry V that he should supply his archers with stakes.[9] For obvious reasons we find little confirmation of this activity in the English records; but the Chaplain certainly refers to the capture of prisoners in his account of the journey from Harfleur to Agincourt; and these could have proved especially useful in finding a way to cross the Somme.

In the early Tudor period, the Scottish poet William Dunbar wrote of London as 'the flower of cities all'; but the capital was well-known for its size and wealth a century earlier. Its importance was noted by the Greek historian Laonicus Chalcocondyles, who was in a position to make comparisons with Constantinople – a far larger city at the time. He wrote that 'in populousness and power, in riches and luxury, London, the metropolis of the isle, may claim a pre-eminence over all other cities of the West'.

Parliament granted subsidies but it took months to collect the money, whereas the Crown's need for money was immediate: supplies had to be purchased and soldiers paid. The only way of reducing the fiscal deficit was to borrow the shortfall; and the lenders who were nearest to hand were the merchants of the City of London. London had 23,314 tax-payers, whereas there were only 7,248 in York, and 3,000 in each of Norwich, King's Lynn and Boston. When Bishop Beaufort negotiated terms for the repayment of two very large loans in 1421, he agreed to take the customs of Southampton as security in the first instance, but insisted on those of London as a guarantee. If the Battle of Waterloo was won on the playing fields of Eton, there is a good case for saying that Agincourt was won in the counting-houses of London.

In July 1413 the draper John Hende lent £1,000. In 1415 the Corporation of London advanced 10,000 marks and several other large loans were made by individual London merchants, though they may have been acting on behalf of syndicates. Other towns and cities throughout England were also prepared to lend, but the amounts were small: Bristol, £582, Norwich, £333 6s 8d, King's Lynn, £216 13s 4d, Newcastle, £216 13s 4d, York, £200, Boston, £80, Beverley, Canterbury, Exeter, Northampton and Nottingham, £66 13s 4d, Bridgwater, £50, Gloucester, Maidstone and Sudbury, £40, Bury St Edmunds and Faversham, £33s 6s 8d, Plymouth, £20 and Dartmouth, £13 6s 8d. These loans pale into insignificance when compared to the amount advanced by Roger Salvyn, treasurer of Calais, which was a staggering £10,936 3s 8d.[10]

There is a stark contrast between London and a place like Salisbury. The First General Entry Book of Salisbury records that at an assembly, held in the presence of the Duke of York and the Chancellor on 2 March 1415, the Mayor John Moner and the leading citizens of the town considered a letter from the King, requesting a loan of £100 'to be raised by the citizens and other competent inhabitants of the city', and there follows a list of around 100 men who contributed. The total advanced was £102 13s 4d. Judging by their surnames (Mercer, Mason, Tanner, Goldsmith, Potter, Needler) the contributors were merchants and craftsmen. The Mayor contributed the largest sum, which was £10, the next largest loan being £2. The smallest contribution was one mark.[11]

The Crown Jewels, and other private treasures belonging to the King, kept in the Tower of London and in the Jewel Tower near the Palace of Westminster, played an important part in raising the war chest. The fact that Henry was prepared to 'pawn the family silver' shows the lengths to which he was willing to go in pursuit of his objective.[12]

The foreign merchants in London were also made to pay: those of Lucca, Venice and Florence were committed to the Fleet prison before paying over £200, £1,000 and £1,200 respectively. At around the same time, Richard Whittington and John Hende were lending a further £700 and £4,666 13s 4d. Steel's figures for Henry V's reign as a whole (1413–22) were £32,096 13s 4d for the burgesses of London and £6,786 13s 4d for those outside the capital, which means that the Londoners were lending five times as much as the rest of the country put together.[13]

The King knew how important London was and he cultivated its leading citizens. On 10 March 1415 he summoned the Mayor, Aldermen and other citizens to the Tower of London, told them that he had decided to invade France to recover the territories which had been withheld from him 'by enormous wrong', and said he would send his brothers into the City to make the necessary preparations. The Archbishop of Canterbury and the three Royal Dukes then visited the Guildhall and flattered the Mayor and Aldermen. The City agreed to advance 10,000 marks, to be secured on the customs of the port of London, and temporarily guaranteed by the pledge of 'a great collar of gold, composed of crowns and antelopes richly enamelled and bejewelled'. All this was done as a preliminary to the meeting of the Great Council in the Palace of Westminster, where matters were discussed in public.[14]

Much of the money raised must have come back to London relatively quickly. At various dates in the spring and summer of 1415 numerous payments were made out of the royal coffers to London merchants, variously described as grocers, mercers or simply as citizens, for supplying quantities of saltpetre, the principal ingredient in the manufacture of gunpowder, or for the grinding of saltpetre, or 'for cannons, and other necessaries of war'. By the end of October 1414, 10,000 gun-stones had been forwarded to London, for onward transmission. London was also the place where many of the ships needed for the invasion fleet were commandeered, hired or assembled, before being taken around the coast to Southampton. Yet the Crown was not prepared to allow the City to make unlimited profits. On 12 April the King summoned the Mayor and some of the leading aldermen to the Tower once more and told them that the price of armour must be reduced within three days.

The preparations for war were a stimulus to economic activity in many places. Great herds of cattle had to be collected for the use of the army's butchers, at Titchfield, Farnham, Southwick, Alresford, Romsey, Beaulieu and Lymington. Some 100 masons were ordered up to London with their tools by 17 June. On 1 May, twenty-five London cordwainers were engaged to serve for six months at 6d a day. Farriers, turners, carpenters, smith and carters were hired in large numbers. On 27 May, the Sheriff of Southampton was ordered to cause proclamations to be made in Winchester, Southampton and all other market towns and hamlets where he had jurisdiction, commanding his subjects to 'bake and brew against the coming of the King to those parts with his retinue'. Luxury goods were also in great demand: spices and confectionery to be supplied by the London merchants, especially the grocers. Thomas Chaucer, who was Speaker of the House of Commons five times and Chief Butler of England for around thirty years, was paid a staggering £1,214 for wine.[15]

What was London's contribution in terms of manpower? In 1642 the London 'trained bands' helped to stop Charles I's advance into London, at Turnham Green; but in 1415 these bands were not yet in existence. The Londoners who fought in Henry V's army did so as individual members of various retinues, and for that reason the part they played has been obscured; but some of their names can be found in the French Rolls printed by the Deputy Keeper of the Public Records in 1883, because the king issued 'letters of protection' (or passports) to allow men to travel abroad. Letters were issued to

John Spicer alias Cook, of Stratford at Bow, in the retinue of the Earl of Huntingdon.

John Hugge of London, notary, in the retinue of Hortauk Van Clox (alias Hartung von Klux).

John Lynton of Gravesend, Kent and John Elys of London, grocer, in the retinue of the Duke of Clarence.

John Everard and Rob. Gray of London fishmonger, in the retinue of the Earl of Dorset.

Thomas Kynot, of London, grocer, in the retinue of John Cornwall, knight.

William Atte Mersh, workman in the Tower of London, in the retinue of the King.

Here we see the potential of the teeming mass that was London, with its wide range of trades and occupations, to fill up the ranks of the army, and also the way that the army was organised according to retinues and personal loyalties rather than ties of geography or class.

In the Plea Rolls of the City, we find occasional glimpses of Londoners who played their part in the battle. In July 1415 a youth from Wigan in Lancashire called William Marshall complained to the Mayor that he had been brought to the City on the 3rd of the month by a man called William Bradshaw, and put in the charge of John Chesterford, who was a leather-seller in the Parish of All Hallows, Honeylane. Originally, he had been told that Bradshaw was 'about to cross the sea in the company of the king' and that he would only have to stay with Chesterford until Bradshaw returned; but he complained that 'after the said William's departure' for France, Chesterford had bound him as an apprentice for eight years, against his will, though he was not yet fourteen.[16]

Shakespeare was right when he wrote of the intense activity which must have preceded the Agincourt expedition

Now thrive the armourers, and honours thought
Reigns solely in the breast of every man;
They sell the pasture now to buy the horse,
Following the mirror of all Christian Kings.

What he did not make clear, perhaps, is the dominant role played by London in all this activity; but I would argue that it was partly this which enabled the English to put a more effective army in the field in 1415 than the French, notwithstanding the natural advantages which favoured the defence.

The importance of the Tower of London in Henry V's war has also been overlooked, because no great dramatic event happened there at the time. In 1821 John Bayley wrote that:

> The reign of Henry IV furnishes us with no information regarding the Tower which is worthy of particular notice and that of his glorious successor is equally silent and uninteresting. Neither kept court there for any length of time and the principal use to which it was put seems to have been as a prison for offenders against the state.[17]

In fact the Tower was the central arsenal in 1415. St Thomas's Tower, the Wakefield Tower and the Lanthorn Tower, which have now been restored as part of 'the Medieval Palace', were all built in the thirteenth century and an audience room in the Wakefield Tower was being used for the storage of documents even before Edward III died. In Henry V's time, the Tower as a whole was no longer required as a residence, but it was used as an arsenal, prison and armoury. The King's smith worked there, and the Master Provider of the King's Bows had a special workshop and residence there too, while many bowyers lived in Ludgate, later known as 'Bowierrowe', making longbows, crossbows, arrows and bolts. Throughout 1413 and 1414 Henry had been buying bows, bowstrings and arrows and stockpiling these in the Tower, where he also ordered guns to be made. He also kept old-fashioned siege engines, scaling-ladders and battering rams there, as well as several large new cannon, including one called 'London'.

London reaped its rewards from the Agincourt campaign and in particular from the capture of Harfleur. Her tradesmen and merchants received increased orders for goods and supplies of all kinds and interest on loans made to the Crown, despite the medieval Church's prohibition on usury.[18] The Letter Book of the City of London records that during the siege London merchants were urged to 'speed to the king' with all manner of victuals, sheets, breeches, doublets, hose, shoes, clothing, armour and artillery; and the French Rolls contain a fascinating entry which confirms that, in some cases, they were richly rewarded. On 28 December 1415 one

Richard Bokelond received a grant of an inn called The Peacock' in Harfleur, 'on account of his having assisted the King at the siege'.

'Dick' Whittington (c. 1354–1423) first appeared on stage in 1605, when an engraving shows him holding his cat, though the pantomime which celebrates his rise from rags to riches did not become popular until the nineteenth century.

> *Turn again, Whittington,*
> *Thrice Lord Mayor of London!*

In Whittington's case fiction is not far from truth. He was one of the merchants who helped to pay for Henry V's wars; and the author of the *Libelle of English Policy*, written around 1436, was a great admirer.

> *And in worship now think I on the sun*
> *Of merchandy, Richard of Whittington,*
> *That lode star and chief chosen flower.*[19]

The historical Whittington made his fortune as a mercer and wool exporter; but also as a royal financier. He was a member of the Mercers' livery company, becoming the chief supplier of Richard II's Great Wardrobe. He *was* Lord Mayor of London three times, in 1397, 1406 and 1419, and Mayor of Calais twice. He financed a number of public projects in the capital, including a drainage system in poor areas and a hospital ward for unmarried mothers; and he bequeathed a large fortune to a charity which still exists; but at the time it was his loans to the Crown which mattered. He made some fifty-eight of these between 1388 and 1422. He lent the Crown £2,000 in 1413 and advanced £466 13s 4d 'to maintain the siege of Harfleur' in 1415. He acquired a share in the ransom of at least one French prisoner, 'Hugh' Coniers, taken at Agincourt, though he sold it later to an Italian merchant.[20]

Did Whittington make a profit from his moneylending? Caroline Barron could find no evidence that he charged interest on his loans to the Crown, nor that these were made to secure trading or other privileges. At the same time he did not aim to acquire an estate in the country, as merchants often did, because his wife died around 1402 and he had no children. Barron thinks that the predominant motive was to gain influence at court. Whittington served briefly on the royal council and on royal commissions, and was consulted by the great and the good when he was mayor of London and Calais.[21]

France

The Armagnac lords in charge of the French army had good reason to feel confident on the eve of Agincourt. Divided as the country was, they had still put a much larger army into the field than the English, and substantial numbers of Burgundians were rallying to the cause, albeit late in the day. Unlike the historians, they did not see the greater degree of independence they enjoyed from the Crown as a source of weakness, nor did many of their countrymen. The Frenchman who wrote the *Debate between the Heralds* thought that the French nobility was *more* powerful than its English counterpart, not less.

In sharp contrast to the English kingdom, France was in some ways a federation of great fiefs, rather than a centralised kingdom. The greatest of these were Brittany and Flanders in the north, Foix, Armagnac and Béarn in the south-west, and Burgundy in the centre but, even within the French royal domain, there were minor lords with equivalent privileges. The great fiefs were to a large extent self-governing. They had their own courts, courtiers and servants, their own laws and customs, and sometimes their own legislatures. If and when they obeyed the king's summons to war, their rulers recruited their own troops, at their own rates of pay and under their own command.[22]

Aquitaine was an obvious problem for the French King, since the Duke of Aquitaine was also King of England; but the Duke of Brittany had also acted independently throughout the Hundred Years Wars and, in 1412, he had negotiated a ten-year truce with the English. When he received the French royal summons to arms in 1415, he purported to comply, but marched only slowly into Normandy. On reaching Rouen, where the royal army was assembled, he demanded the cession of St Malo before advancing any further. By the time the Battle of Agincourt was fought, the Duke had only reached Amiens and the only Breton contingent present at the battle was the one led by Arthur, Count of Richemont. This kind of behaviour would have been considered treasonable in England.[23]

But it was the Duchy of Burgundy which came to present the gravest danger to France. This was richly ironic, since the origin of the Valois Duchy was King Jean II's creation of an *appanage*, in 1363, for his youngest son Philip 'the Bold'. Jean's successor Charles V had helped it to grow by arranging Philip's marriage to Margaret, Countess of Flanders; and, when Margaret's father died in 1384, she and Philip the Bold had inherited the Duchy and County of Burgundy, as well as the counties of Flanders, Artois, Nevers, and Rethel. Their son Duke John the Fearless took only a share of their inheritance when his parents died, but this still included the two Burgundies and the counties of Flanders and Artois.[24]

By 1415 the Duke of Burgundy had thus become the quintessential 'overmighty subject'. He had his own capital in Dijon, and his own court and army, several thousand strong. His vassals owed allegiance to him in priority to the King of France. He also ruled extensive territories which had never been part of the French kingdom. (Flanders was technically part of the Holy Roman Empire though, in practice, the Duke needed to co-operate with the 'Four Members' who represented the burghers of Bruges (and district), Ypres and Ghent.)

John the Fearless behaved like an independent sovereign but he was also a member of the French royal family. He retained ambitions in France, especially since his first cousin, the French King Charles VI, was periodically insane, though never totally incapable. Yet, from the moment he became Duke in 1404, John had a rival for power and influence in the shape of his cousin, Louis, Duke of Orléans, Charles's younger brother. In 1407, John resolved his difficulty by arranging for Louis to be murdered in the streets of Paris. He admitted his crime but, extraordinarily, sought to justify it as lawful tyrannicide. The murderer and the victim each had their supporters and the hatred between them soon degenerated into full civil war.[25] John was formally absolved of his crime in 1409, but never forgiven. The murder led to the formation of a league in 1410, headed by the Count of Armagnac and soon named after him. In 1419 the Armagnacs took their revenge for the murder of Orléans by murdering John the Fearless on the bridge at Montereau in 1419. The civil war lasted until 1435 and the Treaty of Arras.

The civil war greatly weakened France. Rival factions and armies fought each other regularly, and in several regions. There were major campaigns in the Principality of Liège in 1408, and in Valois and Picardy in 1411 and in 1414.[26] In 1413 John the Fearless even allied with the lower orders, taking control of Paris in conjunction with the *Cabochiens*, the rebels who followed Simon Caboche. Reaction soon set in and royal control was re-imposed by the Armagnacs. Duke John fled the city and did not return until 1418. In the interim the Duke of Alençon, who had once inclined to the Burgundians, joined their opponents. When the Dauphin asked the Duke of Burgundy for assistance in resisting the English invasion, he specified that the Duke should not participate himself. Duke John was offended and stayed away, refusing to provide a contingent at all and doing nothing to encourage his vassals in Picardy and Artois to respond to the royal summons. As we have noted, some Burgundians rallied to the national cause nonetheless but this was far from full participation.

In addition to this feudal disorder, the French kingdom suffered from several other disadvantages. There were at least two different systems of law in operation, and a mass of competing customs. Several different currencies were in use, and there were many internal tolls. Commercial wealth was largely concentrated in Flanders, and mostly benefited the Duke of Burgundy rather than the King of France. The French kings could not reap the benefit of the country's abundant agricultural wealth because there was no effective system of national taxation. There was no institution equivalent to the Westminster Parliament for the whole of their kingdom. The regional and Paris *Parlements* were courts, not Parliaments in the English sense. There were regional estates, but the States General met only rarely and lacked the authority which the House of Commons, House of Lords and the two Convocations of the Church enjoyed in England. The result was that taxes were slow to come in and difficult to collect, and there was a financial crisis every time there was a war. In the fourteenth century the Crown had debased the French currency on several occasions. In the fifteenth, the Duke of Burgundy prevented the King of France from raising a national tax in his dominions.

It has sometimes been said that the French army was more 'feudal' than the English, but in broad terms the French assembled their army in much the same way, by issuing a personal summons to the nobility (*semonce des nobles*), and a Commission of Array (*arrière-ban*) for the rest, and by signing contracts or indentures (*lettres de retenue*) with many. The *lettres de retenue* were drawn up in similar terms to English indentures, except that they did not usually specify a fixed term of service, and provided for two men at arms to every *homme de trait* (missileman), whereas the English usually provided for a ratio of 1:3. Paradoxically, the main difference between the two armies was that the French made more use of town militias. The men of Amiens, Senlis, St Omer, Abbeville and Corbie were called out to defend their towns, and some of those from Amiens fought at Agincourt itself, while Duke Anthony of Brabant summoned men from his towns of Louvain, Brussels and Antwerp.[27] But Philippe Contamine is clear that the French did not lose the Battle of Agincourt because of defects in their system of military obligation. On the contrary, in some ways they lost because they had too many men, given the nature of the ground on which the battle was fought.[28]

Shakespeare's play leaves us with the impression that the French were led by a few aristocratic fops. Yet, throughout the Middle Ages, France was widely regarded as the bulwark of Western Christendom, just as French was the language of chivalry. Shakespeare's myths about the French army of 1415 are therefore both insulting and historically inaccurate. In *Henry V* he mentions the French King Charles VI, the Dauphin Louis, Duke of Guyenne (not the same prince as later became Charles VII), the Duke of Berry, the Duke of Bourbon, the Constable Charles d'Albret, the Sire de Rambures, the Duke of Orléans, the Count of Grandpré and the Duke of Burgundy; but, as with his cast of English dignitaries, this is a list of the great and the good, rather than an accurate roll-call of those who fought at Agincourt. In reality, key members of the royal family remained in Rouen, on the advice of the King's uncle, the Duke of Berry, who stayed away on grounds of age (he was 75). The Duke of Bourbon had been late to join the muster, because of his discontent with the conduct of the Dauphin. On the other hand, the Dukes of Bourbon and Orléans, the Constable, Rambures and Grandpré were all present, and indeed paid a heavy price: the first two were captured, the last three were all killed.

The English were mustered for service overseas, while the French were summoned to defend their homeland. This ought to have given the French an advantage, but by 1415 the English had acquired a good deal of experience in mustering, transporting and landing expeditions. Smaller forces had been sent to Northern France in 1411 and 1412. In addition, by October 1415 the English had been 'blooded' at Harfleur and had marched together for several weeks. By contrast, the French army was a coalition, put together at short notice and composed of many different contingents. In the nineteenth century Otto von Bismarck was to compare his homeland of Prussia to a smart little frigate, and her rival Austria to a rusty old battleship. A similar contrast might have been made between the two armies and the two countries which fought each other in October 1415. Monstrelet paints a vivid picture of the confusion which reigned amongst the French only a few days before the battle. Orders had been given to all captains and noblemen throughout the kingdom, to assemble and fight the invader; and the chronicler seems mildly surprised that a force as disparate as the French army was able to concentrate in Picardy at all. The result was there were around thirty-five different potential commanders. When the army did form up, each division had several: the rearguard had five, the main 'battle' no less than eight. It was a case of too many captains, rather than too many cooks.

The French commanders had been appointed some time before the battle, in different places and for different purposes. They were unable to help beleaguered Harfleur. Such resistance as there was to the English invasion was provided the lords of Normandy, not by the central command, which was also slow to devise a plan for dealing with Henry's army, even after it had set off for Calais. Although the Constable and the Marshal were technically in charge, they could not control their aristocratic colleagues; and the position was not assisted by the stand-off between the Burgundians (who were strong in Paris) and the Orléanists (who were influential at court). There were conflicts and differences of opinion which were not present on the English side. The professional soldiers were in favour of letting Henry march on to the Channel, rather than risk a major battle, whereas the Princes of the Blood wanted to fight.[29]

The civil war in France affected Paris, more so even than the rest of the kingdom. Whereas London played its part in full in the English war effort, Paris could not do the same for the French, since it was riven by faction. John the Fearless had regularly resided in Paris during the years 1408–11 and constructed a tower there, in the *Hôtel d' Artois*, though he had to flee after the suppression of the *Cabochien* rebellion.[30] No Parisian levies were at Agincourt, though they could at least have provided some companies of expert crossbowmen, if political circumstances had allowed. The failure is usually blamed on the contempt which French aristocrats had for 'rude mechanics'. The Monk of St Denis has a story that the Parisians offered to send 6,000 men and that the offer was rejected because of a perverse kind of snobbery; but there is a more convincing reason for the failure to deploy Parisian troops in Picardy. This is that the French royal family were afraid that, if they did so, the Duke of Burgundy might make another attempt to capture the capital. Outnumbered as they were, the English did not have to face the full might of the French kingdom or capital, in 1415.[31]

Chapter 7

Strategy, Tactics & Morale

Strategy

In 1415 there was no tradition of writing manuals and treatises on warfare and chivalry in English: the Fastolf Memorandum of 1435 appears to have been the first. There were treatises in Latin and French, but these were somewhat academic works and there is no evidence that Henry V read them, though he was literate and might have done so. Advice about strategy was given in the privacy of the council chamber, or around the camp fire, but this was not recorded and it is not clear that Henry was listening. We have to judge his intentions by what he did.

The first priority was to secure the homeland, in particular the border with Scotland. In Shakespeare's *Henry V* the Archbishop of Canterbury advises that the Scots pose a local threat, one that can be left to local forces to deal with; but Henry says that he is worried about a large-scale invasion. Canterbury makes light of this, but Westmoreland advises the King to take it seriously.

> *But there's a saying very old and true,*
> *'If that you will France win,*
> *Then with Scotland first begin.'*

Exeter and Canterbury then advise Henry to take steps to safeguard the North with part of his own forces; but the playwright is exaggerating the danger posed by Scotland. In 1415 the King of Scots had been a prisoner in English hands for almost ten years, while the Scottish Regent Albany's son, Murdoch Earl of Fife, had been held in England since 1402. By virtue of the Auld Alliance, the Regent still felt bound to help the French; but he was unwilling to jeopardise the chances of obtaining his son's release by engaging in all-out war. The result was that, although Henry did make provision for the defence of the Borders, by negotiating a truce with Albany and reinstating the Percys as wardens of the Eastern March, he had much less to fear in that quarter than Edward III. Two Scots armies did invade England in July 1415, but they did not penetrate very far and the larger of them was relatively easily defeated, at Yeavering by the Constable of Alnwick Castle.[1]

Henry also issued a writ to his bishops, ordering a muster in every diocese, of both secular and regular clergy. The Bishop of Lincoln was ordered to assemble 'the able and fencible clergy' to include both those who were 'exempt and not exempt'. In the diocese of Lincoln around 4,500 men were arrayed this way, 4,000 of them as archers; but these men did not sail for France. They stayed in England, to act as a kind of 'Home Guard'.[2]

The next question was where to land the invasion force. The English had at one time or other held several 'barbicans' in France, for example at Cherbourg, Brest, St Malo and La Rochelle, while St Sauveur-le-Vicomte in Normandy had been a private fief of Sir John Chandos, but all these strongholds had been lost years before. There were now only three ways to invade France: via Normandy (as Edward III had done in 1346), Bordeaux (as the Black Prince had done in 1355) or Calais (as Edward IV was to do in 1475). Why did Henry choose Normandy in 1415, when Bordeaux and Calais were both in English hands, and no part of Normandy was? In particular, Calais had become a major garrison and arsenal, a key part of the English military establishment, with a considerable hinterland, guarded by a series of forts. This would have been the obvious place to land, and the crossing was of course short; but there was a major political objection: much of the territory adjoining Calais and its March was now controlled by the Duke of Burgundy, who was also Count of Flanders and Artois.

Henry V had good reason to avoid alienating the Duke of Burgundy, as he would have done if he had marched through his territories without permission. French domination of Flanders in the mid-1380s had enabled France to threaten England with invasion, and send an expeditionary force which helped the Scots to take the castle of Wark in Northumberland in 1385. Moreover, Henry had always favoured the idea of a Burgundian alliance, and between 1413 (when he lost Paris) and 1419 (when he was murdered) Duke John the Fearless's star was in the ascendant. Burgundy looked to him like a 'better bet' than the Armagnacs and in 1414 he tried hard to negotiate an agreement with the Duke.[3] Indeed, when Henry landed in Normandy in the summer of 1415, he may still have been hopeful that John would ally himself with England, or at least stay out of the fighting. Some of the Armagnacs presumed (wrongly) that such an alliance had been formed.

In fact the Duke of Burgundy maintained diplomatic relations with the princes of Germany, Bohemia and Hungary, the Teutonic Knights, the Hanseatic League, Castile, Aragon and Portugal, the Count of Savoy, the republics of Venice and Genoa, the King of Navarre, the Papacy and Scotland. His policy in relation to England was unusual, for had the interests of both Flanders and of Burgundy in mind. The need to please the Flemings did not always make him pro-English – between 1405 and 1407 he was notably hostile, and even assisted in a plan to attack Calais – but throughout the whole of his ducal reign there were regular negotiations, in Calais and Gravelines, between the English, Burgundians and the Four Members of Flanders, which resulted in a series of truces for the Flemings, and the continuance of commercial relations. Nevertheless, he had been unwilling to sign a treaty with the English in 1414. He would have been willing to do so as long as the alliance was solely directed against the Armagnacs, but he was unwilling to go further. Ultimately, he placed his loyalty to Charles VI above his wish to promote the commercial interests of Flanders, or any attachment to England.[4]

Despite the length of the voyage from English ports, Bordeaux was a possible point of disembarkation until the very eve of the invasion of Normandy. The city had been in English hands for centuries and had important economic links with England, particularly because of the wine trade. The men of the South-West were traditionally loyal to the English Crown, and Henry had been made Duke of Aquitaine in 1399, as soon as his father became king. Indeed, there are indentures of war, signed in 1415, which refer to the rates of pay payable for military service in Aquitaine, as well as 'French' rates (which implied service in northern France); and an expedition to Gascony was expressly referred to as a possibility in the negotiations which took place between England and Burgundy in 1414. There is also evidence of a last minute diversion of troops in June 1415, for in that month two Norfolk squires – John Fastolf and Henry Inglose – who had been retained for Aquitaine, were transferred from one commander to another, indicating that the invasion was now definitely aimed at Normandy.[5]

There were several good reasons to attack Harfleur. For the French the port had become the 'great arsenal of the West', and was therefore an important objective in itself, as well as a safe haven for pirates. It was described by Bishop Beaufort as 'the king's lieges' greatest enemy'. It had been used as a naval base when the French sent assistance to Glyndwr and the Scots, and it could also be used to invade England directly. Situated at the mouth of the Seine, it was the potentially the gateway to Normandy (one of the richest of French provinces) and, indeed, to Paris and the Valois heartland. Moreover, Henry had a considerable advantage over Edward III during his invasions of Normandy in that he had effective cannon, much-improved in the last half century. (They were at least useful in siegecraft, though not yet on the battlefield.) Lastly, if Autrand is right, the French were expecting any attack on Normandy to start in the Cotentin peninsula. Edward III had landed there and Sir John Chandos had maintained a fortress there in the 1360s. Henry took everyone by surprise in landing at Harfleur.[6]

As Vale pointed out, Henry V adopted a northern strategy in France, and there was no 'Gascon Agincourt'. In the King's eyes, the correctness of this decision was confirmed by God's verdict, delivered on the battle-field. Indeed all three Lancastrian kings campaigned almost exclusively in the north of France and took the allegiance of the Gascons for granted. Henry V never sailed for Bordeaux to receive the homage of his vassals, despite the fact that English Aquitaine was constantly under the threat of French invasion. When he wrote to the citizens of Bordeaux in October 1414, calling on them for financial assistance, Henry even had to apologise for the fact that he had never sent them any reinforcements. The only mention of Agincourt in the Westminster Parliament Roll which also mentions Bordeaux dates from 1429. In that year, Parliament asked the Gascon authorities to repay a grant of taxation, made to the town in the aftermath of the battle, on the grounds that the money had not been used for the purposes for which it was voted. Instead, it had filled the pockets of the leading Bordelais. Doubtless the Crown felt short-changed by the Gascons; but the feeling was probably mutual.[7]

It is Henry's northern strategy which enables critics to accuse him of being a warmonger. The English kings had enjoyed their title of Dukes of Aquitaine for centuries, but they had long since ceased to rule Normandy. Henry's revived claim, backed up by force of arms, was bound to look like aggression, whatever his diplomats might argue.

Did Henry seek battle in 1415, as McFarlane and Clifford Rogers argued and argue?[8] If we look at the early stages of the Agincourt cam-paign, when Henry had the initiative and the French were struggling to organise their defences, we might well think so; but, by the time the King made the decision to march for Calais, and certainly by the time he reached the Somme, the situation had changed. His original numbers were much depleted, and he had had to abandon any ideas of attacking Paris, or marching for Bordeaux. Moreover, in contrast to Edward III, he had been forced to march many miles out of his way before he could cross the Somme.

Given the civil war in France, Henry V may at one stage have thought that, when he reached the County of Ponthieu, he might have received a friendly reception. Several towns and fortresses there had once owed allegiance to Edward, and were now under Burgundian control; but, if such were his hopes, Henry was to be disappointed. There was no residual loyalty in Ponthieu and local commanders rallied to the French national cause when the English presented themselves outside their gates and asked for assistance. At the town of Boves, near Amiens, the garrison actively resisted, and the Count of Vaudémont was to fight and die on the French side at Agincourt. Similarly, when the English entered Picardy, Jacques III de Heilly, lord of Créquy, joined the French host, despite being a principal lieutenant of Burgundy. Several members of the de Heilly family, including Jacques III, also died for the French cause at Agincourt.[9]

While Henry was trying to cross the Somme, part of the French royal army left Rouen in pursuit of the English and substantial French reinforcements continued to swell the enemy ranks. By the time he turned north once more and reached the vicinity of Hesdin, it is difficult to see that Henry could have maintained any ambition he may originally have had, to provoke a battle, though – as he said – he was prepared to fight, if the French would not let him pass. There is therefore little room for the view that Henry remained a battle-seeking general, if he had ever been one. Françoise Autrand is probably right in taking the view that the siege of Harfleur had proved a 'crushing burden' on 'the small English kingdom'; and Henry's goal in marching for Calais was simply to get home without encountering the French army.[10] The purpose of the march was merely to 'show the flag'.

Tactics

Agincourt was a 'pitched' battle. Once the French caught up with the English, the two parties agreed to fight, the battle lines were drawn up in an orderly way and the conflict took place in half a day. It was not an accidental encounter and the victory owed nothing to the element of surprise.

> The French, in their blind and chivalrous unwisdom, gave up their sound tactics of holding fords and blocking rivers. Each side was bound by the etiquette of chivalry to take no unfair advantage of the other, but each to be in his allotted place by appointment to start fair

together at the word and fight square according to the rules of the game.[11]

In Wylie's view Agincourt was one vast tournament rather than a battle; but it may be doubted whether the rules of chivalry really dictated that neither side should take advantage of the other, where this became possible. After all, there was no equality of arms here, as there was supposed to be in a tournament, or as there has to be in a court of law. The rules of chivalry probably had more influence on the way the narrative of the battle was constructed afterwards, than on the tactical decisions which were taken on the day, when life, limb and liberty were at stake.

Agincourt was a victory for the infantry and English cavalry played very little or no part in it, though Henry is said to have lost twenty-five horses, of which six were palfreys and nineteen were trotters (interestingly, neither of these types of horse was a warhorse). The point is worth making, because the illuminators of medieval manuscripts were fond of showing horses, and some French narratives of Agincourt do mention English cavalry. In fact, though thousands of animals were transported to Normandy, and many must have ridden all the way from Harfleur, the English men at arms fought on foot at Agincourt, in accordance with their usual practice. As for the mounted archers, these had not been trained to shoot from the saddle, as the horse-archers of the Steppes were and so they too formed part of the infantry.

The French threw away their natural advantages and René de Belleval gave a whole series of reasons for their defeat. The Constable drew up his superior numbers in a confined space, between the woods, with little room to manoeuvre. His three 'battles' were lined up one behind the other, so that he was unable to outflank the enemy at any point, or at any time. It was probably also a mistake to keep his men waiting for several hours on the morning of the battle. Discipline, morale and courage were all weakened by allowing the initiative to pass to Henry.

The English made better use of the ground. We know that their three 'battles' were drawn up side by side, between the two woods, and with their backs to Maisoncelle, which made it unlikely that they would be outflanked; but there is room for debate as to how precisely they did form up. The Chaplain described Henry's tactics in a sentence: 'He mixed wedges of archers with each battle-group and had them drive in their stakes close by.' Jean Le Fèvre tells us that in the original order of battle the archers were placed 'on both sides of the men at arms'; and that just before the battle, Sir Thomas Erpingham was directed by Henry 'to draw up his archers and put them in a forward position on the two wings'. This would accord with contemporary practice: Christine de Pisan, a prolific authority on medieval warfare, wrote the French army was usually drawn up in three divisions, with the vanguard consisting of

> A long train of men at arms, all close together and ranged full smoothly, that the one pass not the other ... and at the foremost sides are made wings, in which be all manner of shooters ranged, and in good array, as well gunners as balesters and archers.

So far so good; but do these accounts mean that the archers at Agincourt were drawn up on either side of the men at arms as a whole, and therefore in two main groups, or that they were divided into four (or perhaps six) groups placed on either side of each of three 'battles'? Were they grouped in wedge-shaped formations? Were any detachments of archers placed in the adjacent woods, as suggested by one of the sources cited by Nicolas?

It is impossible to be sure;[12] but in the late nineteenth century, there was a lively controversy, in the *English Historical Review*, as to the meaning of the Chaplain's word 'wedges' (*cuneos*). In 1895 the Reverend Hereford B. George speculated that the archers must have been placed in wedges on either flank of each of the three 'battles', and not in a continuous line in front of the men at arms – since the medieval practice was to regard each of the three battle groups as a separate unit. Two years later J. E. Morris supported the Reverend George. He thought that English battle tactics had not changed since Crécy, where there had certainly been three 'battles', ranged one behind the other. What was different at Agincourt was that Henry had so few men, and therefore deployed one line of men at arms, not three, 'plugging the gap' between his line and the woods of Azincourt and Tramecourt on either side with archers. This is certainly the view of many modern historians, including Anne Curry; but in *The Great Warbow* Strickland and Hardy have three diagrams, showing three possible formations: (1) all the archers on the wings, and with the men at arms in the centre; (2) most archers on the wings, but some in two central blocks, placed between three groups of men at arms in the centre; and (3) most archers in the centre, placed *in front of* three groups of men at arms, but also with some archers on the wings.[13]

If there were archers between each battle, as well as on the flanks, this may have had serious consequences for French tactics. Morris cited another passage in the Chaplain's account, which states that 'The French divided into three columns [*turmas*], attacking our line of battle, at the three places the standards were.' Morris thought that, when they charged the English line, the French must have been compelled by opposing fire to 'huddle blindly' into the spaces of least resistance, which were three, because they came under fire from 'the points of the two intermediate wedges, as well as from the outside wings'. In other words, the enemy was prevented from charging the English line as one mass by the English tactic of placing the archers to guard each English 'battle'.

The idea that the French charged in columns was popular in the nineteenth century, because this was thought to be the tactic they adopted during the Napoleonic Wars; and it has had a long life. In a letter written to *The Times* from the Carlton Club on the 500th anniversary of Agincourt and published the following day, 26 October 1915, Sir Herbert Maxwell (1845–1937) claimed that 'The Battle of Agincourt is memorable as the first recorded instance of the success of line formation against column.' He published a seventeen-page article on the same subject in *The Cornhill Magazine*. The idea remained part of conventional military wisdom: in 2005 Strickland and Hardy could still write that Agincourt was 'a battle of line against column in which the former held the key advantages'; but it seems to be based on very little.

It is also generally agreed that the English provoked the French into starting the battle, but there is little agreement as to how this was done. The ambiguity is present in the earliest of chronicles, since the Chaplain tells us simply that 'the King decided to move against them' and Tito Livio says that 'the whole army set aside their burdens and with only their arms and each one with a great sharp stake moved towards the enemy', though 'Pseudo-Elmham' agrees that the entire army moved forward but says that the archers left their stakes behind them. Woodford, Kingsford, and Allmand all write of a first and second position, and have the archers moving forward with their stakes; but, as Michael K. Jones pointed out in 2005, it would have been highly dangerous to uproot the stakes, march or run with them up the battlefield in full view of the enemy, replant them and then open fire – especially if the French decided to charge before the manoeuvre was complete. Jones therefore suggests an alternative scenario, in which the English move forward but only by a limited distance, taking only some of the stakes with them (and that some of them laid an ambush for the French in the woods). On the other hand, Strickland and Hardy thought that, given the recent rains and the nature of the soil at Azincourt, it may have been relatively easy to drive the stakes into the ground a second time.

Did the English deploy archers in the woods on either side of the two armies, as well as on the battlefield? This would have enabled them to some extent to ambush the French and provoke them into mounting a charge. The use of such tactics was 'vigorously denied' by English chroniclers because it was not considered to be honourable.[14] Likewise Le Fèvre wrote that he heard reports of this ambush: 'But I have heard said and certified by a man of honour who was there on that day in the company of the King of England that nothing like this happened.' But, if Henry was the callous 'Machiavellian' prince he is sometimes said to have been, he would not have thought twice about laying an ambush for his opponents; and Strickland and Hardy think that there is little reason 'to doubt the essential plausibility of Henry's attempt to offset the great odds ranged against him by the use of surprise'.[15]

When Lord Strathclyde, leader of the Conservatives in the House of Lords for fourteen years, resigned from that post in January 2013, he remarked that his reason for leaving was that debates in the Lords had become 'more like cage-fighting than Agincourt'. Presumably he meant that Agincourt was a more chivalrous and respectable form of combat than politics; but if so he was mistaken. The conventional story tells how common English archers defeated French knights by means of their unique skill with the longbow. Agincourt has never been regarded as a series of chivalrous jousts and the idea that archery was the principal reason for English success is very old. It dates back to the earliest of the ballads celebrating the victory, and it was powerfully reinforced, even before Shakespeare put pen to paper, by the desire of Tudor propagandists to sing the praises of a uniquely English weapon and thereby prolong its life, even in the age of gunpowder weapons and the so-called 'military revolution'.[16]

Medieval crossbowmen commonly carried large shields known as *pavises*. English bowmen did not have shields but the Chaplain tell us that, as they were making their way from Harfleur to Calais, Henry ordered them to provide themselves with stakes as a form of defence.

As a result of information divulged by some prisoners, rumour went the rounds of the army that the enemy command had assigned squadrons of cavalry, many hundreds strong and mounted on barded [armoured] horses to break the formation and resistance of our archers when they engaged us in battle. The King therefore had it proclaimed ... that every archer was to prepare and fashion for himself a stake or staff, either square or round, but six feet long, of sufficient thickness, and sharpened at both ends, and he commanded that whenever the French army drew near to do battle and to break their ranks by such columns of horse, all the archers were to drive in their stakes in front of them in line abreast and that some of them should do this further back and in between, one end being driven into the ground pointing towards themselves, the other end pointing up towards the enemy above waist-height, so that the cavalry, when their charge had brought them close and in sight of the stakes, would either withdraw in great fear or, reckless of their own safety, run the risk of having both horses and riders impaled.

This was not the first time that the idea of providing the bowmen with some means of defence had occurred to English commanders. In 1342, the archers at Morlaix in Brittany had dug pits. During the Peasants' Revolt of 1381, rebel militias had tried to protect their positions with barricades and ditches, in one case reinforced with stakes. Excavations at Aljubarrota in Portgual have confirmed Froissart's account, which says that the English who fought there in 1385 dug potholes before the battle. The archer Paul Hitchin has even proposed that stakes were a standard part of the archer's equipment; but Strickland and Hardy think that the most likely origin for the use of stakes in 1415 is that the English were copying tactics used by the Ottoman Turks at Nicopolis (in modern Bulgaria) in 1396. It has also been suggested that Henry learned the tactic, not from the Turkish Sultan, but from his uncle John Beaufort, who commanded a contingent of around 1,000 English crusaders there.[17]

What was new at Agincourt was that the stakes were portable. Indeed, de Belleval was so impressed that he suggested that the archers, having cut the stakes some five days before the battle, had time to practise how to use them. Allmand also suggests that the stakes were used offensively, once the supply of arrows had run out, but this seems improbable. A stake which was six feet long (and very heavy) would be an encumbrance not a weapon, though not so much of an encumbrance as a stake which was eight feet long (as suggested by Steve Beck) or eleven (as once proposed by Desmond Seward).[18]

At the time of the battle of Montlhéry in 1465, the French counsellor and historian Philippe de Commynes (1447–1511) wrote: 'My advice is that archers are the most important thing in the world, but only if they are present in large numbers. In small numbers they are useless.' The Chaplain tells us there were 5,000 English archers at Agincourt, but Waurin and Le Fèvre each mention 10,000. As we have already seen, the archives show that there were 4,128 mounted archers and 3,772 foot archers who embarked at Southampton, but the number present at Agincourt cannot be known for certain.

The Burgundian chroniclers tell us that the archers operated as a corps, commanded by Sir Thomas Erpingham. Supposedly, Erpingham spoke personally to his troops, urging them 'to fight with vigour'; and he gave the signal to attack by throwing his baton in the air and shouting the mysterious command *Nestroque!* In England this has at various times been thought to mean *'Now Strike!'* or *'Now Stretch!'* and even *'Menée stroke!'* (the order to blow a hunting horn), while in France it has been thought to be a chivalric motto or battle-cry. If it was the latter, the family in question has not been identified.[19]

There is little doubt about the devastating effects of the arrow-storm. Waurin and Le Fèvre both say that the archers shot volleys of arrows 'for as long as they could pull the bow'. Also

> [the French] horses were so troubled by the arrow shot of the English archers that they could not hold or control them. As a result the vanguard fell into disorder and countless numbers of men at arms began to fall. Those on horseback were so afraid of death that they put themselves into flight away from the enemy. Because of the example they set many of the French left the field in flight.

Gilles Bongrain takes the view that the rate of shooting produced by English archers in 1415 was not equalled by firearms until 1866–70.[20] French losses as a result of archery have also been compared to those inflicted by the British on the Madhi's army at Omdurman in 1898, when they used machine-guns.

How did the archers draw their bows? Excavation of the skeletons of the men buried at Visby in Denmark, after a battle fought there in 1361, showed that many of the dead had been killed by missiles which fell vertically from above, splitting the links of their mail hoods and penetrating the skull. Illustrations of the Battle of Shrewsbury (1403) show medieval archers pulling their drawstrings back as far as their right shoulders, rather than to their mouths or chests or ears; but it is possible that not everyone was trained in the same way. A dummy in the Royal Armouries which I saw in 2008 portrayed a man leaning backwards onto his right leg as he aimed for the sky. However, much depends on the range; and if it is right that the archers ran up the field of battle to shorten this before firing, the problems posed by firing over a great distance would have been reduced.

The maximum range of a longbow is thought to have been around 400 yards, but it is said to have been 'effective' at 200, and lethal at 80.

It took great strength to pull a longbow; and indeed it has often seemed as if the force required was incredibly large; but we have recently learned that the strength was there – the result of long years of training and practice. When Henry VIII's ship *Mary Rose* was discovered and excavated in the 1970s, several hundred bow staves were found in or near the wreck and, although the vessel sank in 1545, there is little doubt that these staves are of the same type as would have been used at Agincourt, 130 years before. Marine archaeologists and other scientists have been able to reconstruct longbows of this type, and archers were able to test them, establishing that the draw-weight was as much as 170lbs. This is truly amazing. (For comparison, a Yorkshire archer whom I met while researching this book told me that, for practice at short range, he uses a bow with a draw-weight of only 26 or 28lbs.) But the English acquired their expertise at some cost to their health. Some of the skeletons found at Towton in Yorkshire in 1996 were found to have significant musculoskeletal changes in the arms and the back.[21]

Archery was deeply embedded in English culture, long before Agincourt. It was a popular sport and – unlike football – it was encouraged by the authorities. It was practised by boys and men from the age of 12, throughout the length and breadth of the kingdom, and from the fourteenth century a series of statutes, ordinances and local legislation sought to discourage other sports. Christine de Pisan wrote that:

> In this art young Englishmen are still instructed from early youth, and for this reason they commonly surpass other archers. They can hit a target from a distance of 600 feet. Vegetius says that this art must be practised constantly even by skilled masters ...

But we may ask how an arrow, fired by a longbow, could penetrate armour, some of which was made from steel in 1415? John Lydgate did not find it difficult to answer this question at the time.

> *Our archers stood up full heartily*
> *And made the Frenchmen fast to bleed.*
> *Their arrows went fast, without any let,*
> *And many shot they throughout;*
> *Throughout habergeon, breastplate, and bassinet*
> *An eleven thousand were slain in that rout.*

Some modern experts are sceptical; but much depends on the type of arrowhead which is used, the force which is applied and the trajectory of the arrow, as well as on the type of metal used to make the armour and the skill of the armourer. Given the dearth of archaeological finds on early fifteenth-century battlefields, and the almost complete absence of them at Azincourt, any ballistic tests on reproduction armour with reproduction arrowheads are likely to be of limited value. Nevertheless, such tests have been carried out, for example in 2002, for the TV programme *Agincourt's Dark Secrets*. These purported to show that even the bodkin type of arrowhead was incapable of penetrating armour made of best quality steel; but, in Gilliot's book *Azincourt* (2007) Gilles Bongrain set out the results of other trials, and purported to demonstrate the opposite.

Even if the ability of the arrow to penetrate armour was as poor as some tests suggest, the fact remains that a horse cannot be totally protected by armour; and an 'arrowstorm' was undoubtedly capable of breaking up formations of infantry and cavalry, in particular of creating chaos amongst the horses. In 1976 John Keegan argued that the main damage must have been done to French horses rather than Frenchmen: armoured only on the head, many horses would have run out of control when they were struck in the back or flank.[22]

Some accounts suggest that the archers provided their own longbows; but in fact this had ceased to be so in the time of Edward III. By 1415 it was the Crown which commanded the making of bows and arrows, and this was a skilled business, controlled by guilds of bowyers, stringers, fletchers and arrowsmiths. It was in everyone's interest that quality goods be produced, and in 1405 Henry IV had legislated against arrowsmiths who produced arrowheads which had not been properly tempered.[23] On 20 April 1415 Henry V ordered Nicholas Frost to provide workmen, at the King's expense, to make and repair the King's bows as required, and for that purpose to procure bow staves from any place he thought proper, except from the property of the Church. Frost and five other bowyers formed part of the royal retinue. A few days later, Nicholas Mynot, the master fletcher, was ordered to commission twelve other fletchers to make arrows (and crossbow bolts). Doubtless, these men would have their work cut out to make enough for the king's own retinue, but there is no reason to think that the captains in charge of other retinues did not employ similar professionals, as Thomas Mowbray, the Earl Marshall, is known to have done. Despite the traditional view that the best staves were made from English yew planted in churchyards, it was common practice to import yew staves from Spain, Italy and Scandinavia.[24]

The English archer has sometimes been endowed with almost supernatural powers. Wylie wrote of his 'swift and unerring skill': apparently, he 'shot never arrow amiss'. In 1976, Robert Hardy appeared to think that this skill was heritable.

> At his best there was no man in the world to beat him, no matter the odds against him; and his breed lasted long beyond the longbow; he used the musket and the rifle; he endured in 1915 the same, and worse, than his forefathers had suffered in 1415 ... He will never entirely perish because for all the sloth and the cantankerous emulation that lie side by side in his nature, he shares with the best of mankind, courage, clear sight and honesty.

In *The Adventure of English* (2003) Melvyn Bragg could still write that 'it was the English bowmen with their hearts of oak who turned the battle'. This is stirring stuff but it is scarcely serious history.

In *Agincourt* (1964) Christopher Hibbert wrote that the French knights decided to charge the men at arms rather than the archers, because it was only the former who were worthy opponents. There was, he argued, 'no reputation to be won in fighting archers'. It seems unlikely that snobbery dictated tactics in this way, but something of Hibbert's view remained in John Keegan's highly-acclaimed *Face of Battle* (1976), which suggested that the French third line was never committed because some French noblemen thought it beneath them to join the fray; but what class of men were the archers, exactly? There is no simple answer.

The chroniclers all describe the archers as commoners. Some were even barefooted, while

> most were without armour, dressed in their doublets, their hose loose about their knees, having axes or swords hanging from their belts. Many had bare heads and were without headgear ... [though some had] *hunettes* or *cappelines* of boiled leather and some of osier on which they had a binding of iron ...

In the novels written by Michael Cox and Bernard Cornwell, Jenkin Lloyd and Nicholas Hook are landless peasants, and Cox's hero tells us that his friends are of the same ilk. The economic historian M. M. Postan (1964) wrote that when he studied medieval court rolls, peasant genealogies and inheritance cases, he often found that peasants were missing because they were 'absent, missing or slain in their lord's or the king's service'. The longbow was certainly an ancient weapon, and one which was never considered a noble one; and the archers were certainly inferior socially to the men at arms. They were paid less; they were treated very differently when it came to military discipline, and the code of chivalry did not apply to them. When Henry gave that fateful order to slaughter the French prisoners, the men in charge of the prisoners refused and it was the archers who were ordered to finish the job.[25] Supposedly, they were less squeamish, because they were unversed in chivalrous ways; but, if the English archer was relatively low-born, how lowly was he?

These same archers have also been described as the backbone of English society. Shakespeare seems to have thought so

And you, good yeoman,
Whose limbs were made in England, show us here
The mettle of your pasture; let us swear
That you are worth your breeding; which I doubt not.

This English yeoman – a man like Shakespeare's Michael Williams – had appeared in Chaucer's *Canterbury Tales* at the end of the fourteenth century and in Roger Asham's *Toxophilus* (1545), while Charles Dickens was also enthusiastic about him.[26] He even re-appeared in the opera *Merrie England*, in the early twentieth century.

Who were the Yeomen –
The Yeomen of England?
The freemen were the Yeomen,
The freemen of England!

Where are the Yeomen –
The Yeomen of England?
In home-stead and in cottage
They still dwell in England!
Stained with the ruddy tan,
God's air doth give a man.

This was untrue even in 1902, when most Englishmen already lived in towns. Yet the myth that Agincourt was won by the yeomen, indeed by sturdy *Saxon* yeomen, was expounded in detail in an article written by Major-General Sir Frederick Maurice for the *Cornhill Magazine* as late as 1908.[27] For some years after the Second World War, schoolboys still sang about *The Yeomen of England*, though there were not many us who lived in cottages and, if there were any ruddy tans amongst us, they must have been acquired in Mallorca.

The truth is that yeomen were commoners but they were not at the bottom of the pile. In the earliest ballads about Robin Hood the 'merry men' are described as 'good yeomen', despite being outlaws. In Chaucer's *Canterbury Tales* the Knight has two attendants, the squire and the yeoman, and the yeoman has a horse of his own, though he is the other's servant. In 1413 Parliament enacted a statute which required anyone who brought a lawsuit to describe himself; and the terms men most commonly used were 'knight', 'squire', 'gentleman', 'yeoman' and 'husbandman'. The French Rolls for 1415 contain several references to 'yeomen of the household' or 'yeoman usher of the household'; and these were clearly men who enjoyed relatively high social status. In the 1460s the Lancastrian jurist Sir John Fortescue, described the English yeoman in glowing terms: it was he who was responsible for the fact that England was a comparatively prosperous country, compared to France; and the system of trial by jury, which Fortescue revered, depended upon the verdict of the 'twelve good men and true', all yeomen farmers.

Yet there was also an association between archery and crime. The tales of Robin Hood predate Agincourt by more than a hundred years; and the term 'Robinhood', 'Robehod' or 'Hobbehod' seems to have become official shorthand for any fugitive or outlaw. The first literary reference occurs in William Langland's late fourteenth century *Piers the Plowman*, where Sloth, the lazy priest, confesses 'I know not perfectly my Paternoster, as the priest it singeth, but I know rhymes of Robyn Hood, and Ranulf Earl of Chester'.

Edward Powell showed that some of those who fought at Agincourt – admittedly not very many – were pardoned criminals. This was because Henry V went to great lengths to restore law and order in England *before* embarking for France in 1415. He instituted an unprecedented number of enquiries, assizes and trials of all kinds and even issued a general pardon, in December 1414. Powell's conclusion was that

> It would perhaps be an exaggeration to say that the battle of Agincourt was won in the court of King's Bench; but there is no doubt that in order to explain Henry's successes in France, we must first look to his achievement in restoring order in England.[28]

This puts a fresh complexion on the traditional tales of the 'noble' yeoman archer.

The French context of Agincourt is important. In France, the bulk of the English army, composed as it was of archers, was seen as socially

Henry V's chantry at Westminster Abbey.

Portchester Castle, the Palace of Richard II.

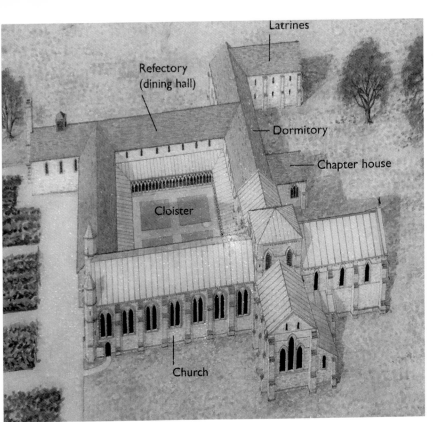

Titchfield Abbey.

Latrines

Refectory
(dining hall)

Dormitory

Chapter house

Cloister

Church

Titchfield Abbey, the Tudor gatehouse.

Wolvesey Castle.

The Somme near Voyenne.

The battlefield, 2009.

The Calvary, *La Gacogi*

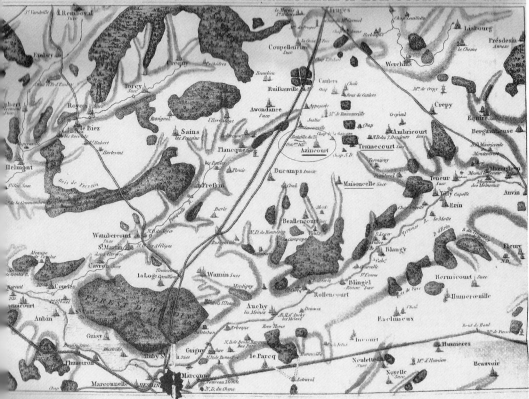

Nicolas's map of area, 1827.

Nicolas's map of battlefield, 1827.

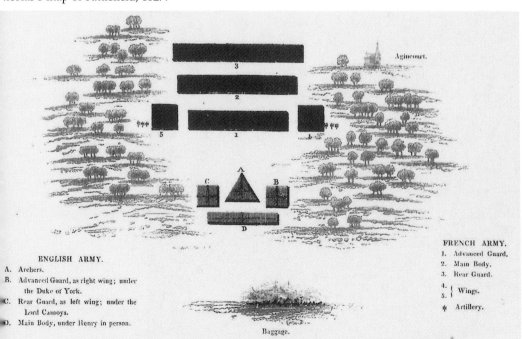

ENGLISH ARMY.
A. Archers.
B. Advanced Guard, as right wing; under the Duke of York.
C. Rear Guard, as left wing; under the Lord Camoys.
D. Main Body, under Henry in person.

FRENCH ARMY.
1. Advanced Guard.
2. Main Body.
3. Rear Guard.
4. } Wings.
5. }
✣ Artillery.

Agincourt.

Baggage.

Maisoncelles.

POSITION OF THE ENGLISH AND FRENCH ARMIES,
ON THE MORNING OF THE 25TH OF OCTOBER, 1415.

The Agincourt Museum, 2009.

Sir Lewis Robessart,
Westminster Abbey.

The Jewel Tower, Westminster.

The Guildhall, London.

The Tower of London.

Henry V, York Minster

Henry V in Cassell's *History*.

Owain Glyndwr, Pennal.

The Castle of Vincennes, Paris.

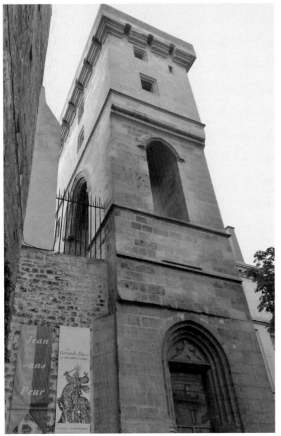

The Tower of Duke John the Fearless, Paris.

Thomas Chaucer, Ewelme.

Henry V's shield (Westminster Abbey).

Henry V's achievements (Westminster Abbey)

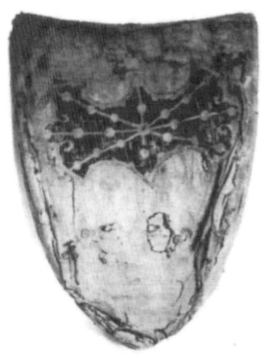

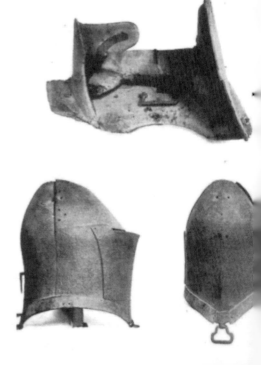

Gloucester's chantry,
St Albans Cathedral.

Cardinal Beaufort,
Winchester Cathedral.

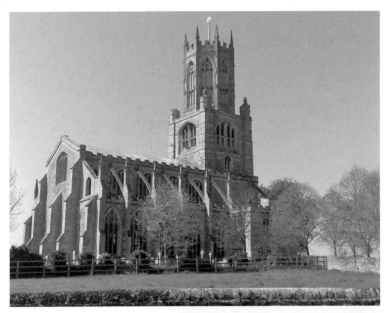

Fotheringhay.

The 2nd Earl of Suffolk, Wingfield.

William ap Thomas, Abergavenny.

The Erpingham Gate, Norwich.

Sir Simon Felbrigg, Felbrigg.

Sir Roger Vaughan, Bredwardine.

Lord Bardolph, Dennington.

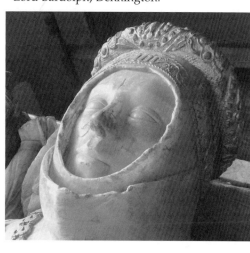

John de Roos, Bottesford.

The Albert Memorial Chapel, Windsor.

The Royal Window, All Souls College, Oxford.

Archbishop Chichele, All Souls College, Oxford.

Lyme Hall, Cheshire.

Groombridge.

An archer, Royal Armouries, Leeds.

Auchy-lès-Hesdin.

Henry V, Strawberry Hill.

inferior because there was no real equivalent to the yeoman class there. The Monk of St Denis lamented the fact that, on the day.

the nobility of France were taken prisoner or else perished under the blows of a faceless soldiery. O eternal dishonour! O disaster for ever to be deplored! If it is usually a consolation for men of heart and a softening of their sadness to think that they have been beaten by adversaries of noble origin and of a recognised valour, it is on the other hand a double shame, a double ignominy, to allow oneself to be beaten by unworthy and vile men.

All writers agree that the repeated 'arrowstorms', shot at a rate of around ten arrows a minute, had a devastating effect on the French. Some think that they shot so rapidly that the English must have run out of arrows quite quickly; but Wylie was confident that 'the supply was enormous and cartloads were always kept at hand in readiness for refills'. This is also the line taken by Robert Hardy, who found it incredible that the high command would have risked the 'paralysis' brought on by the lack of ammunition. Juliet Barker writes that each archer had around seventy-two arrows. The more usual view, taken for example by Paul Hitchin, is that he had two quivers, with twenty-four arrows in each.[29] Even if there were only 5,000 archers, this is still enough to produce a tremendous hail of arrows; but the arrows would still have run out, and probably within a matter of minutes. If that is right, the question is what the archers did next.

The Chaplain gives us an answer:

When the arrows were all used up, seizing axes, stakes and swords and spear-heads that were lying about, they struck down, hacked and stabbed the enemy.

Le Fèvre and Waurin agree.

And soon afterwards, the English archers, seeing the breaking up of the French vanguard, came out from behind their stakes all together and threw down their bows and arrows, taking up their swords, axes and other arms and weapons (swords, hatchets, mallets, axes, falcon beaks and other weapons). They struck wherever they saw breaks in the line. They knocked down and killed the French ...

The tactical significance of the actions described here is enormous, because at Agincourt the archers had already carried out their main task, which was to defend the men at arms; but, evidently, they had not been able to prevent the enemy from reaching the English line. The secondary function which they now performed, when they joined their more heavily-armed compatriots in hand-to-hand fighting, was therefore of vital importance.

This is not something which could easily have happened in a French army, where the missile arm was usually composed of crossbowmen, who were either foreign mercenaries (as at Crécy in 1346), or were provided by the town militias; but it was a necessity in the case of the English army, where the knights and men at arms might well be outnumbered. Further, according to the Monk of St Denis, the English archers wielded a new type of weapon: 'They had lead-hammers [*massues de plomb*] which, with a single blow, were capable of killing a man, or at any rate of laying him out unconscious.' This has the ring of truth. The excavations at Towton confirm that in the fifteenth century it became common to use weapons which were designed to crush and pierce armour, rather than swords, which might bounce off. This was partly the result of the improvements which had taken place in plate armour. For whatever reason, the English bowmen now used hammers to batter their opponents. They may also have made use of their notorious 'kidney' or 'bollock' daggers.[30]

The question posed by Strickland and Hardy is whether the archers joined the *mêlée* by chance – because they had run out of arrows – or whether this was a deliberate (and rehearsed) tactic, designed to enable the English army as a whole to mount a counterattack, once the French vanguard had been disrupted by archery. The second is the more likely explanation, and it is suggested in the accounts provided by Monstrelet, Le Fèvre and Waurin, though as usual the Chaplain only has eyes for the hand of the Lord.

Morale

The Chaplain's account is suffused with the idea that God was on the side of the English, a view which was clearly shared by Henry V, as well as by Oliver Cromwell two centuries later. The surprising thing is that this view is still held today, though it takes a modern form. It is often argued now that the English army enjoyed superior morale, something which is impossible to prove and takes little or no account of the morale of the French, without which any comparison is meaningless.[31] This is also an unnecessary argument (and should rightly be cut down by Ockham's razor) in view of the many other explanations for the victory of the English and the defeat of the French. It also relies too heavily on Shakespeare's Anglocentric vision and the speeches he put in the mouth of Henry V.

Both sides were fighting for their king; but the French were probably more deeply attached to Charles VI in 1415 than the English were (as yet) to Henry. Charles had been king since 1380, whilst Henry had only ascended the throne in 1413, while his father had been regarded by many (in both kingdoms) as a mere usurper. The change of dynasty in 1399 still cast a pall over the Lancastrians' claim to the English throne, let alone their right to the French. Moreover, the French had a higher notion of the sacred nature of the monarchy, whereas the English had deposed their monarch not once but twice. Oscar Wilde might have had something to say about this, and many Frenchmen did say it, at the time. Although Charles VI is known to history both as Charles 'the Well-Beloved' (*Charles le Bien-Aimé*) and 'Charles the Mad' (*Charles le Fol*), he was always known by the former nickname in France; and the evidence suggests that his people did not stop loving him because he suffered from mental illness. Many regarded him as a Christ-like figure, who suffered long and in silence, along with his country.[32]

It is often said that loyalty in the modern British Army is based on the regiment; but there were no regiments in 1415. There was the Order of the Garter, but that was a small elite; and the French had their orders of chivalry too, though none so famous. They also had numerous 'fraternities', the basis of loyalty and high morale at a lower level. Unlike the English, they were fighting in defence of their homeland. Both sides were devoted to St George, who had not yet become the exclusive property of the English. Each side also had its military heroes. The English could look back on the achievements of Edward III and his captains, but the French had a living legend in their ranks, in Marshal Boucicaut, and they could look back with pride on the achievements of Bertrand du Guesclin, a commoner who had become Constable of France and was regarded by some French as the 'Tenth Worthy' of chivalry. All the great literature of the late Middle Ages about war and romance was written in French; and the French were also known for having the largest and one of the oldest universities in the world, in Paris, as well as having provided Christendom with many more famous saints, bishops, abbots and even popes, than the English had ever done.

Henry V may have believed that he had a mission to punish the French for their vices; but there is no evidence that the English shared that sense of purpose and, though they offered up prayers for his success, the French also prayed for their King and nation. The Monk of St Denis mentions organised processions. Both sides were brought up to believe that they were descended from Trojans who had fled Troy when it was sacked by the Greeks, centuries before Christ. The English believed they were descended from Brut, while the French traced their ancestry to Francion, son of Hector.[33]

The historian must regretfully conclude that the English and the French disliked each other – they had probably done so since the Norman Conquest – and that this antipathy probably played a part in motivating the troops on each side at Agincourt. England had been almost continuously at war with France since 1337 and there is evidence of English dislike of the French in the poetry of Laurence Minot (1300–52).[34] On the other side of the xenophobic coin, some of the French thought that the English were a perfidious race who had murdered their own kings in 1327 and 1399, and inflicted untold damage on France, a view amply confirmed by the great Catholic writer Henri Denifle, when he published his magisterial *La Désolation des Églises, Monastères, Hôpitaux* in the nineteenth century. Others thought that Englishmen were born with tails, a myth which had originated in the twelfth century. Soldiers on both sides were told by their comrades that

> *One of us is worth four of them*
> *Or, at least, well worth three.*

Tudor historians tell us that, on 24 October, the French were confident of victory and spent the night carousing and gambling on the fate of the English prisoners they would take next day. There are stories which suggest that they even expected to take Henry prisoner and parade him through the streets of Rouen and Paris in a cart. On the other hand, Le Fèvre tells us that the French troops (and horses!) comported themselves well on the eve of battle.

> Although the French numbered 50,000 men and had a great number of wagons, carts, canons, *ribaudequins* and other military equipment, they had very few musical instruments to cheer them up and hardly any of their horses neighed during the night, which some saw as amazing and a sign of things to come.

Shakespeare wrote of the 'little touch of Harry' which served to boost morale on the eve of the battle; and this metaphor has appealed to some historians though, if Desmond Seward is right and the King ordered his men to maintain silence at night, this too must be a myth.[35]

Did Henry V speak to the troops? Some chroniclers have him rousing his men immediately before the battle, others have him giving them a 'pep-talk' the night before; but Hardyng's brief account has no reference to a speech. In Walsingham's version the speech is mundane and could have been made before any battle. In 1992 Christopher Allmand referred to a shout – *In the Name of Almighty God and St George, avaunt banner! And St George this day thine help!* – which would certainly have provided the basis for a battlecry, and one which invoked the patron saint of England; but in a footnote he also refers to a phrase used in one version of the *Brut* chronicle which is a command rather than a battlecry – *Felas, let's go!* and this was also cited by Juliet Barker, almost fifteen years later.[36]

There is a much more eloquent speech in a contemporary English text.

And then he said to his lords and to his army, 'Sirs and fellows, the yonder army thinks to stop us, but they will not attack us, let every man prove himself a good man this day, and advance banners, in the best time of the year, for as I am a true king and knight, for me this day England shall never ransom pay.'

Le Fèvre has the following

[the king] made very fine speeches, encouraging them to do well, saying he had come to France to recover what was [his] rightful inheritance, telling them that they could fight freely and securely in this quarrel and that they should remember that they had been born in England where their fathers and mothers, wives and children, were at this moment ... The kings of England, his predecessors, had gained many splendid victories over the French ... In addition, he told them that the French had boasted that if any English archers were captured they would cut off the three fingers of their right hand so that neither man nor horse would ever again be killed by their arrow fire.

This is a very clever speech, combining appeals to patriotism, history and the instinct for self-preservation; but it differs markedly from Shakespeare, not only in its lack of poetry, but in the fact that it was evidently delivered more than once. Le Fèvre refers to 'speeches' in the plural, which makes good sense when we remember that there were no megaphones or microphones in the fifteenth century. As to the French threat to chop off the bowmen's fingers (and in other versions, to sell them at six a penny), there is no supporting evidence for this. Indeed, it is unlikely that the French would have wasted their time in mutilating worthless prisoners, when they could kill them outright; but the threat may of course have been repeated, to stiffen their resolve.[37]

Why did the archers fight so fiercely? Superstition was as strong as religious faith in medieval times, and there is a very old story that each man took a piece of earth in his mouth before going into battle; but the English *Brut* tells the tale in more pedestrian terms. According to this, the English merely made the sign of the cross on the ground and kissed it, in remembrance of Christ's sacrifice. Dominique Paladilhe thinks that the traditional account does not indicate Christian motivation: he thinks that, when they embraced the sod, the English were merely accepting the possibility that they might finish the day lying under it.

When the *Bourgeois* de Paris was in xenophobic mood, he wrote that all Englishmen were murderers and thieves (*murdriers et larrons*), and it seems that many Parisians shared his view, at least during the English occupation of the capital between 1420 and 1437; but there were good reasons for the English to fight hard on 25 October, apart from a criminal propensity to violence. After all, they were on their way home, but had been stopped in their tracks. If they were to survive, they had to fight their way out. Moreover, the life and liberty of the King – and therefore the kingdom – was at stake. The English were invaders but there may have been a 'backs to the wall' mentality at work, such as Field Marshal Haig famously sought to invoke during the *Kaiserschlacht* of Spring 1918. From the French point of view, Charles VI was safe in Rouen, the English were not on their way to Paris and this was not a situation where the French needed to draw a line and proclaim *Ils ne passeront pas!*, as they did at Verdun in 1916.

After the battle was over, the French had cause to examine their souls and various writers reflected a profound sense of disappointment and demoralisation. When Alain Chartier's four ladies talk about Agincourt in their *Quadrilogue Invectif*, it is the ignominious flight at the end of the day which is the focus of their attention

> *Their ugly and notorious flight*
> *Awarded victory to our enemies*

Similar sentiments appear in the verses of Robert Blondel (c. 1390–c. 1460), a poet from the Cotentin, described by Contamine as a Norman patriot:[38]

> *The fields of France are empty of men*
> *Because all the French have gone*
> *The good are dead, the others have fled*

Françoise Autrand has pointed out that Pride, Avarice, Indiscipline, Cowardice and even Dame Stupidity, all had a part to play in the French defeat.[39]

The great French historian Jules Michelet (1798–1874) confused morale and morality. Writing twenty-five years after the defeat of Napoleon I, he reflected that Henry V resembled Oliver Cromwell in his sanctimoniousness. The most galling experience which the French prisoners taken at Agincourt had to suffer was to be lectured to by him, and he solemnly told them that they were sinners, and the authors of their own misfortune. At one point Michelet even seems to agree, because there had never been a time when France witnessed 'so much disorder, hedonism, sin and vice'. Yet, when he examined the state of the French medieval soul more carefully, he cited numerous examples of chivalrous and Christian behaviour. Michelet concluded (unsurprisingly) that there was no truth in the notion that the French sinned more than the English. This stands in stark contrast to the view which Charles Dickens conveyed in his *Child's History of England* (1851–3) when he assured his young readers that the French nobility was 'proud and wicked'.

Is there anything left of the idea that English morale was higher on the day? From Roman times onwards, writers emphasised the importance of training, discipline and experience and therefore of the role played by veterans. While the French must have had their veterans too, it is likely that the English had more, or proportionately more. Matthew Bennett believes that many of the men enrolled in English retinues were professional soldiers in all but name, men who went from contract to contract and were very used to war, and to fighting in each other's company; and this conclusion is supported by a study of the database recently established by the ICMA Centre and Southampton University.[40] Some of the soldiers who fought with Henry in 1415 had also participated in the expeditions of 1411 and 1412. They were linked by pre-existing ties of locality and household;[41] and, by the time the army reached Agincourt, they must have become used to marching and fighting together, to common discipline, and common training. The French had the advantage of numbers, but they were essentially a 'scratch' force.

Chapter 8

The Memory of Agincourt

Why do we remember Agincourt, when the Chaplain also tells the story of other miraculous victories, won the following year, which are now almost entirely forgotten? The only territorial gain in 1415 was Harfleur, and this was only preserved because of the Duke of Exeter's successful defence of the town during the winter of 1415–16, and Bedford's victory at sea in the spring of 1416. For that matter, why remember Agincourt in preference to Verneuil, the Duke of Bedford's great victory of 1424? Verneuil allowed the English to invade and conquer Maine, and then advance to the Loire.

The answer is that Agincourt was a royal achievement, rather than a ducal one, and it was the first major English victory won on the Continent since 1367. It was a triumph for the King and the country, and one which the authorities wanted to celebrate, both in London and throughout the counties of England. The Chaplain spends more time describing the festivities in the capital than he does in describing the battle itself.

There was also something intensely dramatic about Agincourt, where the fate of two kingdoms turned upon a bloody confrontation which lasted a few hours. In the cold light of day we might choose to remember Henry V's role in founding the Royal Navy. As a result, the ports of Normandy fell into his hands and remained under English control for a generation. The Dauphin was reduced to using La Rochelle on the Atlantic when he wanted to bring in Scottish reinforcements; and for some years English sea-captains were able to cross the Channel without fear of molestation by foreign vessels or pirates; but, in a chivalric world, his achievements at sea did not win the same kind of fame for Henry V as his victory on land.

Celebration and Lamentation

Of its nature, the march from Harfleur to Calais was a risky business and the English feared for the fate of their army. Rumours must have abounded, and the Letter Book of the City of London records a 'lamentable report, replete with sadness', received in the capital on the very day of the battle, that the King had met with disaster.[1] Conversely, a rumour

reached Abbeville that the French had won a great victory, and a cele-
bratory feast was arranged. The festivities must have been distinctly
muted when news of what had really happened arrived.

Agincourt was fought on a Friday, and accurate information did not
arrive in London until the following Tuesday, 29 October (the day Henry
arrived in Calais). About a month later the Londoners welcomed Henry
back to the City, an event which was recorded in the *Brut* and in the
London chronicles. This is the Chaplain's triumphant account.[2]

> And the citizens, having heard the greatly-longed for, nay indeed
> most joyful news, of his arrival, had in the meantime made ready
> themselves and their city ... for the reception ... and on that eagerly
> awaited Saturday [23 November 1415] they went out to meet the king
> as far as the heights of Blackheath, that is the mayor and the twenty-
> four aldermen in scarlet and other citizens of lower degree in red
> gowns with parti-coloured hoods of red and white, to the number of
> about 20,000 on horses. All of them, according to their crafts, wore
> some particularly rich-fashioned badge which conspicuously distin-
> guished the crafts from one another.[3]

Londoners were used to staging processions – the Mayor and Aldermen
paraded through the city several times a year; but the festivities on this
occasion were unusually elaborate. The City fathers spared no expense.

> When the tower at the entrance to [London] bridge was reached,
> there was seen placed high on top of it, and representing as it were the
> entrance into the city's jurisdiction, an image of a giant of astonishing
> size who, looking down upon the King's face, held, like a champion, a
> great axe in his right hand and, like a warder, the keys of the city
> hanging from a baton in his left. At his right side stood a figure of a
> woman, not much smaller in size, wearing a scarlet mantle and adorn-
> ments appropriate to her sex; and they were like a man and his wife
> who, in their richest attire, were bent upon seeing the eagerly awaited
> face of their lord and welcoming him with abundant praise.

At London Bridge the King encountered a giant, whose message was very
clear.

> *Upon the gate there stood on high,*
> *A giant that was full grim of sight,*
> *To teach the Frenchmen courtesy.*[4]

When the procession reached the 'the conduit in Cornhill', the tower here was covered with crimson cloth, and displayed the arms of three saints held in high esteem by the English – St George, St Edward and St Edmund; and there was a company of prophets with 'venerable white hair', their heads 'wrapped and turbaned', who released a flock of sparrows and other small birds as the king came by, 'of which some descended on to the king's breast, some settled upon his shoulders, and some circled around in twisting flight'. At the tower of the conduit at the entrance to Cheapside, there was a group of old men dressed as the Apostles, together with twelve English kings, martyrs and confessors, 'girt about the loins with golden belts', with sceptres in their hands and crowns on their heads, singing psalms. They gave the king loaves of silver intermingled with wafers of bread and wine from the pipes and spouts of the conduit – for the gutters were literally flowing with wine that day. When the procession reached the cross in Cheapside, there was a mock castle, a mock bridge and a gatehouse, with:

> a choir of most beautiful young maidens, very chastely adorned in pure white raiment and virgin attire, singing together with timbrel and dance, as if to another David coming from the slaying of Goliath (which might appropriately be represented by the arrogant French) this song of congratulation: 'Welcome Henry ye fifte, Kynge of England and of France'.

All the way from London to Westminster were dense crowds, with people of all classes. Thomas Walsingham tells us that:

> It is impossible to describe the joy, rejoicing and the triumph with which [Henry] was welcomed by the Londoners, because the elaborate arrangements, the enormous expenditure, the variety of spectacles would need a short book to themselves. [He] was met by an extraordinarily large crowd – it seemed to comprise everyone in London. The abbot and convent of Westminster received him with a magnificent procession and led him to [Westminster Abbey].

Henry V was musical,[5] but various chroniclers tells us that when he made his entry into London he would not suffer any songs to be sung in his praise, because the victory was God's. Whether this injunction was seriously intended or universally obeyed may be open to question, since the King had taken minstrels with him on the Agincourt expedition and Rymer's *Foedera* contains confirmation that he always rewarded them well.

We cannot know what Henry V was thinking; but in 1947 the historian Ernest Jacob, who had served in the First World War, concluded that Londoners noticed his 'sober and reserved expression'; and he speculated that Henry might well have been reflecting on 'the narrowness of his escape [at Agincourt] and the need for different tactics next time'. Pugh suggested that the King 'may well have been contemplating his plans for the conquest of France and for seizing its Crown', while Seward added that 'other spectators may have attributed his restrained bearing to his known piety and humility'.[6] All this is speculation, apparently based on a single remark made by the Chaplain, who merely wrote

> From his quiet demeanour, gentle pace, and sober progress, it might have been gathered that the king, silently pondering the matter in his heart, was rendering thanks and glory to God alone, not to man.

Agincourt gave rise to a number of poems, ballads and songs, for example the *Agincourt Carol*, which was probably composed in Henry V's own chapel or in a monastery connected with the royal house.[7]

> *Our King went forth to Normandy*
> *With grace and might of chivalry*
> *There God for him wrought marvellously;*
> *Wherefore England may call and cry*
> [Chorus]
> *Deo gratias*
> *Deo gratias Anglia redde pro victoria!*

Ballads may well represent the authentic voice of the English people (and they evidence a visceral dislike of the French). Adam of Usk included the following verse in his chronicle

> *People of England, cease your work and pray,*
> *For the glorious victory of Crispin's day;*
> *Despite their scorn for Englishmen's renown,*
> *The odious might of France came crushing down.*

Another manuscript contains a dialogue between a Frenchman and an Englishmen. The Frenchman displays the outrage of the innocent victim of an unprovoked attack. He also refers to the old myth that at least some Englishmen were born with tails:

The Verse of the French

Oh you people of England, is this the sum of all your achievements?
Why do you destroy what belongs to the people of France?
Those you have sinned against are the servants of Christ . . .
Break off that poisonous tail which you have always carried around
with you.[8]

In France, news of the catastrophe reached Boulogne on the same day, and the royal family at Rouen heard of it within four days. Several provincial churches held ceremonies of mourning immediately, while the French members of the University of Paris held a service at Martinmas (11 November). Some Parisians were reluctant to take in what they heard. It was over a month before Nicolas de Baye, *greffier* (clerk) to the *Parlement*, mentioned Agincourt, and even then he did not do so by name: he merely referred to 'the affair that the English had against the king' (*la besoigne que ont les Anglois contre le roye*). Later on, he included a poem about it in his Journal, attempting a brief analysis of the causes of French failure.

Piteous outcome . . .
When the house is so divided,
There is no remedy . . .
Counsel is infected with party spirit
A nation is destroyed by prodigality,
The people are reduced to beggary
And each man looks after his own interests.[9]

The poets were even more critical. In Alain Chartier's *Livre des Quatre Dames* (1416–18), the writer attacked those who had failed to do their duty, claiming that they were not the men their fathers had been. Some of them only knew 'how to get their arses out of a tight corner'. Chartier also reproached French knights for their pusillanimity and disloyalty in his *Quadrilogue Invectif* (1422). Christine de Pisan wrote consoling verse, dedicated to Marie de Berry, in which she described the suffering the battle had brought to the great families of France. Marie's third husband, the Duke de Bourbon, was captured and died a prisoner eighteen years later, without ever returning to France. The son she had by her second husband, the Count of Eu, was also captured and only released twenty-three years later; and her son-in-law the Count of Nevers was killed, as were several close cousins.[10]

Wylie wrote that, as each Englishman who had fought at Agincourt reached his home, he was feasted by his friends and the story of the glorious victory spread with songs and music throughout the whole country – echoes of Shakespearean verse here, but there is evidence that it reflected the truth.[11]

> *He that shall live this day, and see old age,*
> *Will yearly on the vigil feast his neighbours.*

News and Propaganda

Henry V wrote to the Mayor and Aldermen of Salisbury on the day of the battle, telling them of his decision to leave Harfleur for Calais 'on account of the grievous pestilence that was prevalent' and how he had no more than 10,000 men when he encountered the French army, some 100,000 strong. He included a long list of the French dead, and said that some 4,000 had been killed, not counting commoners. He contrasted this with fifteen English casualties, and only two members of the nobility. Lastly, he told the men of Salisbury of his triumphal return to London.[12] He also wrote to the authorities in Bordeaux, in a letter which reached them on 23 November 1415. Since Bordeaux was the capital of English Aquitaine, it was ordered that processions should be held and that the people should be convened, to hear 'the good news that has come from the King of the victory in Picardy'.

News of the victory was given to Parliament, and conveyed to the regions by means of speeches, letters, sermons and proclamations. It was proclaimed in every county court and marketplace in the country and spread by chroniclers, poets, storytellers and songwriters, priests and sheriffs. Henry V's appointment of a new 'Agincourt Herald' may have assisted the process (though the title seems to have been dropped during the conquest of Normandy between 1417–19, when Henry was keen to appease local French feelings).[13] The State and the Church controlled the means of communication, so the message was laced with propaganda from the very beginning: the King's cause was just; the French were to blame for the war, because they had refused to agree to his legitimate demands; and God was on the side of the English.

The Church played its part. It was routine for bishops to order parish priests to offer up prayers and give thanks for military success. On 29 October, Bishop Beaufort announced the news of the great victory in St Paul's Cathedral. The message was relayed throughout the 10,000 parishes in England, and prayers were doubtless said in monastic houses too, especially at the royal foundations of Sheen and Syon.[14] Sermons commonly contained 'a note of strong national feeling against the particular enemies of England, be they Frenchmen, Scots or Welsh who happen to have been troubling her peace'; and at least one preacher now referred to 'King Harry' (for so he was often called) as captain of the ship of state.

> At the fierce battle of Agincourt he well nigh oversailed the great cog of France. To many dangers our peerless prince exposed himself for right of the realm. Many bitter storms hath he abided; many sharp showers hath he sustained for the salvation of our ship; and in all perils God hath preserved him ... Many glorious princes and worthy warriors were rulers of our ship before the [Norman] Conquest and after; but none with so few folk passed so tearful a war with the palm of victory as he, at the fierce storm of Agincourt.[15]

A story is told that there was a monastery of French Celestines, in Isleworth Manor, where the monks refused to pray for Henry V, and which was dissolved by him on this account; and this may have some foundation in fact. Because of the long war between England and France, and the animosity which this engendered, the Crown had taken action to expropriate so-called 'alien priories'. These were said to be nests of spies, guilty of trading with the enemy; and, in 1414, Parliament urged that, even if Henry were able to recover his French lands and titles by peaceful negotiation, he would be ill-advised to restore any confiscated property to the French monasteries in England.[16] Henry is known to have used the proceeds of sale of alien priories to fund his new foundations.

A study of the Parliament Rolls for the years 1415–21 shows that Agincourt was used very effectively by the Crown, as an aid to raising revenue for further expeditions. When a session of Parliament was convened in early November 1415 – only two weeks after the battle – Bishop Beaufort (who was Lord Chancellor and Speaker of the House of Lords) lavished extravagant praise on the King.

> God in his great mercy gave him the victory and the Adversary was killed and undone, and it was clearly demonstrated that, by this gracious beginning, his just pursuit of his rights was and is approved by God Almighty.

Beaufort pointed out that the King had only just begun his work and that the French were still recalcitrant; and Parliament's grateful response was to accelerate the collection of money granted in 1414 and vote another grant of money, together with the appropriate customs duties at generous rates, for the rest of his life. Though it stated that this was not to be taken as a precedent by other kings, this was nonetheless a remarkable step. Henry was being treated in the most favourable way, both in relation to direct and indirect taxes. In 1373 Parliament had granted Edward III the same customs duties, but only for the duration of the war; and, although a lifetime grant had been made to Richard II in 1398, no such generosity had been shown to Henry IV.[17]

The parliamentary proceedings in March 1416 were recorded by the Chaplain. Parliament was told that God had now intervened in the long war on each of three occasions, and every time he had favoured the English: at Sluys (the great naval battle off Flanders in 1340), Poitiers,

> and now, thirdly, by our most serene king on the field at Agincourt; where, the unwarlike host of the French having been put to flight, the sword of the French yielded to the sceptre of England in the third avenging sentence, their leading men being captured and their nobles done to death.

By these victories, the English had achieved three important objectives. Firstly, they had deprived the French of their 'chief ports', Calais and Harfleur. Secondly, French morale had been badly shaken.

> As a result of their being infected with fear by the terrible and irreparable disasters befalling them when their men were butchered in those encounters, and especially now, most recently, at Agincourt.

Thirdly, there was the effect of attrition on French military resources.

> as a result of their losing their nobles and brave men in all these battles, and especially in that last dread sentence of God at Agincourt.

In October 1416 it is said that, despite the victory at Agincourt, the French are still refusing to negotiate. They are 'full of pride and thinking nothing of their said defeat and weakness'. Consequently, further taxes are required. A double subsidy of two fifteenths and two tenths is granted but, as the editor of the Roll notes, the 'shoe is now clearly beginning to pinch'; and the taxes are not ordered to be accelerated. It is much the same story when we look at the Roll for the Parliament held in November 1417. Harfleur and Agincourt are mentioned, but only briefly – as 'noble deeds and a marvellous victory' – and the Lord Chancellor also sees fit to remind M.P.s of Henry's previous military success in Wales, and in putting down domestic rebellion. It would appear that mentioning the great battle cuts less ice than it used to. Parliament votes two fifteenths and tenths, but does not order that the money be accelerated.[18]

No Parliament is held in 1418. In that held in October 1419 there is only a brief reference to the 'glorious victory over the French people'. This is doubtless because it has been overtaken by other events. The Duke of Burgundy has been assassinated on the bridge at Montereau, apparently on the orders of the Dauphin. The Commons loyally vote a tenth and a fifteenth payable in February 1420 and a third of a fifteenth and tenth payable in the following November; but this is less than the Crown had hoped for

By the time the Parliament of December 1420 comes to meet, the Treaty of Troyes has been signed. Humphrey, Duke of Gloucester – who was wounded at Agincourt himself and has since distinguished himself during the conquest of Normandy – is in the chair, though the Lord Chancellor does the talking. Since the King has apparently achieved all that he could have hoped for (having won the reversion to the Crown of France, which will fall in when Charles VI dies), no subsidy is asked for and none is granted. Instead the Chancellor recognises the 'great out-pouring recently of money from the land' and asks the Commons to look at other matters. It is striking that no mention at all is made this time of Agincourt. Perhaps this is in deference to the French, who are also to become Henry's subjects, under the Treaty of Troyes. Instead the Lord Chancellor praises the King for 'the suppression of Welsh rebellion in his youth' and for

> the destruction and crushing of heresies and Lollardy here within the kingdom, as well as in the ancient rights pertaining to his Crown of England overseas in the parts of France, and also in the welcome conclusion of peace and unity between him, on behalf of his kingdom of England, and his former adversary of France.

Events move on. There are other triumphs to celebrate and other events which it is more politic for the English to emphasise. Yet the battle remains important to individuals. As Shakespeare realised, 'old men forget', but Agincourt is not easily forgotten by men who were there, and others may have reason to mention it, even when they were not there. When Bedford triumphs at Verneuil in 1424 this is called 'the greatest deed done by Englishmen in our day, save the Battle of Agyncourte'. In 1427 a parliamentary memorandum recalls the service performed by the Duke of Gloucester 'in his happy battle of Agincourt': the reference is part of a campaign by Gloucester (and Salisbury) to obtain payment of arrears of wages still owed to them. Likewise, in 1450 the Duke of Suffolk complains that he is defamed throughout the whole of England, despite the fact that several members of his family lost their lives in the King's service: his father at Harfleur, his eldest brother at Agincourt and two other brothers at Jargeaux in 1429. He adds that he spent a total of seventeen years in the French wars himself, 'without coming home or seeing his land'.[19]

Agincourt was widely, though inaccurately, reported throughout Western Europe. In his *Scotichronicon*, the Scotsman Walter Bower compressed what he must have heard much later into a few garbled lines.

> Henry V king of England ... captured a heavily fortified port in Normandy called Harfleur, then Montvilliers, Honfleur, Caudebec, Tancarville, Caen and Rouen, and subsequently nearly all Normandy. Thereafter, following the appointment of certain keepers to guard the towns and castles, and considering that many of his army had died of dysentery, he planned to move with his army of 12,000 men to England for a time to recover themselves. But on the way they were surrounded by a host of Frenchmen and there was a clash which was bitterly fought at Agincourt near St Pol, where 200,000 Frenchmen were defeated.

News of the battle reached Constance in Switzerland some three weeks after the event. The Venetian chronicler Antonio Morosini heard that the French had responded vigorously to the invasion and that the English had been forced to retreat to Calais with their tails between their legs. He also heard reports predicting that the French, having prevented the enemy from crossing the Somme, would soon overwhelm them. Then he heard that a battle had been fought in the county of Artois 'between France and Picardy', and the French had suffered a terrible defeat. Morosini listed the chief members of the French nobility and high command who had been taken prisoner. He listed twenty-six who had been killed, while noting the reports that a total of between 10,000 and 12,000 others had also perished. He reported no English casualties. The kingdom of France was desolated, 'a prey to the anger of God'. The survivors were divided among themselves. In Morosini's view, the French were finished if they did not change their ways.[20] The Greek writer Laonicus Chalcocondyles remarked that the English were 'renowned in arms and victorious in war ... the use of the longbow is [their] peculiar and decisive advantage', though there is no evidence that he ever heard of Agincourt specifically.

Memory and Commemoration

Given the scale of the English victory, we might have expected that we would still have some monument of it in England, some medieval equivalent of Nelson's Column or Waterloo Station; but in fact there is nothing of that kind. Henry V founded no less than three monasteries in the neighbourhood of the palace which he intended to build at Sheen on the Thames (though only two were ever built). He spent around £10,000 on the project. He also left books to Syon and Sheen; but not a trace of these foundations can now be seen. Likewise, we can no longer view the pavilion, or 'Pleasance in the Marsh' at Kenilworth Castle, which he built in 1417. All these buildings were pulled down in the reign of Henry VIII.[21]

Henry V died at the age of 36, in 1422, in the castle of Vincennes, on the outskirts of Paris. According to Pseudo-Elmham, his body was so emaciated that it did not require evisceration, prior to embalming. It was taken to the burial place of the French kings at St Denis and thence to England, to be buried at the east end of Edward the Confessor's Chapel in Westminster Abbey; but there was not enough room and it was decided to place the tomb in the ambulatory. Henry had made a will with detailed directions regarding the prayers to be said, masses to be sung, and candles to be burnt.[22]

The royal tomb is entirely typical of its time, with effigy, tomb-chest and canopy. It is part of a chantry chapel which forms a miniature building within the main body of the Abbey church. The inscription reads

Henry V, scourge of the French [*Gallorum mastix*] lies here. Henry was put in the urn 1422. Virtue conquers all. The fair Catherine finally joined her husband 1437.

Henry's effigy shows a young, clean-shaven man, not dissimilar to the well-known Tudor profile.

The Clerk of the King's Works was paid £12 to purchase Caen stone for the chantry and a further £23 6s 8d was paid for labour. The tomb supporting the effigy was of Purbeck marble. Henry's effigy was made of wood plated with silver gilt, but the head and hands were made of solid silver. Some of the more precious parts had disappeared by 1467 and the entire head was stolen in Tudor times. Some years later, the antiquary William Camden, in an essay entitled 'Of the Antiquity of Epitaphs in England', deplored this burglary and vandalism but, when Joseph Addison of *The Spectator* visited the tomb in 1712, he found that Henry was still 'without a Head'. His fictional Tory friend Sir Roger de Coverley was told by the custodian that it had been stolen, and quipped 'Some Whig,

I warrant you, You ought to lock up your Kings better. They will carry off the Body too, if you don't take care'. But the missing head was never found and it was only replaced in 1971, with one made of polyester.[23]

Henry V's funeral 'achievements' – the saddle, shield, sword and helmet which once hung on a beam above his tomb – are kept in the Abbey Museum at Westminster. The helmet has a dent in it high above the right ear and Monstrelet, the *Liber Metricus* of Thomas Elmham and Shakespeare all referred to 'the king's bruised helmet'. The late John Keegan (writing in 1976) still thought that this was the very helmet which was dented at Agincourt, and when this was lent to the British Museum for an exhibition in 2012 there was no suggestion there to the contrary; but this cannot be right.[24] The helmet in question is very obviously a great helm, of the kind used in tournaments and often depicted in coats of arms, which would have been totally unsuitable for use on the battlefield.

Bishops and abbots were present in great numbers when a solemn funeral service was held on 1 December, for Edward, Duke of York, Michael, Duke of Suffolk and all those, English and French, who had fallen at Harfleur and Agincourt. The king's uncle the Earl of Dorset came to this service from Harfleur, though the town was still under siege by the French. There was a requiem mass the following day.

Henry particularly wanted to ensure that Agincourt would be remembered on the anniversary of the battle; and we are told by the Chaplain that he celebrated St Crispin's Day privately in the chapel royal on the first anniversary, 25 October 1416.

> There came round in due course the Feast of Saints Crispin and Crispinian, on which feast, the year before, God had shown His Clemency to England in her resistance to the rebellious people of France at Agincourt, the king, not unmindful of God's goodness, renewed praises to Him in the hymn *Te Deum laudamus*, which was solemnly chanted in his chapel before Mass.

Henry wanted the anniversary of the battle to be remembered much more widely and he consulted with the Church as to how this could most suitably be done. The problem was that there were several competing candidates for veneration. October 25th was the Feast of Saints Crispin and Crispinian, but it was also special to St John of Beverley, who had the advantage of being English (or at any rate Anglo-Saxon) and was an important focus of loyalty in the North of England. It was said that the shrine at Beverley had oozed drops of holy oil, resembling sweat, on the day that Agincourt was fought, which indicated the great exertions which the Saint had made in Heaven on behalf of the English army. Clearly, Archbishop Chichele and his advisers had to be sensitive to the wishes of the whole country in framing legislation for the English Church.

So it was that on 16 December 1416 Henry ordered the Bishop of London to celebrate the feasts of all three Saints on 25 October each year, throughout his diocese and in perpetuity, in commemoration. The Bishop duly referred to the battle in extravagant terms.

> O inexpressible consolation, above all in our own time, but in all times worthy of rejoicing, and always to be remembered, THE FAVOUR-ABLE VICTORY of our most Christian Prince Henry V King of England and his army AT THE BATTLE OF AGINCOURT, recently won in the district of Picardy.

Similar instructions were issued throughout the South of England, indeed all parts of the country forming the Archdiocese of Canterbury.[25]

By the time Shakespeare came to write his history plays in the 1590s, the Protestant Reformation had fatally undermined the way in which the Saints were venerated; and it is noticeable that when John Stowe (1525–1605) and Ralph Holinshed (1529–80) wrote their accounts of the battle, they mentioned that Agincourt was fought on St Crispin's day, but gave credit for the victory to God alone, not to the saints involved. The history written by Edward Hall (1498–1547) is also essentially Protestant, so much so that his book was later placed on the Papacy's index of proscribed works. (Hall gave an account of Henry V's religious celebrations which focuses on psalms rather than saints.)

As for the shrine of St John of Beverley, this was destroyed in 1541, on the orders of Henry VIII, and what remained of the saint's relics was buried under the floor of the Nave in Beverley Minster. Today St John is still venerated in Beverley, but on the day of his death (which was 7 May), not on 'Agincourt day' (25 October), which was the day of his 'translation'. Yet, ironically, Saints Crispin and Crispinian's Day remains a 'Black Letter Saints' Day' in the Anglican Church, though it was removed from the Roman Catholic calendar in the early 1960s, on the grounds that there was no good evidence that either Crispin or Crispinian had ever existed! On the other hand, there is evidence that St George's Day, 23 April, which had been declared a national feast as early as the thirteenth century, was celebrated with renewed vigour after Agincourt, and this celebration has undergone something of a revival in recent years.[26]

It is easy to overlook the fact that All Souls College, Oxford, was founded as a Lancastrian war memorial as well as a chantry chapel and college. It was planned, built and endowed by Henry Chichele, who had become Archbishop of Canterbury the year before Agincourt was fought. Its foundation charter was granted by Henry VI in 1438 and portions of the building, including the Chapel, were ready for occupation by 1442. The new foundation was made for educational purposes, but also a place of prayer for the souls of the founders, Henry V, Thomas, Duke of Clarence, and *all other English captains and subjects who had drunk 'the cup of bitter death' in the French wars.* All English chantries were suppressed in 1548, ten years after the monasteries had met with the same fate; but All Souls remains as one of the glories of Oxford University, and its Chapel still has statues of Chichele and Henry VI, and a Royal Window, with a stained-glass image of Henry V.

It is less well known that Archbishop Chichele also founded, or helped to establish, a fund to assist poor scholars at New College Oxford, and another for the University at large; and he established at least three other colleges, including one at Higham Ferrers. Divine service was to be celebrated there each day, for the good estate of Henry VI, Henry V and his Queen, and the archbishop, and for all those who had fallen in 'the long wars with France'.[27]

Traditionally, we were taught that the Hundred Years War ended in 1453; but at the time, Englishmen did not see it this way. No peace treaty was signed after Sir John Talbot's defeat and death at Castillon that year. Indeed there was not even a truce, either with the French or with their allies, the Scots. Calais remained in English hands but all the rest of the English possessions in France had been overrun; but the memory of Henry V was kept green by old soldiers, such as Sir John Fastolf of Caister Castle in Norfolk, and by his literary circle. Fastolf died in 1459, and the last of the survivors of Agincourt must have died by 1470; but the memory of the great English triumph lived on.[28]

Indeed, it was difficult to forget, given the continuing level of defence expenditure and the refusal of the English Crown to give up Henry V's claims in France altogether. The lawyer and judge, John Fortescue (c.1394–1476) included in his list of the Crown's regular charges the 'keeping' of the Scottish marches, the maintenance of the king's 'works' (fortifications), the keeping of the sea, the maintenance of a fleet, and the keeping of Calais. For his part, the French king Charles VII continued to have designs against both England and her former ally Burgundy, and he lived until 1461. In August 1457, the French burnt Sandwich, while in 1458 and 1459 they threatened invasion. Charles's successor Louis XI

(1461–83) governed his kingdom on the not-unrealistic assumption that the English were likely to renew the war if they could.

Yet, outside the Church and the cloister, 25 October did not find a lasting place in the Christian calendar in England. In other words, it is not clear that there was ever an 'Agincourt Day'.[29] The day was certainly never as important as Queen Elizabeth's Day became in the late sixteenth century, or as Guy Fawkes's Day has been since 1605; and there was no national celebration in 1515, or indeed on any later centenary. There is very little evidence of celebrations on 25 October, other than a reference to a 'solemn triumph', which included a procession, hymns, the shooting of guns, the sound of trumpets and other musical instruments and general rejoicing, held each year in Calais and the Calais Pale in Henry VIII's time.[30] It may well be the case that the Day ceased to be celebrated as early as the reign of Henry VI, since he took a very different view of the aims of foreign policy from his father. This said, there must have been some residual celebration in the following centuries, to explain Dr Johnson's lament of 1765.

It may be observed that we are apt to promise to ourselves more lasting memory than the changing state of human things admits. The prediction is not verified: the feast of Crispin passes by without any mention of Agincourt. Late events obliterate the former: the civil wars have left in this nation scarcely any tradition of more ancient history.

It could be said that Agincourt is not much remembered today, except by academics and military historians; but this is not strictly true, since there is a thriving industry in battlefield walks, and there are even companies of Frenchmen prepared to dress up as the Crossbowmen (*Arbalétriers*) of St Omer or Hesdin, when required for a pageant. Back in England the battle is still celebrated in a different fashion by two livery companies in the City of London – the Worshipful Companies of Bowyers and Fletchers. They hold commemorative dinners, listen to speakers and stage an annual 'Shoot in the Tower' (of London). In addition, the Bowyers maintain a website, with a page referring to the Agincourt Memorial Window in Groombridge, in Sussex.[31]

In France, on the presumed site of the battlefield, a Calvary (which can still be seen) was erected near La Gacogne in the 1860s and a commemorative monolith was erected nearer to Maisoncelle in 1963; and there was a parade and a pageant when the second of these monuments was consecrated. Several speeches were made by local and national dignitaries. General Hassler said

> We are here, not to celebrate the English victory or the French defeat but to honour those who fell on the battlefield. We have chosen the date [12 May] to reduce the pain which the memory of Azincourt bring us, and in order to recall the Maid [Joan of Arc] who, fourteen years later was to chase the English out of France and forge us once more into a united nation.

Nowadays, the village of Azincourt has a splendid museum, whose architecture incorporates motifs of longbows and stakes, and which very fairly emphasises the cultural importance of Agincourt for the English nation – above all, in the Shakespearean version; but there are no visible memorials of the battle in adjacent villages. The village of Fressin has a ruined fifteenth-century castle and a fine fifteenth-century church, but these were both built after the battle, when the local lord reverted to Burgundian allegiance and evidently became very wealthy and powerful. There are monuments here to Joan of Arc, but none to Henry V, or even Charles VI; and, although there was a time when French noblemen who were killed at Agincourt were commemorated at the abbey church of Auchy-lès-Hesdin, their monument there has long since disappeared underneath a factory. Saddest of all, the medieval coats of arms which were once displayed in the citadel of Montreuil-sur-Mer – headquarters of Field Marshal Sir Douglas Haig during the First World War – have recently been stolen.

Chapter 9

A Decisive Battle?

The idea that Agincourt was 'the worst disaster in a thousand years' from the French point of view, overlooks the fact that at Nicopolis in Bulgaria, only twenty years earlier, an entire Franco-Burgundian army of between 7,500 and 16,000 men had been almost completely destroyed by the Ottoman Turks. To suggest that every noble French family lost a member at Agincourt, or that the French lost 'half their nobility', is simply wrong. France had a larger population than any other Christian state apart from Russia, and a single battle could not have had a very serious demographic effect. It may be the case that there was a heavy toll of casualties amongst members of the 'officer class', especially in Normandy and Ponthieu, Picardy and Artois; but Henry V admitted to Parliament in 1416 that the French were not finished yet. Indeed, this was why he undertook a second expedition to Normandy the following year.[1] If we look further afield, and in particular beyond the borders of France and Britain, Agincourt cannot compare with the battles of Kosovo (1389) and Nicopolis (1396) or with the siege of Constantinople (1453), which delivered large parts of the Balkans to Ottoman rule for several centuries.

Likewise, Agincourt was not a débacle on the same scale as those suffered by the Second French Empire in 1870 or by the Third French Republic in 1940. France did not 'lose everything' on 25 October 1415. The French army was defeated, but it was not interned, nor was the country occupied, nor did the state collapse, nor was the national spirit broken. The Armagnacs still held Paris. The French king remained at liberty, as did the entire royal family. The victorious English army went home, having captured nothing more than Harfleur. The French monarchy was left with large territories and resources to draw on; and the law of inheritance still worked in its favour, even in the aftermath of defeat. Agincourt had temporarily removed the Dukes of Bourbon, Alençon and Orléans from the inner councils of the French court; but in 1416 the death of the old Duke of Berry without male issue saw his Duchy revert to the

French Crown. Henry V claimed to have God on his side; but only the worst of French pessimists believed him at the time.[2]

Nevertheless, there is room for disagreement about the importance of the battle. Sir Harris Nicolas concluded that Agincourt was not decisive, even in the short run: 'neither the spirit nor the resources of France were exhausted by the heavy wound inflicted upon them on that occasion'; but the Victorian editor of the Latin *Deeds of Henry V* of 1850 wrote that 'there have been three great battles which changed the face of Europe, those of Crescy [*sic*], Poitiers and Agincourt'. Sir Edward Creasy did not include it in his *Fifteen Decisive Battles of the World* (1851), nor did J. F. C. Fuller in his *Decisive Battles of the Western World* (1954–6), nor did Lt-Col. Green, in his *Famous Engagements and their Battlefields Today* (1969). More recently, Anne Curry expressed surprise that 'Agincourt has not been seen as one of the decisive battle of the western world' (though she was writing only about the boost which it gave to Henry V's career). Juliet Barker gave her book about Agincourt the subtitle 'the Battle That Made England'. Ralph Griffiths's view was that Agincourt was not decisive, but at the same time marked 'a turning point in Henry V's life and in his quest for the Kingdom of France as well as England'.[3]

France

It is sometimes argued that Henry achieved more, after five years of fighting, than Edward III had achieved in twenty-five. Instead of an enlarged principality in Aquitaine, he had won the entire French kingdom, becoming Regent and prospectively King, in place of Charles VI. His soldiers occupied a large swathe of Northern France and even held fortresses in Paris, for the one and only time in medieval history; but how far was this due to the events of 25 October 1415?

The Monk of St Denis wrote of the 'eternal dishonour' suffered at Agincourt and referred to a 'disaster forever to be deplored'; and there has been no shortage of other writers who agreed. Pierre Cochon saw it as 'The ugliest and most wretched event that had happened to France over the last thousand years'.[4] The *Bourgeois de Paris* thought that France had never suffered such a defeat before, not even in the Dark Ages, when the Saracens had raided the Mediterranean coasts. He reported a serious collapse of morale: 'it was commonly said that those who had been taken prisoner had not proved true and loyal to those who had died in battle.' In 1419, when the English captured the towns of Mantes, Vernon and Pontoise near Paris, the *Bourgeois* still thought that their progress owed something to the defeat suffered four years previously.

So many lords of the blood were still held prisoner by the King of England, since the time of the Battle of Azincourt, fought on the day of Saint-Crispin and his brother ...

Françoise Autrand tells us that Agincourt was a turning point for Charles VI because, when he heard the news that the royal army had been destroyed, he finally descended into madness, 'losing all contact with reality, even during remission'. Towards the end of his life, he was less prone to violent seizures, but had ceased to care about worldly affairs.[5]

There is a view that the high number of deaths amongst the nobility and gentry of Picardy and Normandy contributed to the difficulties of mounting an effective resistance during Henry's conquest of Normandy between 1417 and 1419; and it is certainly true that the French government was unable to put an army in the field in those years. Although the conquest consisted of a series of sieges, some assistance, by the French Crown to the besieged, might have made a considerable difference. As it was, the English met with little resistance and they took the towns and fortresses of the Duchy one by one. Henry V's reputation as a great conqueror, acquired at Agincourt, went before him. Christopher Allmand, a particular authority on Lancastrian Normandy, wrote:

Not all those who fled before his army between 1417 and 1419 were the patriots whom French historians of the late nineteenth and early twentieth century thought them to have been, but men and women fleeing before the army of the man with the greatest military reputation of his day.

This is an authoritative view; but in linking Agincourt with the conquest of Normandy which followed two years later, historians tend to ignore other factors, including the Duke of Bedford's victory at sea in August 1416. While Henry V devoted that year to diplomacy rather than war, the French maintained their siege of English Harfleur, and this was only broken by the Duke, who relieved the port and crushed the French navy in the process. Naval historians regard Bedford's victory, rather than Henry's, as the event which paved the way for the conquest of Normandy.[6]

In one way the consequences of Agincourt had definite limits: it did not even put an end to the civil war in France. Bernard, Count of Armagnac, was appointed Constable. He did not accept that the defeat suffered in October 1415 was fair or that it decided anything; and his followers refused to accept what the English regarded as the verdict of God. The Count had always been bitterly opposed to the Burgundians and he

rejected any idea of compromise. The Armagnacs had suffered disproportionately and there was a fear that the defeat would enable the
Burgundians to recapture Paris; but, although John the Fearless took up
a position some 20 miles east of the capital, at Lagny-sur-Marne, in
December 1415, the capital remained firmly under Armagnac control. In
July 1416 Duke John met Henry V at a conference in Calais and parties
signed a 'treaty of abstinence' from war in Picardy and Flanders; but no
further agreement, secret or otherwise, was entered into.

The defeat failed to drive either the Armagnacs or the Burgundians into
the arms of the English. Negotiations were begun with the Dauphin
but they proved abortive. The French still refuse to cede any territory
unless the English king agreed to do homage for it – a position which
French diplomats had maintained since 1370.[7] Even in 1419, when all
Normandy had fallen to Henry, the French Queen made it clear that there
was no question of a return to what had been agreed at Brétigny in 1360.
The country at large would not stand for it.

Shakespeare depicts Agincourt as leading directly to the Treaty of
Troyes in 1420, while others have claimed that it 'laid the foundations for
the resurrection of an English empire in France';[8] but these views fail to
take account of the fact that Agincourt was fought in 1415 and that the
Treaty followed the assassination of the Duke of Burgundy in 1419, which
led to the conclusion of a full Anglo-Burgundian alliance between John
the Fearless's successor and Henry V. The majority of French writers have
always thought that it was their civil war which gave the English their
greatest opportunities. Monstrelet's Chronicles are mainly concerned
with this *Cruel Civil Wars between the Houses of Orléans and Burgundy*, and
by comparison English activities in general are made to look small. It may
be true that Louis XI (1461–83) still retained a healthy respect for English
arms, half a century after Agincourt – his adviser Philippe de Commynes
wrote that Louis would never have risked a pitched battle with the
English, as Charles VI had done – but it was also Commynes who wrote
that, in the end, God had punished the English for what they had done.

> All have been killed in battle. Their fathers and their followers had
> destroyed the kingdom of France and possessed the greater part of it
> for many years; but they all killed each other [in the Wars of the
> Roses].[9]

When we look at the French response to the events of 1415, it is also
worth remembering the story that when Francis I visited Dijon in 1521, a
monk presented him with the skull of Duke John of Burgundy and,

pointing to the gaping hole in it, explained 'this is the hole through which the English entered France'. No reference was made on that occasion to Agincourt.

Importantly, Charles VI still had allies in 1415. Despite the loss of Harfleur (and the remaining Norman ports between 1417 and 1419), the Valois retained harbours and ports in the south and the west of the kingdom; and Charles's ministers negotiated a renewal of the 'Auld Alliance' with Scotland. This brought much-needed reinforcements, in the form of two Scottish armies, which disembarked at La Rochelle in 1419 and 1424. Individual Scots had fought for the French before, but the arrival of these new forces, each of which may have numbered as many as 6,000 men, was something new. It was these Scotsmen who enabled the Dauphin to win his first victory in the field, at Baugé in 1421 (when the Duke of Clarence was killed); and this intervention was seen as decisive by Daniel Defoe in his *Essay* of 1706 on the proposed Act of Union between England and Scotland. He wrote that, if Scotland had been united with England in the 1420s, the conquests of Henry V would have been secured, France would have been 'entirely subjected to the English power' and 'Britain would have given Law to all these parts of the World'. By implication, Agincourt settled nothing.

French historians have long been able to portray the defeat in 1415 as a low point, from which the nation soon recovered. In his book on Agincourt, Dominique Paladilhe has a chapter entitled *De l'Abîme à l'Espérance* – 'from the Abyss to Hope'. Françoise Autrand pointed out that the French had recovered from worst defeats in the past – notably Poitiers in 1356, when the French King had been captured. Seen through French eyes, what Henry V had achieved at Agincourt was to secure a bridgehead for the invasion of Normandy, which he (and the Duke of Bedford) then managed to bring under English rule for some thirty-five years. This was hardly 'decisive' in the long run, or even in the medium term. It was not a victory to be compared with Hastings in 1066, which entirely changed the course of English history, or Philip II's victory at Bouvines in 1314, which had long-lasting effects in France, England and the Holy Roman Empire. French schoolboys whom I knew in the 1960s had never heard of Crécy, Poitiers and Agincourt, but they had all heard of Bouvines (and Fashoda, which is scarcely remembered here).

Europe

In his *History of the English-Speaking Peoples* Sir Winston Churchill (1874–1965) wrote that 'Agincourt ranks as the most heroic of all the land battles

England has ever fought.' Henry V had 'before all Europe, shattered the French power'. The King 'stood at the summit of the world' and 'ascended without dispute the throne not only of England, but very soon of almost all Western Christendom'. What did Churchill mean by this extraordinary claim? Specifically, that Henry married the daughter of the King of France; that he persuaded the Queen of Naples to adopt his brother Bedford as her heir; that he arranged for his brother Gloucester to marry Jacqueline of Hainault. For Churchill the result was that 'the pedigrees of southern and western Europe alike met in the house of Lancaster, the head of which thus seemed to be the common head of all'.

This was, to say the least, a very Anglocentric view. When we examine the threads of Churchill's dynastic tapestry, we find that there was no master weaver at work. It is true that Henry V married Catherine of Valois in 1420; but Joanna II, the childless Queen of Naples (1414–35) only considered adopting the Duke of Bedford as her heir for a short while (in March 1419), when she was in desperate need of support. She turned away from England the next year, before performing a complete volte-face and finally looking to France for protection.[10] As for the marriage between the Duke of Gloucester and Jacqueline of Hainault, this may have been planned by Henry V but it took place after his death and was much disapproved of by the Regent Bedford, since it seriously compromised England's alliance with Burgundy.

The truth is that Henry V had no pan-European foreign policy: he was fixated on the Anglo-French war, though paradoxically he saw that war as a means of achieving peace. The result was that his military triumphs, and even his conquests, had little impact outside France and England. As for our performance in the royal marriage market, English candidates were consistently outclassed by the French – notably in Flanders and Italy. In addition, Henry's short reign did little to enhance his country's economic and commercial power. As a trading city, London remained the only serious player on the international stage, but was still in the shade compared with Milan, Venice, Genoa, Bologna, Florence, Rome, Naples and Palermo. Finally, Churchill's account obscures the enduring diplomatic importance of France and the French royal family in the Italian theatre, in Naples, Milan and the Papal States, despite the setback of Agincourt.[11]

Yet Churchill has not been alone in exaggerating Henry V's influence in Europe; and we need to consider why. Monstrelet tells us that, on his deathbed, Henry sent for his confessor and his chaplains, and ordered them to chant the seven penitential psalms.

When they came to *Benigne fac, Domine*, where mention is made of the walls of Jerusalem, he stopped them, and said aloud, that he had fully intended, after he had wholly subdued the realm of France to his obedience, and restored it to peace, to have gone to conquer the Kingdom of Jerusalem, if it had pleased his creator to have granted him longer life.

This was easily said. Yet, on account of these words, Henry is sometimes compared to Richard the Lionheart, though Richard spent several years in the Holy Land, while Henry never went there.

Henry V's last statement of intent was surely no more than wishful thinking: it resembles nothing more than Richard III's statement to a German visitor to Yorkshire in 1484, that he wished England was situated on the borders of Europe, so that he could drive out the Turks.[12] But it has led several historians to speculate as to what might have been achieved, if Henry had not died prematurely. The Victorian J. R. Green wrote about this with Jingoistic, if counterfactual, enthusiasm.

Dreams of a vaster enterprise filled the soul of the great conqueror himself; he loved to read the story of Godfrey of Bouillon and cherished the hope of a crusade which should beat back the Ottoman and again rescue the Holy Land from heathen hands. Such a crusade might still have saved Constantinople, and averted from Europe the danger which threatened it through the century that followed the fall of the imperial city. Nor was the enterprise a dream in the hands of the cool, practical warrior and ruler.

Fifty years later K. B. Mcfarlane, normally so devoted to detailed and patient prosopography, wrote in a similar vein.

It is possible to believe that Henry might have bridged the gap that divides Napoleon and Godfrey de Bouillon, and have succeeded where Richard I and St Louis had failed ... Had he been living in 1450 there is no reason why he should not have rolled up the map of Europe as in nine years he had rolled up that of France. Indeed it is hard to believe anything else.

This merely shows that the most sceptical of English historians can get carried away when writing about Henry V; and it is fair to point out that McFarlane originally said this in a lecture he gave to the Workers' Educational Association (W.E.A.) in 1954, only a decade after the defeat of Nazi Germany; but there is no reason to think that it was not also his considered view.[13] However, a French historian might well respond that the French in fact played the major role in all the Crusades. In the late Middle Ages, the House of Lancaster may have dreamed the Crusading dream; but it was their French enemies, inspired by Philippe de Mézières, who actually intervened and fought Islam, both in Barbary (1390) and Bulgaria (1396).

In general, medievalists tend to admire Henry V, and his victory at Agincourt is seen as his crowning achievement. McFarlane also told the W.E.A. that by 1422 Henry was 'the arbiter of Christian Europe, dwarfing Emperor and Pope'. Pugh wrote that 'Henry ... profoundly altered the balance of power in Europe'. Anne Curry has claimed that Agincourt put Henry V and England 'on the international map'; and Ralph Griffiths has stated that Agincourt 'transformed the reputation of England and its ruler'.[14] Yet, when we examine what Henry actually achieved in European terms, the answer is very little. In particular, the Treaty of Canterbury (1416) and English participation at the Council of Constance (1414–17) seem relatively little to boast about, when compared with the grandiose claims that are sometimes made.

The Holy Roman Emperor Sigismund (1368–1437) was the greatest ruler of the Christian West. Though few English people ever hear of him, his fifty-year reign overlapped with those of numerous English and French kings. His dominions stretched from the Baltic to the Mediterranean and from the Rhône to the Black Sea. They included what we now know as Germany and the Czech Republic. Though he could not drive the Turks from Europe altogether, Sigismund was able to contain them, at a time when they presented a real danger to Christian Europe. We forget that, after Nicopolis, the Ottoman Sultan had threatened to march on Rome and 'let his horse eat corn upon St Peter's altar'; and that Mehmet I, whose reign (1413–21) more or less coincided with Henry V's, is honoured in Turkey as 'the second founder of the Ottoman Empire'.

If Sigismund ever heard of Henry's belated wish to re-conquer Jerusalem, he might have concluded that the English king had, to say the least, got his priorities badly wrong. In Sigismund's eyes, the Anglo-French dispute, which Henry supposedly wanted to settle before setting off for the East, must have seemed like Neville Chamberlain's 'quarrel in a faraway country between people of whom we know nothing'. When the Italian Morosini heard that the English and the French had failed to reach agreement, he exclaimed *Dio faza Christiany*! ('God help Christendom!').[15]

From Sigismund's point of view, the entire Anglo-French war was an unwelcome distraction, as was the Treaty of Canterbury, signed by Henry and Sigismund in 1416. The Treaty was a treaty of friendship entered into because, when he visited the West, the German Emperor concluded that the French were not serious about the idea of a negotiated peace. He then left for England, where he was admittedly impressed by Henry. Under the terms of the treaty, Henry was left free to pursue his 'just rights', while Sigismund was also allowed to recover lands, rights and inheritances lost by the German Empire to France. But little enough came of the pledges of mutual assistance, except that at the Council of Constance, Anglo-German co-operation resulted in the election of a new Pope, Martin V, thereby ending the Great Schism which had so damaged the Church. It is difficult to see why some historians write of this as changing very much in terms of European politics, let alone as if it upset the 'balance of power' (surely an eighteenth century concept, if ever there was one).[16]

The main success at the Council of Constance, from the English point of view, was the vindication of the right to sit as a separate 'nation', when we had previously sat with the Germans. The French opposed this bid for independent representation, but in vain; and, in the late eighteenth century Edward Gibbon thought that the English delegation won this new right by the force of rhetoric, but also because 'the victories of Henry V added much weight' to their arguments. The point has been repeated ever since.

Yet, when we look at what actually happened at Constance, it is hard to detect the influence of Agincourt. The most prominent members of the English delegation were Robert Hallum, Bishop of Salisbury (d. 1417) and Thomas Polton, Bishop of Worcester (d. 1433). They seem to have deployed several (mostly spurious) arguments for separate English representation, based on the size, geography, history and languages used in Britain; but neither Agincourt nor the Anglo-French war in general was directly referred to. Indeed it was unlikely that a battle would be mentioned in an international gathering composed largely of priests and Churchmen. In any case the English success at Constance was again short-lived: during the Council of Basle held between 1431 and 1449, the practice of sitting as nations was abandoned.[17]

There were other events which occurred at this time which were far more significant in European terms. In 1410 a Polish-Lithuanian army had defeated the Teutonic Knights at Tannenberg in East Prussia, while in 1415 Sigismund granted Brandenburg to the house of Hohenzollern. The former brought 200 years of German expansion in the East to a halt, whilst the latter was the first stage in the rise to power of one of the most powerful dynasties of modern times. Also in 1415, a Portuguese expedition set sail for North Africa. Leaving home on 24 July, it captured Ceuta by assault on 21 August. The Battle of Ceuta was hailed by the Council in Constance as a victory for the whole of Christendom, since the port had been in Muslim hands for 700 years. It remains in Iberian hands to this day, though it is claimed by Morocco. The consequences were therefore long-lasting. The contrast with Agincourt could not be more stark.

In *The Great Warbow* (2005) Matthew Strickland wrote: 'The first half of the fifteenth century witnessed a far more sustained period of emulation of, or reaction to, English tactics and military prowess than had occurred in the late fourteenth', but the evidence he presents does not prove his point. The Scots tried to use archers on the battlefield, in much the same way as the English, from the time of their defeat at Homildon Hill in 1402; and, when James I was released from his English captivity in 1424, a Scottish Parliament made it compulsory for all able-bodied Scotsmen to practise with the longbow. (Football was also forbidden, as a distraction, as had long been the case in England.) Yet the outcome was not what James hoped for. The chronicler Walter Bower recorded sadly what happened after the King's murder in 1437.

> After, and as a consequence of, his sad death nearly everyone gave up bows and archery equipment without a thought, and devoted themselves to riding with lances, with the result that now at a meeting of magnates, you usually find out of one hundred men some eighty lances and scarcely six archers. For this reason the English can now truly say with the Psalmist about the Scots, 'the bow of the brave has been overcome'.

In France, the Burgundians attempted to copy English tactics, and they recruited limited numbers of English archers in the process but the Burgundian 'state' crashed into oblivion in 1477; and the attempt to emulate English tactics in Valois France was likewise unsuccessful and short-lived. Charles VII enlisted contingents of archers in the *Compagnies d'Ordonnance* which he established in the 1440s but, as Michelet noted, it is doubtful if these owed much to English influence, and Charles's main claim to fame rests on his achievement in sweeping the English out of Normandy and Aquitaine with vastly superior numbers, organisation and co-ordination. The final victory of his forces at Castillon in 1453 owed much to the use of cannon, but nothing to the longbow.

By contrast, English soldiers – and archers in particular – were internationally famous in the late fourteenth century, when they were much in demand as mercenaries, notably in Italy, as the career of Sir John Hawkwood amply demonstrates. At Agincourt, English archers scored their greatest victory to date; but it was not one which even they were able to repeat, except arguably at Verneuil in 1424 and (on a small scale) at the Battle of the Herrings in 1429. Nor were their tactics easily exportable, because other countries lacked a tradition of training their men from youth in the use of the longbow. Michael K. Jones has written that 'it was the highest compliment to our bowmen that, by the early fifteenth century, the Grand Master of the Teutonic Knights began to recruit substantial numbers of English archers' for warfare in Prussia; but he does not claim that this practice continued after the catastrophic defeat of the Knights at Tannenberg; and Strickland and Hardy do not even mention Prussia in their comprehensive study of the longbow.[18]

In fact there was no real diaspora of English soldiers, or English tactics, after the Treaty of Troyes in 1420, comparable to that which had taken place after the Treaty of Brétigny in 1360. One reason for this was that the treaty of 1420 was repudiated by a large part of the French kingdom and did not inaugurate any period of peace. As a result English soldiers were not made redundant in 1420 as they had been sixty years before, because there was still work for them to do in the royal army. Having married his French Princess, Henry V immediately threw himself back into the war with the Dauphin. Although he died young, his brothers took up the challenge and the war went on, for many years. Soldiers like Sir John Fastolf were therefore not given the same opportunities to fight outside France as had been afforded to men like John Hawkwood. Instead, they had to spend almost thirty years in Normandy, Maine and Anjou, locked in a war of attrition.

Within a hundred years, the longbow was overtaken as a common infantry weapon, first by the pike and then by the handgun, though the English monarchy insisted that all men be trained in archery throughout the Tudor period, long after the art had been rendered practically obsolete. The result was that, in the late fifteenth and early sixteenth centuries, Swiss pikemen and German *landsknechts* earned a greater reputation as mercenaries than the English had ever done internationally. As for the development of artillery, Francis Bacon wrote in his *Novum Organum* of 1620 that this, together with printing and the mariner's compass had 'changed the whole face and state of things throughout the world'. Although Henry V made good use of siege guns at Harfleur, there is no evidence that he dragged them behind him to Agincourt, or ever used them as field guns.

England

As we have noted, Henry V started to build warships when he was still Prince of Wales and he continued to do so throughout his reign. He had only two in 1410 but thirty-four by 1417, the core of 'the most impressive royal fleet owned by any medieval English king'.[19] He commandeered large numbers of merchantmen from ports in England and the Netherlands to ferry the army of invasion across the Channel in 1415. His conquest of Normandy made the south coast of England safe from piracy and the threat of invasion for a generation. For the first time since the days of Edward III, the English were masters of the English Channel; but this has been almost entirely forgotten, eclipsed by the temporary glory of Agincourt.

Not the least of Henry V's achievements was to re-establish internal peace, after the plots and rebellions of his father's reign; and Agincourt was certainly regarded as a vindication of the Lancastrian regime, which had only come to power in 1399. The victory clearly showed the efficiency of the Lancastrian war-machine but it was also thought to demonstrate the legitimacy of the dynasty's claims, both at home and abroad. Oldcastle's Rebellion had taken place in 1414, and the Southampton Plot was discovered immediately before the army embarked for Normandy; but there were no further plots against Henry and his brothers after 1415, nor were there any popular or aristocratic revolts before 1450. McFarlane was right in saying that the authority of the Crown stood at its highest between 1415 and 1422. 'Two years [1413–15] had been long enough for Henry of Monmouth to dispose effectively of sedition and rebellion; for the rest of his brief reign the royal will was imposed without challenge.'[20] Further, Henry VI succeeded to the English kingdom without argument in 1422, though he was only a babe in arms at the time. There is no question that his father's prestige helped the new king all through the time of his minority.

Yet heretics continued to be found in many counties. Lollardy, the first major heresy in England since Roman times, had originated in Oxford, in the academic treatises of John Wycliffe (c.1320–84), but his new way of looking at the Church and the Faith had spread throughout the South and the Midlands. Belatedly, the Archbishop of Canterbury acted to drive Lollardy out of Oxford, and then took action elsewhere: all preaching, and all translations of religious works, now had to be licensed by the local bishop. It became heretical to even possess an English Bible. In 1401, the State came to the aid of the Church by enacting the Statute on Heresy

(*De Haeretico Comburendo*), which provided that relapsed heretics should be handed over to the secular authorities to be burned at the stake.

Lollardy, which had gained some currency amongst the upper classes in the time of Richard II (1377–99), ceased to be respectable, especially after Oldcastle's rising, which linked the heresy directly with treason; but it survived nonetheless. This is clear when we look at the career and the writings of Bishop Reginald Pecock (c. 1395–c. 1461). Pecock disagreed with the Lollards, but he did not believe in persecution. He hoped to reconcile his opponents with the Church through the power of persuasion. His patient exposition of Lollard views, made for the purpose of refuting them, demonstrates that the heresy was still shared by significant numbers of men and women.

The Pope also believed that the Lollards were dangerous. Martin V, elected in 1417, regarded them as responsible for the Hussite revolution in Bohemia in the 1420s. When he wrote to the English Church in 1428, urging it to contribute to the crusade he was authorising against the Hussites, he said:

> This wretched and terrible heresy has its roots there [in England] and has created so much scandal and evil throughout Christendom. For the sake of your honour and reputation the English ought to give this matter the highest priority. There exist in England not a few offshoots of this heresy which will continue to grow up quite significantly if they are not quickly cut down. One wonders if England may not suffer the same fate as Bohemia. Similarly we have been informed by a reliable source that frequently representatives of the Wycliffites, hiding in England, go to Bohemia to strengthen them [Hussites] in their pestiferous ways.

Some Lollards maintained a belief in armed resistance, even after Oldcastle's open rebellion; but others were pacifists, hostile to all forms of war, even when English arms were enjoying stupendous success. One Lollard asked

> What honour falls to a knight because he kills many men? A hangman kills more than any knight; a butcher kills more beasts, and to better purpose – and so it were better for a man to be butcher of beasts than to be butcher of his brethren, for that is more unnatural.

Reginald Pecock also encountered Lollards who thought that

> No man should be slain of any other, for any trespass cause or peril, but all slaughter upon Man is reserved to God; and that in no wise

and in no case is battle lawful, neither between Christian and Christian, neither between Christian and heathen.[21]

Yet the rebels and pacifists were in a tiny minority, so far as we know. For orthodox Catholics, the King's cause was just and Agincourt was a great victory, even though the French were fellow Christians. Agincourt blinded the majority of Englishmen, at least for a time, to the political and geographical realities. Whatever revisionists may say, it was a victory won against the odds; but the scale of it fed Henry V's ambition. After it, he believed that he could achieve his wildest dreams. When he came to nego-tiate terms for peace, he overreached himself and demanded too much, with lasting consequences. Even after he died, there were many who con-tinued to believe that the impossible could be achieved. A soldier like John Fastolf believed this all his long life; and Agincourt made it difficult for more sober politicians and diplomats to argue the case for a negotiated settlement. Indeed, this was practically impossible during Henry VI's minority, since any backtracking from the dead hero's plan was seen as a betrayal of his memory.

The French prisoners taken at Agincourt, and especially Charles, Duke of Orléans, posed a particular problem for Henry VI, when he declared that his minority was at an end in 1437. By 1440, the Duke had been kept as a prisoner in England for twenty-five years and Henry, who was a pious man, thought it was time to release him. The difficulty was that Henry V had expressly ordered, on his deathbed, that the Duke should not be released unless and until the whole of France had been reduced to obedi-ence. Henry VI's advisers therefore issued a broadsheet in the king's name, explaining the royal wish for peace and justifying the proposal on the grounds of humanity as well as expediency.

Henry VI's declaration is an extraordinary document. It took a very realistic (some would have said, pessimistic) view of the progress of the war. It had been going on for a hundred years. Even Edward III had not managed to make himself King in France, for all his many victories on the battlefield: he had settled for an 'easy part' of the kingdom at Brétigny. And in any case it was simply impossible to conquer the whole of the French kingdom: it was too 'ample, great, and so mighty in multitude of walled towns, castles and fortresses, in rivers and strong counties'. Most strikingly, Henry VI claimed that

The king's father, had by him and by his victorious battle of Agin-court, and other battles ... by water and by the land, so prospered by the conduct of the said war ... yet not long time before his death ...

he was so *sadded* of the war and disposed in all wises, to have entended to a peace to have be treated and made ...[22]

Of course, the son could not possibly have spoken with the father, about the war or anything else. Henry VI had been less than twelve months old when Henry V died; and it is unlikely that he would have been fed these ideas as a boy by his uncles of Bedford or Gloucester, who were both staunch advocates of their brother's war policy. It is much more likely that Henry VI was giving voice to his own ideas; but Henry V's prestige was still so great that, even when he argued for peace, the new King had to invoke the memory of Agincourt.

There was another way in which Henry V's campaigns in Normandy proved to be a turning point in English history. No King of England ever led an army into that province again, and it is arguable that no King of England ever seriously pursued the lost inheritance in France. At the time, Agincourt was seen as heralding the re-awakening of the spirit of a former age; and for much of the fifteenth century, 'outward werre' continued to be seen by many as the surest road to national revival; but things had changed by the time Edward IV led the expedition of 1475, which proceeded so ignominiously to Piquigny and ended there, on the Somme.

The sober truth is that, as a result of the conquests which Agincourt facilitated, new divisions had arisen between those Englishmen who benefited from the occupation of Normandy and Maine, and those who did not; and the latter resented the cost of that occupation. Accordingly, the conquests of the fifteenth century did not unite the English nation in the same way as the great raids of the fourteenth had done. Even Henry V could not fully rekindle the readiness of English knights and gentlemen to undertake military service abroad, though this had so amply been demonstrated under Edward III.[23] By the time Henry VIII led his expedition to the *Pas de Calais* in 1513, England had ceased altogether to be a serious contender in the European power game. The second Henry Tudor was but a pale imitation of his Plantagenet forebear.

Chapter 10

History, Legend and Myth

The difficulty of finding out what really happened at the Battle of Agincourt can be illustrated by the fog of uncertainty which surrounds the capture of the Duke of Orléans. Legend has it that he was taken prisoner by Sir Richard Waller and kept at Groombridge Place in Kent for many years, but there is no documentary evidence of this and it is not recorded in the chronicles either. The first mention of it seems to have been made by the antiquarian John Philipot (c. 1589–1645), almost 200 years after the battle. Furthermore it seems likely that the Duke of Orléans was moved from place to place at regular intervals, rather than kept at Groombridge for any long period of time.

Nevertheless, there is a strong tradition in Kent, linking Waller to the Duke; and the family still has a coat of arms which seems to confirm the link. The Duke's crest consisted of a crown, indicating that he was a grandson of Charles V of France. His coat of arms consisted of a blue shield with three *fleur de lys* in gold, surmounted by a 'label' with three 'ribbons', indicating that he was the eldest son of Louis, Duke of Orléans, assassinated in 1407. Sir Richard Waller incorporated this coat of arms into his own crest, placing it on top of his own walnut tree. In 1597 there was a monumental inscription in the church at Chartham recording that Sir Richard had brought Orléans to Groombridge, 'where he remain'd a Prisoner Four and Twenty Years', though this is probably an exaggeration. In 1625 John Packer, who had acquired Groombridge Place around 1618, built a chapel at ease and installed stained glass there, incorporating his own coat of arms and those of the Duke and Richard Waller. Subsequently, the Wallers continued to assert their right to bear the Duke's emblems, though this was challenged by the heralds of the College of Arms in 1668, when the family wished to display the arms at a funeral. (Allegedly, the heralds even pulled down the arms, defaced them and carried them away.) The Wallers persisted with their claim but were not alone. According to Burke, the families of Billam (of Billam and Wales in South Yorkshire) and Lenthall (of Hampton Court, Herefordshire and

Besselsleigh Manor in Berkshire) made similar claims, and adopted *Azincourt* as a family motto.

Meanwhile, the tradition has lived on in Groombridge, though the house has changed hands many times since 1415. In the 1890s the owner of Groombridge Place was the aptly-named J. J. Saint, who was also the Anglican curate. He donated the seventeenth-century chapel at ease to the Church, so that it is now the parish church of Groombridge. He also had several stained glass windows made for it by Charles Kempe, incorporating pieces of glass left over from Packer's time. The inscriptions now claim, not that Waller captured the Duke of Orléans at Agincourt, but that he 'rescued' him there; and that the Duke became a 'benefactor to the parish church'. This would have come as news to both men.[1] But this was not the last of the Chinese whispers concerning the French prisoner. There is also a highly improbable story current in Groombridge that it was not the Duke of Orléans who was imprisoned there at all, but his younger brother Jean, who had been taken to England as a hostage in 1412 and was kept there until 1444 – longer even than his elder brother.

The Medieval World

After he died, Henry V became the James Dean of his age in England and Agincourt its greatest achievement. The battle was celebrated in verse and in song in the halls and taverns of every county, as well as in the capital. Although John Lydgate's poetry is nowadays considered to be of poor quality, it was popular in his own day; and Lydgate idolised Henry. He even bestowed a new honour on him. As we have seen, the medieval West had come to recognise Nine Worthies – three pagans (Hector, Alexander the Great and Julius Caesar), three Jews (Joshua and the two Maccabees) and three Christians (King Arthur, Charlemagne and Godfrey of Bouillon the Crusader); but the poet added Henry, describing him as

> *Of knighthood, lodestar*
> *Wise and right manly, plainly to determine.*
> *Right fortunate, both in peace and war*
> *Greatly expert in martial discipline*
> *Able to stand among the Worthies Nine.*[2]

Thomas Elmham, Thomas Walsingham and Tito Livio all compared Henry and his brother Gloucester with ancient warriors and lawgivers. The author of the *Libelle of English Policy* (c. 1435) had an equally high opinion of the King.

If he had to this time lived here,
He had been prince named without peer;
His great ships should have been put in press
Unto the end that he meant of in chief.
For doubt it not but that he would have been
Lord and master about the round sea.[3]

Our direct knowledge of what Henry did at Agincourt is based on some twenty-six chronicles, some in Latin, some in French, others in English. Of these, ten were written in England and sixteen in France (including Burgundy); but only four (three English and one French) were written within ten years of the battle. There is therefore no shortage of chronicles; but they have their limitations. Many are unreliable. The chroniclers wrote with quill pens on sheepskin parchment. They enjoyed no freedom of speech and there were draconian penalties for treason and heresy. Information was delivered by sailors, horsemen and foot-messengers. Monastic chroniclers had little interest in or understanding of strategy, tactics or logistics. Laymen like Monstrelet and Waurin were more interested in individual feats of prowess, as the master Froissart had been. There are mistakes and gaps, and all chroniclers were – from a modern point of view – too interested in portents and marvels, prophesies and moral tales, designed to show that virtue was rewarded and evil punished. They tended to work in round numbers and were inclined to put 50,000 or 100,000 when they meant 'a large number of men'.[4]

Nevertheless, there are three accounts which stand out from the rest, because they were written by eye-witnesses and one was written immediately after the battle. This is the *Gesta Henrici Quinti*, thought to have been written by an anonymous chaplain attached to Henry's household.[5] The Chaplain was not a soldier and he does not mention the terrain or the weather; but his account of the campaign and the battle is generally acknowledged to be the best and most complete. It is also full of vivid detail and emotion. When the English had failed to cross the Somme at Blanchetaque, the Chaplain records their dismay.

> We thought of nothing else but this: that, after the eight days assigned for the march had expired and our provisions had run out, the enemy, craftily hastening on ahead and laying waste the country-side in advance, would impose on us, hungry as we should be, a really dire need of food, and at the head of the river, if God did not provide otherwise, would, with their great and countless host and the engines

of war and devices available to them, overwhelm us, so very few as we were and made faint by great weariness and weak from lack of food.

When the battle lines were drawn up, the Chaplain tells us exactly where he was.

But then, indeed, and for as long as the conflict lasted, I, who am now writing this and was then sitting on a horse among the baggage at the rear of the battle, and the other priests present, did humble our souls before God, and said in our hearts: 'Remember us O lord, our enemies are gathered together and boast themselves in their excellence. Destroy their strength and scatter them.'

The English monarchy did not have an official royal chronicler in the same way as the French did, and the Chaplain's account is the nearest thing we have to an 'authorised version' of the Agincourt campaign. The Chaplain stated explicitly that God was on Henry's side and he evidently believed in his master's view of history, and in the idea that it was necessary to defeat the French before embarking on any Crusade against the Turks. The closing passage of his book concludes with a plea

That the two Swords, the sword of the French and the sword of England may return to the rightful government of an English ruler, cease from their own destruction and turn as soon as possible against the unsubdued and bloody faces of the heathen.

The two later accounts by eye-witnesses were both written by Burgundians. Jean Le Fèvre (c. 1395–1468), sometimes known as 'St-Rèmy', was later King of Arms in the Burgundian Order of the Golden Fleece. He tells us that at the time of the battle he was 19 years old and 'in the company of the king of England in all the business of this time'; and he is thought to have been with the heralds, though he did not begin to write until 1463. Jean de Waurin (c. 1398–c. 1474) later fought with the Burgundians at Verneuil and occupied a high position at the court of Philip the Good, but he was only fifteen when he served with his father in the French army at Agincourt.

The best known French account – again by a Burgundian – was that written by Enguerrand de Monstrelet (c. 1400–53). Deliberately continuing the work of Jean Froissart, Monstrelet wrote a chronicle of the years between 1400 and 1444, containing a large number of extracts from original documents. Unlike the Chaplain, he was interested in military detail. He describes how the French army was drawn up in three 'battles' at Agincourt; and we can readily see how, even at this early stage, there were too many 'chiefs' on the French side. We can see too that Henry's troops had been recruited months before, whereas the French army was assembled in haste. Monstrelet also tells us how the English archers prepared themselves for battle.

> Each archer planted before himself a stake sharpened at both ends. Sir Thomas [Erpingham], in the name of the king, exhorted them all most earnestly to defend their lives and, thus saying, he rode along their ranks attended by two persons. When all was done to his satisfaction, he flung into the air a truncheon which he held in his hand, crying out, '*Nestrocque!*'
> When the [main body] of the English saw Sir Thomas throw up his truncheon, they set up a loud shout, to the very great astonishment of the French. The English, seeing the enemy not inclined to advance, marched toward them in handsome array, and with repeated huzzas, occasionally stopping to recover their breath. The archers, who were hidden in the field, re-echoed these shoutings, at the same time discharging their bows, while the English army kept advancing upon the French. Their archers, amounting to at least 13,000, let off a shower of arrows, with all their might, and as high as possible, so as not to lose their effect. They were, for the most part, without any armour, and in jackets, with their hose loose, and hatchets or swords hanging to their girdles: some, indeed, were barefooted and without hats.

As we have seen, Monstrelet's chief interest was the civil war in France, and Agincourt was therefore a sideshow; but it is clear that Armagnacs and Burgundians were both still French at heart, and each viewed the defeat of the French royal army with dismay. Indeed, each blamed the other for what happened. Armagnacs suspected John the Fearless of half-heartedness and even treachery. Some said he had allied with Henry V, others that he had actively assisted him. More surprisingly, the Burgundians sought to blame the Armagnacs. Some spread the ridiculous rumour that Charles d'Albret and Charles of Orléans had defected to the English during the battle. Others alleged that an Armagnac captain, Clignet de Brabant, had led the attack on the English baggage train, thereby provoking the English to massacre their prisoners.[6]

In the 1440s there was a serious disagreement about foreign policy between those members of the Privy Council, like Humphrey Duke of Gloucester, who were for carrying on the war and those, supported by the King himself, who wanted to make peace, almost at any price. In this context, the Italian humanist writer Tito Livio Frulovisi, who worked for Duke Humphrey and wrote a biography of Henry V, emphasised the Duke's military exploits. Gloucester fought at Agincourt and was therefore in a position to give Tito a first-hand account of the fighting, and the Italian included this scene.

> The most serene brother of the king, Humphrey duke of Gloucester, fought bravely and without caution. Having been pierced by the point of a sword he was thrown to the ground half dead. His brother the King himself put his feet astride the legs of Humphrey. For the renowned Duke fell with his head against the King's feet but with his feet to the enemy. In this position the King fought most courageously for a long time, so that his brother might be carried safely from the enemy to his own men.[7]

There were two writers attached to the household of Sir John Fastolf in the 1450s who wrote about the events of 1415. Peter Basset, who had served in the wars, wrote what has been described as a plain 'soldierly' account. William Worcester, who was Fastolf's secretary, wrote *The Boke of Noblesse*, which he started in the 1450s and finished in 1475, in time to present it to Edward IV on the occasion of the latter's expedition to France. Worcester related that Henry V had 'discomfited' the French 'with a few number'; but he also noted that the King had always ensured that the troops were paid at regular intervals; and thought this was a better way to incentivise the army than offering the men the chance to take booty. He pointed to the example set by Henry at Agincourt.

> The noble prince Henry V counselled [his men] not to seek after treasure, prizes, nor jewels and vessels of gold and of silver, neither in relation to what he had lost there, nor in relation to what could be won [the enemy], but have regard only to what was his by right, and for honour.

This rings a little hollow when we recall how many prisoners were taken in 1415. It perhaps tells us more about the incompetence of Henry VI's government – which Fastolf was keen to criticise – than it does about Agincourt.[8]

Agincourt was still a matter of intense interest when Edward IV seized the throne from Henry VI in 1461. The new Yorkist dynasty had an efficient propaganda machine, which *inter alia* produced elaborate genealogies to prove that York had a better claim to the throne than his Lancastrian predecessors; and history was also now written, or re-written, from the Yorkist point of view. The chronicler John Hardyng changed his allegiance from Lancaster to York between 1457 and 1464; and new versions of the widely-circulated *Brut* chronicle emphasised the role played at Agincourt by Edward of Norwich, 2nd Duke of York, as did some of the equally popular London Chronicles. John Benet's account, written some time before 1471, assured its readers that York had fought honourably at Agincourt and had rightly come to be regarded as 'a second Solomon'.[9]

Some of these late fifteenth-century writers even claimed that York played a heroic role in the battle. They portray their hero as leading a vanguard composed exclusively of archers, when he was only ever in charge of the men at arms. Others give him the credit for the decision to place the archers behind stakes, though Lydgate had given the credit for this to Henry V. The idea was taken up by Michael K. Jones (2005), who suggested that the Duke was inspired by his knowledge and experience of hunting. (York was undoubtedly the author of *The Master of Game*, a translation of the famous *Livre de Chasse* by Gaston Phoebus, Count de Foix, to which he added five chapters of his own).[10]

There are many stories associated with Agincourt which are really no more than legend. Perhaps the most widespread is that the battle saw the first use of the 'two-fingered salute' or V sign, when the archers waved their fingers at the French in an act of defiance; but even Anne Curry has not been able to substantiate the link between the modern insult and the battle. Another legend, which has had some currency in France, is that the archers stripped naked for action, but this is probably a misunderstanding, arising from the English custom of wearing relatively light armour. In *Certain Discourses Military* (1590) Sir John Smyth told how the French of his day alleged that, in former times, the English used to smear poison on their arrows. Of course, Smyth hotly denied the charge; but it is interesting that a similar tale was told by the English in the Pale of Calais, about the Genoese mercenaries in the pay of the French.[11]

There are several legends concerning Sir Peter Legh of Lyme Hall in Cheshire. He undoubtedly fought at Agincourt, but it has been claimed at various times that he was knighted, wounded and killed there; and there is also a story, told by the guides at the Hall, that his mastiff stood over him to protect from further harm, that the dog returned home afterwards to sire the famous breed of Lyme Hall mastiffs, and was afterwards buried in the woods in the Park.[12]

That Agincourt witnessed the 'death of chivalry' was a constant complaint amongst French writers; and it is easy to see why. Thousands of French soldiers, and in particular knights, had been killed or taken prisoner. Prominent members of the nobility had been taken to England, where some of them died and others were kept for years, allegedly in conditions of great hardship. These included Marshal Boucicaut, the most famous French knight of his day, who died in captivity, while Charles of Orléans was kept for twenty-five years and wrote many poems in captivity, lamenting his lost youth.[13]

Yet Agincourt did not put an end to either knighthood or chivalry in France. On the eve of the battle, the French created 500 new knights and they did not cease to create them as a result of their defeat. Despite the extraordinary career of Joan of Arc in 1429–30 and the reforms made by Charles VII in the 1440s, the French army which drove the English out of France in 1449–51 remained aristocratic. To take but one example, the Count of Richemont was captured at Agincourt but, after his release, he became Constable of France and participated in the French victories at Patay (1429) and Formigny (1450). Charles VII still made use of armoured cavalry when his generals put together his new *Compagnies d'Ordonnance*; and this 'new' army included numerous men who were relatives and descendants of the men of 1415. They included Gascons like La Hire and Poton de Xaintrailles, the Count of Dunois (younger half-brother of Charles of Orléans); and the son of the Duke of Alençon, killed at Agincourt. Charles VII did enlist the aid of some 'new men' like Jacques Coeur, the famous financier of Bourges; but the presence of a few 'bourgeois' advisers did not transform French society.

More generally, the late fourteenth and early fifteenth century saw the absorption of the Low Countries by Burgundy, as the citizen militias of the towns of Flanders were defeated by the Valois Dukes. Philip the Bold (r. 1363–1404) defeated the army of Ghent at Roosebeke in 1382 and John the Fearless (r. 1404–19) crushed the citizens of Liège in 1408. Even the so-called 'new model armies' of Duke Charles the Bold (r. 1467–77) were still largely composed of cavalry, not infantry. The real military revolution, when heavy cavalry gave way to massed infantry using firearms and artillery, had to wait for the sixteenth century.

In England too we find a lament for the end of the age of chivalry, in a late fifteenth-century preface written by William Caxton (c. 1415–92).

> Oh ye knights of England! Where is the custom and usage of chivalry that was used in those days? What do ye know but go to the baths and play dice? And some use not honour and good living against all order of knighthood. Leave this, leave it! ... Behold the victorious and noble Henry V and the captains under him, his noble brethren,

Montagu the Earl of Salisbury, and many others whose names shine gloriously by their virtuous and noble acts.[14]

But this is no more than the usual yearning for a lost golden age, which we find throughout history. When we look at the tombs which were built for the heroes of Agincourt, we see no sign of the end of chivalry. These knights stood at the apex of society and they were honoured in their own time.[15]

The Tudor Period

In 1513 Henry VIII invaded France and defeated a much smaller French force at the 'Battle of the Spurs', or Enguinegatte, around 16 miles from Azincourt, before agreeing terms with the French. The expedition was not at all comparable with Henry V's but it did coincide with the completion of a work now known *The First English Life of Henry V*, which hailed the earlier Henry as a hero of the English nation.

Not everyone was lost in admiration. Henry VIII's expedition and by implication, we may think, Henry V's, was roundly (if cryptically) condemned by Thomas More, in his famous *Utopia* (1516). More wrote of a King of Nolandia who

On the strength of some ancient marriage, thought he had a hereditary claim to another kingdom, so his people started a war to get it for him. Eventually they won, only to find that the kingdom in question was quite as much trouble to keep as it had been to acquire. There were constant threats of internal rebellion ... They never got a chance to demobilise, and in the meantime they were being ruined.

The Protestant Reformation wrought immense changes in England but it did not change the way in which the average Englishman looked at Henry V. At the time, Agincourt had restored the name of English arms, and the King's reputation remained unassailable throughout the sixteenth century. The historian Edward Hall (c. 1498–1547), though clearly a Protestant, had no desire to denigrate Henry, though he was critical of Archbishop Chichele and the Church. His section on the early fifteenth century is entitled *The victorious acts of King Henry V*: Agincourt is still described as the greatest of triumphs, while Henry is still 'the blazing comet and apparent lantern in his days, the mirror of Christendom ... the flower of kings past and a glass to them that should succeed'. In his *Actes and Monuments*, popularly known as the *Book of Martyrs*, first published in 1563, John Foxe argued that the Lollards were early Protestant heroes;

but he did not criticise the hero of Agincourt, though Henry V had been a stern persecutor of heresy.

Henry V … of whose virtues and great victories gotten in France, I have not greatly to intermeddle, especially seeing the memory of his worthy prowess, being sufficiently described in other writers in this our time, may both content the reader and unburden my labour herein.

In 1550, John Coke, who was 'clerk of the Statutes of the Staple of Westminster' produced his *Debate between the Heralds of England and France*. This was consciously intended as a vigorous reply to a fifteenth-century French work of the same name, and the views expressed were extreme. Through the character of the English herald, Coke explained at length that England was a much better country than France in every respect, in particular its women, food, climate, wealth and military valour. The French population might be greater, but this was only because most Frenchmen were common peasants 'not able to abyde the countenaunce of an Englishman'. The nobility in France had pretensions to superiority, but only because they were 'braggarts' Agincourt was the supreme example of English superiority on the battlefield.

The mighty and puissant conqueror kyng Henry the fyfte, with 9,000 Englyshmen wan a mighty battayle at Agyncourte in Normandye, against 100,000 Frenchemen, where he slewe the Dukes of Barre, Lorayne and Alaunson, 1,500 knyghtes, with an excedyng nombre of Frenchemen. He toke prisoners the dukes of Orlyaunce, Brytayne and Burbon, the erles of Vendosme and Ewe the Marshall of Fraunce, with many other lords and knyghtes, and wan Harflegte in Normandy, the yere of Our Lorde God M.CCCC.XV [1415].[16]

In the early years of the sixteenth century, England ceased to be a major 'player' on the Continent. The armies raised by Francis I of France and the Emperor Charles V dwarfed those led by Henry V and Henry VIII; and the two Continental powers fought each other for hegemony, especially in Italy, whilst England stood on the sidelines. In 1558, the English lost the last of their territories in France, when Calais was re-captured. In the late sixteenth century, France ceased to be a threat to England, when she fell prey to the Wars of Religion. Her place as 'traditional enemy' was taken by the Spain of Philip II, which dominated the Low Countries. England had to look to her navy, rather than the army, for defence. It is almost certain that, if the Spanish Armada of 1588 had been successful, the troops assembled by the Duke of Alba in the Netherlands would have met with little opposition in England. This is the background to Queen Elizabeth's famous 'backs to the wall' speech to the troops at Tilbury. Since the threat of invasion from Spain did not go away in 1588, it is also the background to Shakespeare's most famous history play, *Henry V*, first staged in 1599.

The Bard took great liberties with the facts. In *Henry V* he telescopes the five years after Agincourt into just one month, so that Henry's conquest of Normandy and the murder of the Duke of Burgundy in 1419 are omitted. The action shifts directly from the battle to Henry's marriage to the daughter of Charles VI, and to the Treaty of Troyes. But not every dramatic trick was necessarily fiction. For example, the episode, prior to the Agincourt expedition, where the French diplomats present Henry with tennis balls as a sign of their contempt is mentioned both by Thomas Elmham and in John Strecche's chronicle, composed only a few years after the battle.

> The Frenchmen, puffed up with pride and lacking in foresight, hurling mocking words at the ambassadors of the King of England, said foolishly to them that, as Henry was but a young man, they would send to him little balls to play with and soft cushions to rest on until he should have grown to a man's strength.[17]

Tennis and tennis balls also feature prominently in Lydgate's poem *The Siege of Harfleur and the Battle of Agincourt*.

Shakespeare helped to create or reinforce several myths: that God was on the side of the English; that a small beleaguered force can triumph over a mighty foe by virtue of superior morale; and that one Englishmen is worth more than several Frenchmen. It is because of his *Henry V* that we remember the King and the battle today; and most people who think they know something about the events of 1415 do so because they have seen his play on the stage, or else one of the film versions made by Laurence Olivier (1944) and Kenneth Branagh (1989). *Henry V* reinforced the traditional image of the King as the supreme English hero and made Agincourt a building block of English history, as conventionally taught in schools, as late as the 1960s. The idea that a few good men can triumph over an ill-disciplined horde can be found in many other works of literature; but there is no-one like Shakespeare for turning the commonplace into the unforgettable. What Englishman (or woman) can fail to be roused, even today, by the speeches made by Henry Plantagenet according to William Shakespeare?

> *And gentlemen in England now-a-bed*
> *Shall think themselves accurs'd they were not here,*
> *And hold their manhoods cheap while any speaks*
> *That fought with us upon Saint Crispin's day.*

The Modern World

English foreign policy changed a good deal when James VI of Scotland became James I of England in 1603. Yet there is little sign of any change in English attitudes to Henry V. English writers continued to refer to him in a reverential way and tended to copy what their Tudor forebears had written, sometimes uncritically, though some of the poet Michael Drayton's lines are memorable. He published an anthology entitled *The Battaile of Agincourt* in 1629, which was 'hurried into print as background-making music' for a campaign which the Duke of Buckingham was about to undertake in France.[18]

> *Fair stood the wind for France,*
> *When we our sails advance,*
> *Nor now to prove our chance*
> *Longer will tarry.*

Shakespeare's *Henry V* was little performed in the seventeenth century; but Samuel Pepys recorded that he had seen a performance of a different play about Henry in August 1664. This was written by Roger Boyle, 1st Earl of Orrery (1621–79) who was a politician as well as a soldier and dramatist.

> 13th August to the new play, at the Duke's house, of 'Henry the Fifth' a most noble play, writ by my Lord Orrery ... the whole play the most full of height and raptures of wit and sense, that ever I heard; having but one incongruity, or what did not please me in it, that is, that King Harry promises to plead for Tudor to their Mistress, Princesse Katherine of France, more than when it comes to it he seems to do.[19]

This tells us little about Agincourt; but the context in which the play was staged is interesting: in 1664 Charles II of England faced the rising power of Louis XIV of France; but perhaps the most intriguing aspect of Boyle's play was the emphasis he gave to the chaotic conditions prevailing in that country at the time of Henry V's invasion in 1415.

As a result of the victories of the Duke of Marlborough in the War of the Spanish Succession (1702–15) the British came to expect victory once more, when they fought the French in a Continental war; and Henry V continued to be regarded in Britain as a 'Worthy'. This is certainly how he is referred to in essays published in the eighteenth century in *The Gentleman's Magazine*, and in the correspondence of Horace Walpole. The continuing enthusiasm for him as a military hero was reflected in the work of historians. Thomas Goodwin's *History of the Reign of Henry the Fifth*, published in London in 1704 – the year of Marlborough's victory at Blenheim – repeated the conventional wisdom. In his preface, Goodwin wrote that 'our Black Prince's and Fifth Henry's wars are now no longer acted only on our theatres, but are revived in the field too'. Bishop William Nicholson (1655–1727) who produced a compendious work entitled *The English Scotch and Irish Historical Libraries* wrote in much the same vein: Henry V was 'a most Heroick Prince; and his single Victory at Agencourt [*sic*] might have afforded Matter for more Volumes'. Likewise, Viscount Bolingbroke (1678–1751), who knew something about faction, wrote, in his *Remarks on the History of England*, that

> in the short but triumphant reign of Henry the fifth, the spirit of faction was awed; and the spirit of liberty had no occasion of exerting itself, at least in any signal manner, under a prince just, moderate, and pious, according to the religion of those times.

The British were therefore devastated when their army suffered defeat at the hands of the French at Fontenoy in 1745 during the War of the Austrian Succession (1740–8). Horace Walpole (1717–97) wrote that

> having learned to spell out of the reigns of Edward III and Harry the Fifth, and begun lisping with Agincourt and Cressy [*sic*], one uses one's self but awkwardly to the sounds of Tournay and Fontenoy.

However, thirty years later, Walpole's letters indicate a loss of interest. In 1774 he wrote to a correspondent, apropos of a literary biography that the latter proposed to publish.

> The history of a dead poet will make no more impression now than the battle of Agincourt. If you can tell us of any news of the assembly of the [American] Colonies we will listen to you with avidity.[20]

This was written some nine years after Dr Johnson's remark that 'the feast of Crispin passes by without any mention of Agincourt'.

Yet the loss of interest seems to have been temporary, or perhaps affected only part of the population. In 1738, after a long absence, Shakespeare's play returned to the stage, when it was performed at Covent Garden. Thereafter, it became a regular part of the London repertoire. A statue of Shakespeare was set up in Westminster Abbey in 1741. During the Seven Years War with France (1756–63) *Henry V* was performed every year. John Kemble, the leading Shakespearean actor of his day, played Henry on no less than sixteen occasions between 1789 and 1792, when the play was received with renewed enthusiasm on the outbreak of war with Revolutionary France. Nelson's favourite Shakespearean play was *Henry V*. In 1799 he quoted from the St Crispin's Day speech and called the officers serving under him at the Battle of the Nile a 'band of brothers', a phrase also used by Sir Walter Scott in a song written in 1802 for his colleagues in the Edinburgh Light Dragoons.

The National Portrait Gallery and the Royal Collection each have around thirty portraits of Henry, by artists such as Renold Elstrack (1570–c. 1625); Jodocus Hondius (1610); William Faithorne (1616–91); Peter Vanderbank; Edward Luttrell (c. 1650–1723); John Faber junior (c. 1731); George Vertue (1684–1756); Pierre Francois Basan; John Carter (1784); James Parker (1790); James Neagle (1793); William Ridley (1793); John Keyse Sherwin (1751–90); Silvester Harding (1745–1809); James Basire (1730–1802); and Henry Hering (1862). Many paintings of the battle of Agincourt also survive from the nineteenth century, for example those done by Sir John Gilbert (1817–97), Charles Blair Leighton (1823–55) and Ernest Crofts (1847–1911). The sheer number of these works shows a high level of demand for heroic representations of the King and the battle, even during periods of scepticism and doubt about the merits of British involvement in Continental entanglements.

The first treatise on archery had been Roger Ascham's *Toxophilus* of 1545, but in the modern period there was a whole series of works in the same genre, by poets, amateurs and antiquarians. These included Gervase Markham (1634), E. Hargrove (1792), Walter Michael Moseley (1792), Thomas Roberts (1801), Samuel Rush Meyrick (1824) Thomas Waring (1824), Thomas Hastings (1831), 'The Old Toxophilite' (1833), George Hagar Hansard (1841), H. A. Ford (1859), Maurice Thompson (1879) and Edward S. Morse (1885). Their popularity testifies to an enduring passion for the longbow, which has lasted down to the present day. Markham's work was written at a time when – implausibly – it was still thought possible to revive the use of the bow in time of war: its title was *The Art of Archerie, Shewing how it is most necessary in these times for this Kingdom, both*

in Peace and War, and how it may be done without Charge to the Country,
Trouble to the People, or any Hindrance to Necessary Occasions. The flavour of
his argument is soon appreciated.

> The bow (next unto God) has carried the honor, witness the Battle of
> Agincourt, where Henry V, with 7,000 fighting men, and many of
> them sick and unable, yet such archers, that (as the Chronicle does
> report) most of them drew a yard, slew all the Chevalrie of France, to
> the number of 40,000 and more, and lost not above 26 of the English.

Yet in the Age of the Enlightenment some historians were already
engaged in deconstructing the patriotic myth. Paul de Rapin (1661–1725)
was a French Huguenot, who had left his homeland as a result of Louis
XIV's persecution of Protestantism.

> The Battle of Agincourt is then the great and almost sole warlike
> Exploit, which can justly afford matter for Panegyrick. In this famous
> Action, [Henry V] gave Proofs of an uncommon Conduct, Resolu-
> tion and Bravery. But this very Battle, the Success of which was so
> glorious, gives likewise occasion to tax him with Imprudence. It may
> be said that, if he was victorious, it was because he had reduced him-
> self to an absolute Necessity, of vanquishing or dying; to which a
> General never exposes himself, whatever the Event may be, without
> causing his Conduct to be severely censured.

In his *Essay at removing national prejudicies against a union with Scotland*
(1706) Daniel Defoe (c. 1659–1731) implicitly downgraded Agincourt,
by referring to the fact that France had soon 'recovered herself' under
Charles VII, by courtesy of her alliance with the Scots. The Scottish
philosopher David Hume (1711–76) emphasised the importance of the
civil war in France and the 'utmost imprudence' of the French commanders in explaining English military success, since he considered that
Henry V acted very rashly and took an unacceptably high degree of risk.[21]
Another Scot, Tobias Smollett (1721–71), better known as a novelist, also
wrote *A Complete History of England.* Here is his assessment of Henry V.

> [He was] chaste, temperate, modest, devout, scrupulously just in his
> administration and severely exact in the discipline of his army ... but
> we cannot be so far dazzled with his great qualities, as to overlook the
> defects of his character ... That his disposition was cruel, appears too
> evidenced from the massacre of the prisoners at Agincourt ... as well
> as from the persecution of the Lollards, which could not have been

countenanced by a prince of humanity ... All his renown was founded upon the most pernicious ambition, which seemed to swallow up every principle of justice, and every consideration of humanity ... he had attacked the kingdom of France without the least provocation; he had filled it with widows and orphans, lamentation, misery, and every species of distress; and yet he died in full conviction of having acted according to the dictates of equity.

In his *Characters of Shakespeare's Plays* (1817) the literary critic William Hazlitt (1778–1830) delivered an even more damning verdict, but one that was to become commonplace amongst radicals and socialists.

Henry, because he did not know how to govern his own kingdom, determined to make war upon his neighbours. Because his own title to the crown was doubtful, he laid claim to that of France. Because he did not know how to exercise the enormous power, which had just dropped into his hands, to any one good purpose, he immediately undertook (a cheap and obvious resource of sovereignty) to do all the mischief he could.

Yet the new readiness to criticise Henry's conduct was offset by the growth of a new kind of military history, as the soldiers involved in the Napoleonic Wars returned home after Waterloo in 1815. Four hundred years had elapsed between the English victory and the British one; but the two places are only 100 miles apart and some officers and soldiers who had fought at Waterloo had their medals presented to them on the battle-field at Azincourt.[22] Sir Harris Nicolas (1799–1848) served in the navy from 1812 to 1816 but subsequently became a barrister, while devoting much of his time to genealogy and history; and his book on Agincourt set new standards. He justified all his judgments by reference to the sources, and included copious extracts from original documents. As a military man, he showed a keen interest in getting things right; but he was by no means an uncritical admirer of Henry V. In his view, the letters written by Henry before the Agincourt campaign contained evidence of 'falsehood, hypocrisy and impiety'.

It seems difficult to reconcile the lawless ambition, much less the hypocrisy, which Henry displayed in his negotiations, with an obedi-ence to the genuine dictates of Christianity.

All through the nineteenth and twentieth centuries, military historians (and others) took a simple pride in the fact that an English expeditionary force had beaten a much larger French army in 1415: the exact numbers did not matter. Whenever there was a war involving the British army, and especially around the anniversary of the battle, there was renewed interest in Agincourt. This happened during the Napoleonic War in 1800 (when an article in *Le Moniteur* which drew unfavourable comparisons between the French and British armies provoked a number of irate letters to *The Times*); during the Crimean War of 1853–6 (when the infamous charge of the Light Brigade took place on 25 October, the anniversary of Agincourt); and later, during the French invasion scare of 1859–60 and the Boer War of 1899–1902.[23]

One of the most unusual histories of England in the early nineteenth century was that written by a Catholic priest, Dr John Lingard (1771–1851); but Lingard agreed with the staunchly Protestant chroniclers of the Tudor period that Henry V was a great king, and he stated unequivocally that

> The splendour which conquest threw around [his] person still adheres to his memory four centuries after his death.

It was left to that pillar of Anglican orthodoxy, Bishop Stubbs (1825–1901), founder of the Oxford School of Modern History, to voice what was to become a regular critique of Henry V in modern times, at least amongst academics.

> The war of Henry V must be condemned by the judgement of modern opinion: it was a bold and desperate undertaking, fraught with suffering to all concerned.

This view was never adopted, however, by populist historians. Henry and his archers remained firmly in favour with them. In *A Child's History of England* (1853) Charles Dickens (1812–70) wrote of the English army at Agincourt as 'a little force' which had a 'good proportion of men who were not gentlemen by any means' while, later in the century, William Morris (1834–96) idealised all things Chaucerian, including the idea of the bowman who was also a yeoman. The narrator's guide in *A Dream of John Ball* (1888) is a 'burly longbowman'. In *News from Nowhere* (1890) Morris admired the fine 'yeomen dwellings' which he came across in his Utopian Hammersmith. In the manner of Sir John Fortescue, the typical medieval Englishman was generally thought to contrast very favourably with his counterpart in France.

Horace Walpole's ghost would have been highly amused when Henry V was remembered once more at Strawberry Hill in Twickenham. In the

1860s Frances Fortescue, Lady Waldegrave, made improvements to Walpole's house which included the installation of stained glass windows in her new Round Drawing Room. Six windows here feature Henry IV, V, VI, VII and VIII of England, together with Henry IV of Navarre and France; but it appears that Lady Waldegrave's reason for this extravagant gesture had little to do with Agincourt, and everything to do with the fact that her great friend the Duke d'Aumale (a prominent exile and a stern critic of Napoleon III) was also called Henri.[24]

English pride in the deeds of Henry V was demonstrated in various ways in Victorian times. English pride in the deeds of Henry V has been demonstrated in various ways since Victorian times. Lord Macaulay (1800–59) liked to recall that he had been born on Agincourt day. There were three productions of Shakespeare's *Henry V* during the season of 1900–01 and the Royal Navy has had a succession of warships called HMS *Agincourt*. Some of this jingoism was misplaced. The steelmen of Sheffield boasted that the English victories at Crécy and Agincourt were attributable to the quality of the arrow-heads made in their city; but when Hallamshire's greatest historian, Joseph Hunter (1783–1861) looked into this claim, he could find no evidence for it, though he was an expert on the battle, as well as the antiquities of South Yorkshire.[25]

The Great War of 1914–18 dwarfed all previous wars in which England and the United Kingdom had been involved. The Kaiser's Germany was more populous than Britain, and she had already outstripped her in terms of industrial production. She had recently constructed a fleet which was a challenge to the Royal Navy; and she possessed an enormous conscript army, whereas the British had only a small professional force – reportedly dismissed by the Kaiser as 'a contemptible little army'. It was predictable that, when war came, productions of *Henry V* would be staged. Sir Frank Benson (1858–1939), who was the most famous actor-manager of his day, revived it and for the performance on Boxing Day 1914 he incorporated a specially rousing Chorus. *The Times* noted that Benson's own performance as Henry was 'marked by an unwonted fervour'. In 1915 Eric Williams produced a film entitled *England's Warrior King*, which featured men from the Royal Scots Greys regiment, stationed at York.[26]

In August 1914 The German Army ran into the British Expeditionary Force (B.E.F.) at Mons in Belgium, around 70 miles from the village of Azincourt. Vastly outnumbered, the B.E.F. gave an honourable account of itself but was forced to retreat. This was the setting for a short story by Arthur Machen (1863–1947) entitled *The Bowmen*, which was published in

The Evening News. This tells how 80,000 British troops are attacked by 300,000 Germans, armed with the most modern weaponry, including artillery. The British fight desperately but are eventually compelled to conclude that all is lost. Then one of the British soldiers remembers a Latin motto, *Adsit Anglis Sanctus Georgius* – 'May St. George be a present help to the English'. As soon as he pronounces these words, he hears shouting, louder than thunder: *Array, array, array!*; *St. George! St. George!*; *St. George for Merry England!* And, as he turns to look, he sees, beyond the trench, a long line of shapes, with a shining around them. It turns out that these are the bowmen of Agincourt, arriving to help their beleaguered compatriots and descendants. The bowmen proceed to shoot down the German hordes in droves, with their trusty longbows. Machen's story was pure fiction, but many readers took it for reportage. As the story was told and retold, it seems that some of the bowmen were transformed in the telling into angels. In April 1915, an account of the Battle of Mons was published in a spiritualist magazine which assured readers that the B.E.F. had indeed been assisted by a supernatural force. Machen's story was widely reported in magazines, from *John Bull* to the *New Church Weekly*, and it became a bestseller, though he was bemused by the whole process. It is likely that it helped to give rise to the legend of the Angels of Mons.[27]

On 25 October 1915 – the 500th anniversary of Agincourt – *The Times* printed long lists of the dead and wounded from the Battle of Loos, the first battle in which the British suffered casualties on an 'industrial scale'; but the paper also carried two items devoted to the events of 1415. First, there was a leading article entitled 'Saint Crispin's Day'.

Five hundred years have come and gone today since England won the last and greatest of her medieval victories on foreign soil. This is the day of Agincourt, when Henry V, with his way-worn and half-famished band of Englishmen, attacked and put to utter rout the vast host that barred their way to Calais and the sea ... [England] has yet greater wars today, and her sons again stand embattled in the very fields where the noble Plantagenet with his 'band of brothers' snatched overwhelming victory from the very jaws of disaster ... 'Every subject's duty is the king's' is the keynote of [Shakespeare's] play, and in none is the sense of duty more strongly portrayed than in the King himself. From Crécy and Poitiers, onwards to the immortal signal at Trafalgar, from Trafalgar and Waterloo to the Marne and Ypres, the English sense of duty is the secret of our discipline and our success.

The writer drew a further parallel between 1415 and 1915.

> [The French] thought the English force 'a contemptible little army', as they had thought it at Crécy and Poitiers and as others have affected to think since.

The spirit of Agincourt was still alive in Britain in 1919, when R. B. Mowat, an Oxford academic, published his book about Henry V. This took a very favourable view of the King.

> He educated the nation, and infused it with the spirit of his own youth and energy ... He left an empire that would crumble, but an ideal that could never die ... Henry's most permanent gift to England is the sentiment of patriotism ...

However, Mowat also drew one very adverse conclusion.

> It was an ill day for [Henry V's] house [when he renewed the French war], for although [it] brought the most glorious days to Henry V, they brought nothing but disaster to his son.

There was widespread reaction against war in all its forms after 1918. As Emma Smith has argued, *Henry V* is a heroic play, but it also has intrinsic ambiguities, and it can be performed so as to reflect the horrors of war. George Bernard Shaw (1856–1950) disliked the fact that Shakespeare had 'thrust such a Jingo hero as Harry V down our throats'. On another occasion, he said that people were 'sick of jingoism and fed-up with Agincourt speeches', while the critic Max Beerbohm (1872–1956) considered *Henry V* 'the mere hackwork of genius'. In 1920 Gerald Gould published an article in *The English Review* which argued that the play had been misunderstood. It was actually intended, said Gould, to be an attack on medieval chivalry, rather than a celebration of it. For whatever reason, *Henry V* ceased to be part of the normal theatrical repertoire in the 1920s and 1930s.[28] Yet *The Agincourt Song*, arranged by Gerrard Williams, appeared as the first item in the *Daily Express Song Book* published in 1927.

Hitler's Germany presented an even greater threat to Britain than the Kaiser's Germany had done. Laurence Olivier had performed the role of *Henry V* on stage at The Old Vic in 1937; but, during the Second World War, he entertained the troops with a one-man show which included extracts from Henry V's speeches. As he later explained

> By the time I got to 'God for Harry' I think they would have followed me anywhere. I don't think we could have won the war without 'Once more unto the breach ...' somewhere in our soldier's hearts.

In 1944 Churchill instructed Olivier to make a film of *Henry V* as morale-boosting propaganda for the British troops who were preparing to invade Normandy, though – by the time the film was released – D-Day had taken place. Olivier's film was dedicated 'To the Commandos and Airborne Troops of Great Britain the spirit of whose ancestors it has been humbly attempted to recapture.' It took even more liberties with the truth than Shakespeare's text had; but it was a tremendous success, both critically and with the public. And it altered the perception of Agincourt for a generation.

The aftermath of the Second World War saw a vast growth in the market for patriotic history. When the Oxford historian A. L. Rowse arranged for E. F. Jacob to write a biography of Henry V for his series *Men and Their Times* in 1947, Jacob's book was entitled *Henry V and the Invasion of Normandy*. This was a scholarly counterpart to Olivier's film, and the parallel between Henry's invasions of Normandy and the D-Day landings of 1944 was expressly drawn. On two occasions, the historian compared the Treaty of Troyes of 1420 to Churchill's proposal, in 1940, for a political union between France and England.

More recently, historians have been less able to agree about the significance of Henry V's remarkable career. Pugh (1988) wrote that 'Henry V was a man of limited vision and outlook' and referred to the 'limited success of his costly first French expedition of 1415.' Harriss (2005) took the view that, although the English enterprise in France ultimately failed, 'multiple kingdoms ... were both conceivable and feasible in this [the fifteenth] and in the following century' and the union of England and France was accepted in 1420 by both sides, though with a degree of reluctance and misgiving on each.

In *Henry V, War Criminal* (2000) John Sutherland, Professor of English Literature at University College London, pointed out that in Olivier's film, the king never gives any command to kill the French prisoners. Instead, he looks at the dead bodies of the English boys whom the French have slaughtered in the baggage park, mutters that he 'has never till this moment in France been angry', and then throws himself into the fray once more. Likewise, in Kenneth Branagh's more sombre film version of the play, the King never issues any command that the French prisoners be killed. The dreadful words are simply omitted. By contrast, in the text of the play, Henry gives the order to kill the prisoners on two separate occasions! As Dr Johnson pointed out, Shakespeare's Henry was clearly in sanguinary mood.[29]

It comes as no surprise to discover that Shakespeare's *Henry V* has not played well in France. In fact it is hardly ever played at all; but in 1999, it was performed in French at the Avignon festival. On that occasion, the director chose to present the French as 'braggarts; jerky feathered puppets; stupefied simpletons; escaped lunatics; and pretentious cretins', all equally ineffective on the field of battle. The critics naturally hated it (one said it was more like Monty Python than Shakespeare) and the play was a spectacular flop.[30] Yet in England, *Henry V* continues to delight the audience, at least when conventionally produced. Indeed, when the writer saw Mark Rylance in the play at the newly-restored Globe Theatre in Southwark in the mid-1990s, the jingoism displayed by the modern-day groundlings from the City was positively embarrassing.

Conclusion: From Bannockburn to Agincourt, 2014–2015

Agincourt was never a *British* victory. It was a victory for an English king and an English army. It was only after 1707 that it became possible for the new British nation to look at matters differently. Between the Act of Union and (say) 1950 English historians wrote the history of England as if it were the history of the United Kingdom and histories of 'the British Army' routinely included its success at Agincourt. Agincourt was still invoked to boost the morale of that Army at the time of the D-Day landings in Normandy in 1944. As Jeremy Paxman pointed out in his book *The English* (Michael Joseph, 1998), the victory of the 'happy few' had become a recurrent theme in English history, whether the battle described took place on the land, at sea or in the air.

Much has changed. The United Kingdom and the French Republic have been allies since the *Entente Cordiale* was signed over 100 years ago. In 2015 we will both have been members of the European Union for over 40 years, though a proposed referendum may put this in doubt.[1] Just as it was impossible to celebrate the 400th anniversary of the Spanish Armada in 1988 in straightforwardly traditional fashion, so it will be impossible to celebrate Agincourt in a narrowly English way. This is not for fear of offending French sensibilities. It is because we are no longer the same country or society that we were in 1415. Nor are the French, though most people would agree that in most respects, things have changed for the better.

There is another reason why Agincourt can no longer be viewed in the same light as it was in 1915, or 1815, or even 1715. For better or worse, the United Kingdom is no longer the unitary state it once was. It is a cliché that we live in a multi-cultural society; but the legal and constitutional changes which have taken place in recent years are, if anything, more significant. The twenty-six counties in the South of Ireland became independent (in all but name) in 1922. Historians there remember the late Middle Ages as a period when the English were in full retreat, in face of the first 'Gaelic revival'. In 1998 Wales was given its own Assembly and government, whose powers have since been increased; and Welsh nationalists have long recalled the reigns of Henry IV and V as the time when Wales finally lost its independence. For their part, the Scots regained their own Parliament and government in 1998. Having recently won a majority of seats in that Parliament, the SNP will now hold a referendum on the question of independence in September 2014, shortly after the 700th anniversary of the Battle of Bannockburn.

Bannockburn is altogether easier to commemorate than Agincourt. Rightly or wrongly, it has long been hailed as the battle which secured Scottish independence for almost four centuries; and it is remembered in the lyrics of *Scots Wha Hae* (1793) and *Flower of Scotland* (1967), patriotic songs which have become anthems of Scottish Nationalism and the second of which is regularly sung at sporting events. By contrast, there are no modern songs which celebrate Agincourt, and medieval ballads like the *Agincourt Carol* are no longer sung at all. The reason is simple: Agincourt was fought on French soil and was the first act in an aggressive war of conquest. Edward III had been invited to invade Normandy in 1346 by a rebellious Norman aristocrat, and the Black Prince had been invited to invade Aquitaine by the Gascons in 1355; but no Frenchman invited Henry V to invade in 1415. It was his idea, conceived at a time when there were not even many in England who agreed with it.[2] Yet for us in 2014–15, an English re-conquest of France is no longer conceivable, let alone desirable or possible. An independent Scotland is a real possibility.

Notes

Abbreviations

Allmand, LN: *Lancastrian Normandy*.

BIHR: *Bulletin of the Institute of Historical Research*.

BON: *The Boke of Noblesse*.

Contamine: Contamine's chapters in Corvisier, *Histoire militaire de la France*.

Curry, S & I: Anne Curry, *Agincourt, Sources and Interpretation*.

De Lannoy: see Lelewel ed.

EconHR: *Economic History Review*.

EFC: McFarlane, *England in the Fifteenth Century*.

EHD: *English Historical Documents*.

EHR: *English Historical Review*.

HV: Seward, *Henry V As Warlord*.

Jones: Michael K Jones, *Agincourt 1415*.

The King's Works: *The History of the King's Works*, ed. H. M. Colvin.

LK&LK: K. B. McFarlane, *Lancastrian Kings and Lollard Knights* (Oxford, 1972).

ODNB: *Oxford Dictionary of National Biography* (2004 edition).

POPC: *Proceedings and Ordinances of the Privy CouncilI*.

The P of K: *The Practice of Kingship*, ed. Harriss.

S & H: Strickland and Hardy.

TRHS: *Transactions of the Royal Historical Society*.

Wylie: volume II of Wylie's *Reign of Henry the Fifth*, covering the years 1415–16.

Chapter 1: Location

1. Nicolas, Appendix VI (n. 2). Wylie, 208 (n. 2).
2. *The Battle of Agincourt Sources and Interpretation* (The Boydell Press), 1 (n. 1).
3. Curry, S & I, 381, citing Charles Labitte's article in the *Revue Anglo-Française*, 3 (1815).
4. The Chaplain states at one point that the battle took place *in dicto campo nominato de Agincourt, per quem erat transitus noster versus Calisium*. In another place, he writes *iter* instead of *transitus*. Either word could mean 'road' or 'route'.
5. T. L. Sutherland, 'The Battle of Agincourt: An Alternative Location?', *Journal of Conflict Archaeology*, I (2006), 245–63.
6. T. L. Sutherland (2009), *Archaeological Evidence of Medieval Conflict – Case Studies from Towton, Yorkshire, England (1461) and Agincourt, Pas de Calais, France (1415)*. H. H. Meller (ed.) *Schlachtfeldarchäologie – Battlefield Archaeology. 1. Mitteldeutscher Archäologentag vom 09. bis 11. Oktober 2008 in Halle (Salle)*, 109–16.
7. Curry, S & I, 388 (and in discussion with me). Nicolas's two maps are opposite pages 264 and 113 in his text.

8. *Recueil des Chroniques d'Engleterre*, Volume 5, Book 1, Chapter XII, 210.
9. Wylie, 229–30, was informed by letter written by the late Duke of Richmond dated 29 March 1902 that this ring was preserved in a glass case at Goodwood House. When I enquired, the Curator of the Goodwood Collection (e-mail dated 29 May 2012) could only say that a privately-printed catalogue dated 1907 referred to a 'Gold Ring, made after one found at Agincourt' as item 24 in Case no. 1, at the foot of the Stone Stairs.
10. Curry, S & I, 462; medieval.mrugala.net/Guerre/Azincourt. I am especially grateful to Professor Curry for the point about Henry's order regarding armour: see Curry (2005), 271 and in discussion.
11. I am grateful to Matthew Bennett of the Royal Military Academy at Sandhurst for pointing this out to me. Dr Bennett commented that 'it is difficult to identify a battle-field with any certainty before the widespread use of gunpowder weapons produced a "fall of shot"'.
12. mrugala.net/Guerre/Azincourt.
13. *The Battle of Crécy, 1346*, ed. Andrew Ayton and Sir Philip Preston, The Boydell Press, 2005.

Chapter 2: English Victory or French Defeat?

1. *Choix de Pièces Inédites*, vol. II, CXI.
2. The Monk of St Denis; Barker, 229–32; Curry, S & I, 141. Monstret tells us that 400 men were sent to reinforce Harfleur; but Le Fèvre and Waurin say the number was 300.
3. S & H, 329–32.
4. Contamine, 179; Barker, 292.
5. Contamine, 181.
6. Kightly's *Agincourt* (New Malden, 1974), cited by Curry, S & I, 405; Jones, 151.
7. Barker, 297; Wylie, 159–60.
8. Curry, S & I, 91.
9. See the *Commentaries of Pope Pius II*. For the Abbey as a museum in Tudor times see *Shakespeare's Britain* (The British Museum Press, 2012), 38–9.
10. Allmand, *Henry V*, 89.
11. I am grateful to Anne Curry for this point. De Lannoy's account is reproduced in the 2nd edition of her *Battle of Agincourt, Sources and Interpretation*.
12. S & H, 337; Barker, 305; Autrand, 534.
13. Allmand, *Henry V*, 95.
14. Curry, S & I, 472.
15. De Belleval, 161–2.
16. Curry (2005), 76–7 and in discussion with me.
17. Rose (1982); N. A. M. Rodger.
18. CCR, 1413–19, 223.
19. Salisbury First General Entry Book, items; 151–3, pp. 68–9; *An Official Account of the Battle of Agincourt*, A. R. Malden, *The Ancestor*, ed. Oswald Barron, No. XI, October 1904. In Wylie's version, four men were killed and fourteen others thrown over the bridge into the River Avon.
20. Wylie, 7.

21. Wylie, 16–17; Barker 158–62; *English Suits, Overton v Fastolf*, 264. See also my biography of Fastolf (Pen & Sword, 2010).
22. Curry, *Participants* (ODNB).
23. Nicolas, 47, 373–89; Wylie, 89 (n. 5); Curry, S & I, 423; Barker, 223, 228; Jones, 69; Curry (ed.), 2000, plates 3, 5 & 6; Earle, 132. Anne Curry has pointed out that soldiers can have horses for transport without being required to *fight* on horseback.
24. Anne Curry has pointed out to me that the date of Henry's Ordinances is far from certain.
25. Basset's Chronicle 45v; Monstrelet, I, 394.
26. Wylie, 158, 162.

Chapter 3: The General and the Army

1. R. Theodore Beck, *The Cutting Edge* (Lund Humphries, 1974), 117–18.
2. Collins, 47; according to Contamine, Clarence indented for 240 men at arms and 720 mounted archers; Helen Castor, *The King, the Crown and the Duchy of Lancaster* (Oxford 2000), 33–4.
3. Curry, S & I, 421, citing TNA E404/31/315; Jones, 45.
4. Seward, HV, 25; see also McFarlane, LK&LK 122.
5. Pugh, 42–3; *Prince Henry of Monmouth – His Letters and Despatches During the War in Wales 1402–5*, F S Flood, TRHS, 1889, 125.
6. Knowles, 145.
7. Inwood, 83; *London Civic Theatre, Anne Lancashire* (Cambridge University Press, 2005), 148, Nightingale, 389.
8. Keen, *Chivalry*, 221.
9. Rowe, EHR 1926, 509.
10. Allmand, *Henry V*, 94. For de Lannoy's experience see de Belleval, 285; Barker, 304–5; Curry, *New History*, 263, 286; Jones, 129.
11. Nicolas, 125.
12. Wylie, 175; Allmand, *Henry V*, 94; Mercer, 56.
13. S & H, 338; Nicolas, 115; Jones, 75; Barker, 56, 301–2. Plate 8 in Curry (ed.) (2000) shows Martel with the banner unfurled; but some artistic licence may have been employed here.
14. Powell (1989), 275.
15. Nicolas, App. II, prints two examples of indentures. The commissions of array served to identify men who were fit to serve: Barker, 128–9.
16. Keen, *Chivalry*, 248, 176.
17. Matthew Bennett (in Curry and Hughes [1994]).
18. *Hunter's Hallamshire* (3rd edition 1875), 61; GHQ, 160(n); Nicolas, 127; De Belleval, 355; Jacob, *Henry V and the Invasion of France*, 30.
19. GHQ, 79; ODNB.
20. Pugh, 78, 104; Leland vol. 1, 5; Barker, 317; ODNB.
21. Collins, 293; Mortimer, 161–3; the ODNB, and at least some editions of Burke's peerage, wrongly state that he was elected K.G. for his services at Agincourt. The present Lord Camoys (2010) of Stonor House in Oxfordshire is descended from the Camoys at Agincourt in the female line: I owe this detail, as many others to Anne Curry.

22. While in the Holy Land, he may well have acquired the material for the rich red and gold chasuble, now in the Victoria and Albert Museum, which has motifs of a camel and which bears his coats of arms.

23, Erpingham paid for the Erpingham Gate in Norwich Cathedral, the rebuilding of the church of the Dominican Friars, a new East window for the church of the Augustinian Friars and the West Tower of Erpingham parish church. In Curry (ed.) (2000), Anne Curry doubted whether Erpingham was in command of the archers.

24. Nicolas, App. 60; Wylie, 188, 189; Jones, 118; Powell (1989), 200.

25. Curry, S & I, 422.

26. CPR, 3 Henry V Part II, 395.

27. *First English Life*, 28; Tito Livio's account appears in Nicolas, 35(n).

28. TNA E 101/44/30, roll 1 no 1, membrane 10; TNA E 101/46/24. See Scrope's *History of the Manor and Ancient Barony of Castle Combe*, which exploded the myth that Fastolf fought at Agincourt as long ago as 1852. John Phelip, brother of William, died at Harfleur, not at Agincourt.

29. Nicolas, 75 and 109; Wylie, 142; Curry, S & I, 12 (Table 1); *Political Poems and Songs*, II, 124. Appendix B to Curry (2005) contains a complete list of Army Sizes According to the Chroniclers.

30. Delbrück and Lot's arguments are more fully explained in Curry, S & I, 394–7; Contamine, 178.

31. 'Historians Reassess Battle of Agincourt', *The New York Times*, 24 October 2009.

32. See Curry's article on *Participants in the Battle of Agincourt* in ODNB.

33. Calmette, *Les Grands Ducs de Bourgogne*; McEvedy, *Penguin Atlas of Medieval History*. Charles Ross (*Richard III*, Yale, 1981) wrote of Burgundy as a 'virtually independent state' but he was writing about the reign of Duke Charles the Bold (1467–77).

34. Barker, 239, 294, 301; Curry (2005), 109–11, 219, 227; Autrand, 530; de Belleval, 204.

35. Vaughan (2002), 39, 58, 140 and Chapter V generally (*The Means to Power*).

36. Autrand, 530; Vaughan (2002), 148, 151.

Chapter 4: Casualties and Survivors

1. Rogers, *Infantry Revolutions*.

2. Cited by Wagner, 43.

3. Pernoud, 37.

4. Wylie, 186, 184; Autrand, 536.

5. The ODNB states that Harrington was the royal standard-bearer at Agincourt; but Jones, 14, favours Strickland, who made that claim in 1424 (Nicolas, 171), though Wylie (147–8) had evidence that he returned to England after Harfleur. It is sometimes claimed that Sir Lewis Robsart was standard bearer, when in fact he seems to have held that office under Henry VI. Nicolas, 383, 333, 370; Wylie, 89 (n. 1).

6. Curry, S & I, 432.

7. ODNB (York); www.fordsfarm.co.uk/ewelme (Suffolk). It is Michael's father, the 2nd Earl, who died at Harfleur and is buried in St Andrew's Church Wingfield.

8. Nicolas, Appendix, 60; *Paston Letters and Papers of the Fifteenth Century*, ed. Richard Beadle and Colin Richmond (Early English Text Society, OUP, 2005), Part III, 62.

9. Nicolas, 174, Appendix, no. XIV; ODNB (Vaughan family).

10. The tomb effigy in Bredwardine church contains no indication of who is buried beneath; and the use of alabaster may suggest a late fifteenth-century date.

11. Champion, 158; Rymer (1740) Tome IV, Part II, 163; Wylie, 130, 171.
12. De Belleval, 119 (n. 4).
13. Collins, 47. Nicolas's list (174–5) is not the same; ODNB (Mowbray). Anne Curry has pointed out that we cannot be certain that election as a Garter Knight for service in France means the same as service at Agincourt; and also that the 'Agincourt Roll' is itself a term which was coined at a late date. The roll of 1417 was prepared in connection with the payment of the troops, not as a roll of honour. See also Curry, S & I, Chapter 5.
14. *English Suits Before the Parlement of Paris 1420–36*, Camden Fourth Series, vol. 26, Appendix II; ODNB (Popham & Assheton).
15. ODNB (Grey & Holland).
16. Nicolas, 369; Harper-Bill, 143; ODNB (Gam, Phelip & Bourchier).
17. The matter is of some complexity: see Squibb, 181–2 and Curry (ed.) 2000, 137.
18. The Yorkshireman Sir Robert Babthorpe, controller of Henry V's household in 1416 and again in 1418, cited his presence at Agincourt: Bates & Curry, 274, 278.
19. Allmand, LN, 67; www.entwistlefamily.org.uk.
20. Nicolas, 165–6; POPC, 4 Henry V, 229.
21. Nicolas, 91, 228 (n); Wylie, 115; Jones, 82; Barker, 246; Curry, *New History*, 140.
22. www.thehistoryofparliamentonline.org. He was buried at Launde Priory, the site of the present (Elizabethan) Launde Abbey; Keen, *Origins of the English Gentleman*, 33, citing BL Cotton MS Titus C1, folios 191^v–192^r.
23. The Battle of the Seine in 1416.
24. Nicolas, 171, 173; Mortimer, 352.
25. Two indentures were printed by Nicolas in App. II. Michelet is perhaps the basis for Steve Beck's assertion that 1,500–1,600 prisoners were taken to England where many, unable to pay their ransoms, never returned.
26. Nicolas, Appendix XV.
27. The P of K (Catto), 103.
28. Selden Society, volume X, 1896, *Select Cases in Chancery*, 110; Mercer 56–7; Rose, 59.
29. POPC vol. 2, 355.
30. Michelet, IV, 243. For the Tower see Harrison, 94. The Count of Vendôme's ransom was mentioned in Parliament: RP vol. 4, 300b; see Rymer, vol. IV, II, 188–9 for the events of 1417. For Orléans in the 1430s see John Watts' article on the Duke of Suffolk in ODNB.
31. Nicolas, 165; Wylie, 256.
32. Barker, 369.
33. He is pictured in Cassell's popular illustrated *History of England* first published in 1902.
34. Jacob, *The Fifteenth Century*, 204; Nicolas 177; Barker 373.
35. Calendar of Plea and Memoranda Rolls, 1413–37, ix; and Nicolas.
36. Wylie, 125; Harrison, 92; Bellamy 130 (n. 4); Barker, 74, 370
37. Melbourne Castle was demolished by its owner in 1637.
38. Barker, 373; Barron and Burgess, ed. (2010), 134 (n. 72); Harrison, 92.
39. *Choix de Pièces Inédites*, vol. II, XXXIV.
40. Cup-bearer.
41. Agincourt.
42. *Pocquet de Haut-Jussé*, items 247, 249, 291.

43. This was not the same man as Pierre des Essarts, a prominent member of the Duke of Burgundy's household, who is mentioned in the Journal kept by the *Bourgeois* of Paris and was Provost of Paris between 1408 and 1410, since the latter was executed in 1413.
44. *Choix de Pièces Inédites*, vol. II, XXIV.
45. Wylie, 130, 188 (n. 3); Barker 267; Curry, *Participants* (ODNB, 2102); Barker, 370. De Gaucourt's account of this episode is reproduced in full by Nicolas, Appendix No. VI. It says that the English prisoners in question were 'gentlemen, merchants and soldiers'.

Chapter 5: Who Started It?
1. CCR, 1413–19, 214.
2. BON, 28, 37.
3. Nicolas, Appendix I, 5; Allmand, *Henry V*, 275–6; Harriss, *Shaping the Nation*, 181.
4. Lenfant, 454; Welsh, 171.
5. Curry & Bates, 239, 243.
6. Allmand, *Henry V*, 62; Jacob (1947), 14–15.
7. TRHS, 1979: *Piracy or Policy, The Crisis in the Channel, 1400–1403*.
8. Don Pero de Niño, 115–30, 158–63; Richmond, FW 79 (n. 97); M, I, 37(n).
9. The Parliament Rolls, Henry V, 7; *The King's Works*, 237–43, 434, 436 and the maps at 239 and 242.
10. Sutherland and Watts, 122.
11. Seward, HV, xix. Seward's anti-Lancastrian view is based on Thomas of Walsingham, and partly on French sources such as the Monk of St Denis and Jean Fusoris.
12. Seward, HV, 36–7, 47, 93. Ian Mortimer's thesis in *1415: Henry V's Year of Glory* is much the same as Seward's.
13. Vale, *English Gascony*, 29–30.
14. The contemporary ballad referred to is printed in *Political Poems and Songs*, II. SS Crispin and Crispinian. They were supposed to have been beheaded during the reign of the Roman Emperor Diocletian, in 285 or 286 CE.
15. *Religieux de St Denis*, vol. 5, 311–29; Autrand, 508.
16. Barker, 58, 237; Jones, 27, 91.
17. Powicke, 382; Nicolas, Appendix XVI.
18. Labarge, 59, Keen mentions de Lannoy in this context too, in *Chivalry*.
19. French *Wikipedia* [January 2013].
20. Morton, 138; Seward, HV, xviii.
21. Vale, *English Gascony*, 70; Harriss, *Shaping the Nation*, 266; Vaughan (2002) for Burgundy and Flanders; Autrand, 520.
22. See articles in the EconHR 1942 (Postan); TRHS 1957 (McFarlane); P&P 1962 (McFarlane); and P&P 1964 (Postan). Rowse's views are in *Historians I Have Known* (1995).
23. EFC, 175.
24. Leland, Part IV, 9; ODNB, article by Richard K. Rose. Streatlam Castle was still (just about) extant when McFarlane wrote his seminal article on the investment of profits of war in 1957 but the ruins were blown up by the Territorial Army in 1959, as a training exercise.
25. Leland, Part V, 72.

26. CPR, 1429-36, 446. There is a complete description, plan, and photographs, of the house in *An Inventory of the Historical Monuments in Herefordshire* vol III (Royal Commission on Historical Monuments, 1934).

27. Nicolas, 128, 381, Appendix, 17; Barker, 215 (of these twelve men, two died at Harfleur and three were sent home sick; and two archers died at the same siege); Curry, *New History*, 289. One cannot necessarily believe Lenthall's 'nil return'. Sir John Fastolf consistently declared no profits of war, though he clearly accumulated great wealth in France.

28. Leland, Part I, 102–3. Nothing now remains of Ampthill Castle, though the site is marked by a cross, in memory of Catherine of Aragon. Hungerford was succeeded by his son Robert 2nd Baron Hungerford, whose effigy is in Salisbury Cathedral.

29. Leland, Part II, 138.

30. ODNB (Charles Kightly); *The History of Parliament*, ed. Roskell and others (Boydell and Brewer, 1993).

31. Leland cites oral traditions current in the 1530s and 1540s. His manuscript was used in turn by Holinshed, Camden, Drayton and Dugdale. His work was published by Thomas Hearne, librarian at the Bodleian in Oxford, between 1710 and 1712: Toulmin-Smith.

32. In *Mad Dogs and Englishmen* (Hodder & Stoughton, 2009), Sir Ranulph Fiennes claims that three of his ancestors fought at Agincourt; but the ODNB only lists James Fenes/Fiennes.

Chapter 6: Kingdom and Capital

1. Allmand, *Henry V*, 16–17; G. L. Harriss in *The Practice of Kingship*; Curry, S & I,

2. Wylie, 253 (n. 8).

3. Wylie, 355 (n. 8); Curry, S & I, 422, 432; Nicolas, 128, Appendix, 62; Wylie, 115.

4. Nicolas 380–1, 384; Wylie, 185 (n. 3), 188; Barker 216; 318–19. Hornby Castle is now a private house; Ashton Hall is now (2012) used by Lancaster Golf Club.

5. Allmand, *Henry V*, 355. For Leche see Roskell, Clarke & Rawcliffe, *The History of Parliament* (Boydell & Brewer, 1993).

6. Sumption, vol. I, Chapter II; Postan, *Medieval Trade and Finance*, 342; Harris, *Shaping the Nation*, 258; Postan, 69; NCMH, 461, citing Harriss in *The Practice of Kingship*; Curry, S & I 412.

7. Harriss, *Shaping the Nation*, 318–19; Steel, 187; McFarlane's essays on Beaufort in EFC; Barker, 112.

8. Wylie, 26–9; Barker, 125; Curry (*New History*), 51. Le Gay was captured by the French on his way to Paris and told all he knew, and Fusoris was arrested and tried for treason.

9. Autrand, 526, 528, 534

10. Barker, 110.

11. Salibsury First General Entry Book, item 146–150, 66–8.

12. Nicolas, Appendix III; Wylie, vol. I, 470; A. J. Taylor, *The Jewel Tower* (English Heritage, 1996), 7. For a loan of nearly £1,000 in July by the Bishop of Durham, the Prior of Durham and the Archbishop of York, against the security of 'a great tabernacle of gold', see CPR 1413–16, 350.

13. Steel, 196; POP, vol. 2, 165–6.

14. Calendar of Letter Books, I, 143; Wylie, I, 454–5; CPR 1416–22, 47; C. T. Allmand in P of K, 123; Inwood, 82.

15. CCR, 1413–19, 217, 218 (oxen); 214 (baking and brewing). Chaucer has a brass in Ewelme.
16. Calendar of Plea and Memoranda Rolls, 1413–37, 28–9.
17. Bayley, vol 1, 44.
18. Inwood, 82; *Cardinal Beaufort: Patriot or Usurer?* G. L. Harriss, TRHS 1970.
19. Anne Sutton, 161.
20. Caroline M. Barron, 'Richard Whittington: the Man behind the Myth', in Hollaender (ed.), 228, 243; *Calendar of Plea and Memoranda Rolls*, 1413–37, 91. Whittington claimed that Turnebois had agreed to pay him £296. The court gave judgment for Whittington but the Italian claimed that some kind of error had occurred in the legal process.
21. Maurice Keen, *English Society in the Later Middle Ages* (Penguin, 1990).
22. Sumption, *The Hundred Years War*, vol. I; but compare Pugh, 138-40.
23. Powell (1989), 203; Curry (2005), 113, 219.
24. Vaughan (2002), Map 1.
25. Joseph Calmette thought that the civil war began in 1405, when the Duke of Burgundy marched on Paris (see *Les Grands Ducs de Bourgogne*, 1949).
26. Vaughan (2002), Maps 2 & 3.
27. Curry, S & I, 461–2.
28. Contamine, 183.
29. Allmand, *Henry V*, 90–1.
30. Vaughan (2002), 85.
31. Barker, 280; C. S. L. Davies, reviewing Curry (EHR 2005).

Chapter 7: Strategy, Tactics & Morale

1. Barker, 70–8.
2. CCR, 1413–19, 218; Barker, 129–30; Goodman, 37.
3. Vaughan (2002), 147.
4. Vaughan (2002), 269, 14–15; 19–29; Curry (2005), 17; Autrand, 506.
5. Vale, *English Gascony*, 70–82.
6. Allmand, *Henry V*, 99; xii, 67; Autrand, 528.
7. RP vol. 4, 345a; Labarge, 32.
8. LK&LK, 126; Jones, 71–5.
9. Barker, 244–5; de Belleval, 204. I also rely on information derived from a visit to Créquy, Fressin and Auchy-lès-Hesdin in March 2013.
10. Autrand, 528–9.
11. Wylie, 186, 209–10.
12. Robert Hardy thought that 'the only sensible suggestion' was that the archers were placed between each of the three 'battle' groups as well as on the wings; but he also believed that 'archers were often placed in front of the whole line during the early stages of attack, and that drills existed for them to move sideways among their fellows on the wings, or back behind the men at arms to re-deploy as needed'. Unfortunately, as he also says, there are no surviving drill-books: Nicolas, Appendix, 24; S & H, 327; Hardy, in Curry & Hughes, 180.
13. Curry, S & I, 471; S & H, 309–10.
14. Steve Beck, www.militaryhistoryonline.com.
15. S & H, 333.

16. *The Times*, Wednesday 30 January 2013; Roger Ascham in *Toxophilus* ('A Lover of the Bow', 1545).
17. S & H, 327; Hitchin in Curry (ed.), 52.
18. Allmand, *Henry V*, 93; Beck, in *Military History Online*.com; Seward, *HV*, 77, though in his *Hundred Years War*, 146, Seward stated that the stakes were only six feet long. One wonders if the 'eleven' was meant to be 'seven'.
19. Wylie, 156; Norfolk dialect, attributed to Matthew Bennett in www.norfolkheraldry. org.uk/Sir Thomas Erpingham; Jones, 108 (hunting call). In Chapter 4 of Curry (ed.) 2000, Curry casts doubt on the role played by Erpingham at Agincourt, which is only to be found in the Burgundian chroniclers; but contrast Simon Walker's article on Erpingham in the ODNB.
20. In Gilliot's *Azincourt* (2007).
21. Hitchin in Curry (ed.) (2000), 44.
22. S & H, 274–8, 334.
23. S & H 277.
24. Nicolas, 389 and 18, citing Rymer's *Foedera* IX, 224; Barker, 89; Curry, S & I, 436 for Mowbray; Curry (ed.) 2000, 42.
25. Jones, 8, 20; Postan, 66; Allmand, *Henry V*, 94.
26. I owe the reference to Dickens to Anne Curry.
27. Curry, S & I, 398, citing the article in the *Cornhill Magazine*, third series, 25 (1908), 789–93.
28. *Kingship Law and Society*, 234–40.
29. Hardy, in Curry & Hughes, 170; Curry (ed.) (2000), 46–7.
30. S & H, 337. It is not clear whether they used the long kind of warhammer used by the Flemings at Courtrai in 1302. For sidearms see Hitchin in Curry (ed.) 2000, 50.
31. See *The Face of Battle* (Keegan) and *Agincourt 1415* (Michael K. Jones).
32. Autrand, 289.
33. Autrand, 38; Barker, 294–5.
34. McKisack, *England in the Fourteenth Century*.
35. Seward, *HV*, 75.
36. Allmand, 91; Barker, 291; Jones, 125.
37. *Political Poems*, 124–5. Also: 'erste many a wyght man schall leve is weddes, for here erste to deth I wil be dyght, and therefore, lordynges, for the love of swete Jhesu, helpe mayntene Inglondes right this day. Allso, archers, to yow I praye, no fote that ye fle away, erste be we alle beten in this felde. And thenke be Englysshemen that never wold fle at no batelle, for ayenste one of us thow ther be tene, thenke Criste wil help us in owre right.'
38. Bates & Curry, 219.
39. Autrand, 532.
40. Curry and Hughes, 1994; www.medievalsoldier.org.
41. Curry, *Participants* (ODNB 2012).

Chapter 8: The Memory of Agincourt

1. *Memorials of London and London Life*, 620–2.
2. *Calendar of the Letter Books of London*, I, 143.
3. GHQ, 101–3.
4, GHQ, Appendix IV (Lydgate's verse).

5. Allmand, *Henry V*, 10.
6. GHQ, 113; Seward, HV, 87.
7. Barker, 380. Curry, S & I probably has the most extensive collection of poetry associated with Agincourt.
8. *Political Poems and Songs*, II, 128; EHD vol. V, 1194, citing *inter alia* Trinity College MSS 39, 40.
9. Wylie, 277 ; *Journal de Nicolas de Baye* (1415), 219.
10. Labarge, 91.
11. Wylie, 253 (n. 8)
12. *Salisbury First General Entry Book*, item 154, 69; *The Ancestor*, No. XI, article by A.R. Malden.
13. Curry, S & I, 278.
14. See A. K. McHardy, 'Liturgy and Propaganda in the Diocese of Lincoln during the Hundred Years War', in *Religion and National Identity*, ed. Stuart News (Basil Blackwell, 1982), though no such prayers are recorded in Lincoln under 1415.
15. Owst, *Literature and Pulpit*, 74.
16. Matthew, 127; Knowles, 181.
17. Jacob, 159; Allmand, *Henry V*, 370; McFarlane, *England in the Fifteenth Century*.
18. The Parliament Rolls; RP vol 4, 70a, 94b, 106a.
19. RP vol. 4, 423a; vol. 5, 176a; Allmand, LN, 259–60. I owe the reference to 1427 to Professor Curry.
20. Gibbon, *Decline and Fall*; Morosini, 71–5.
21. *The King's Works*, I, 245, II, 685–6; The P of K (Catto), 107; CPR 5 Henry V, vol. 2, 103; *Chronicles and Memorials of Great Britain and Ireland*, 10011.
22. Allmand, *Henry V*, 179–81, 274.
23. *The Spectator*, Tuesday March 18, 1712 (ed. Donald F. Bond, O.U.P., vol. III, 216). The tomb and the chantry chapel have recently been splendidly restored (2012).
24. *Shakespeare's Britain*, 38–9.
25. Rymer, IV, II, 187–8; *The Register of Archbishop Chichele*, vol. III, 7, 28–9; *The Register of Bishop Hallum of Salisbury* (Canterbury & York Society, Bell & Sons, 1886), item 926. I originally thought that the compiling of what we know today as 'the Agincourt Roll' was a mark of honour, conferred by Henry V on those who fought with him on Crispin's day; but Professor Curry has convinced me that this was not so. It is not a roll of honour but, more simply, a list compiled for more mundane purposes: see her *Sources and Interpretation* (2000), Chapter 5, 207–8.
26. Jones, 50, citing Adam of Usk.
27. www.all-souls.ox.ac.uk.
28. McFarlane's essay on William Worcester in EFC; Fortescue, *Governance of England*, 96–7. Stevenson, I, 319, II, 2, 477–8, 493–4; Griffiths, 815–16; Vale, *Ancient Enemy* ix, 16; P &V, 13.
29. In Westminster Abbey, the morning communion service is held in Henry V's chantry chapel on 25 October each year, though the procession no longer carries the sword Henry reputedly used in battle: Labarge, 188. Once again I owe the point, about there probably never having been an 'Agincourt Day', to Anne Curry.
30. Curry, S & I, 278.
31. www.bowyers.com/arms/groombridge.html.

Chapter 9: A Decisive Battle?
 1. Steve Beck in www.militaryhistoryonline.com; Jones, 4; Barker; 323; Curry, S & I, 333, 357; Vaughan (1970), 31, 276, 337; Nicolas, 179.
 2. Autrand, 520–1.
 3. Vaughan (Philip the Good), 11; Curry, *Agincourt A New History*, 291; Labarge, 110; Griffiths in Wood (ed.), 91; Jones, 1.
 4. Cited by Jones, 125.
 5. Autrand, 317, 518.
 6. Rodger, 145, 165.
 7. Allmand, LN, 269.
 8. Curry (2005), 280; Harris, *Shaping the Nation*, 87; Allmand; Griffiths in Wood (ed.); Barker.
 9. Seward HV, 219.
10. NCMH, 176.
11. McEvedy (map for 1478), 89.
12. Ross, *Richard III*.
13. *Henry V a personal portrait*, in LK&LK, 127, 4 and 133.
14. LK&LK, 124; Pugh, 142; Anne Curry, Radio 4, *In Our Time*, 16 September 2004; Griffiths in Wood (ed.) 2009, 91.
15. Curry, S & I, 192.
16. Vaugan (2002), 255.
17. Lenfant, tome 1, 455; Welch, 172; John A. F. Thomson, *The Transformation of Medieval England* (Longman, 1989), 76. Vale, *Ancient Enemy*, 68, has a different view.
18. Jones, 8.
19. N. A. M. Rodger.
20. EFC, 78.
21. Fudge; Hudson, 369; V. H. H. Green, 163, 168.
22. Stevenson, II, 2, 440–60.
23. I owe much of this to comments which the late Maurice Keen was kind enough to make on my manuscript in 2011, during his last illness.

Chapter 10: History, Legend & Myth
 1. Barker, 367; Burke's *Landed Gentry* (1952), for Lenthall of Bessels Leigh; G. D. Squibb, *The High Court of Chivalry* (Oxford, 1959), 74–8. *Chartham Church Monumental Inscriptions*, Rev Bryan Faussett, 1757 cited in www.kentarchaeology.org.uk.
 2. Nigel Saul, *For Honour and Fame, Chivalry in England, 1066–1500* (Bodley Head, Kindle edition), 67%, citing Lydgate's *Minor Poems*, ii, 716.
 3. *The Libelle of Englyshe Polycye*, 53.
 4. This whole section owes much to Curry, S & I.
 5. John Hardyng also claimed to be an eye-witness: Curry, S & I, 79; Taylor and Roskell (1975) thought it was impossible to be sure who the author was. They rejected the theory of Max Lenz (1874), accepted by Wylie, and eventually by Kingsford, that it was Thomas Elmham, Prior of Lenton, near Nottingham.
 6. Curry (2005), 252.
 7. Tito Livio (1716), 20. René de Belleval stated that Duke Humphrey was killed at Agincourt.
 8. BON 16, 28, 32, 42.

9. Camden Miscellany vol. XXIV, Camden Fourth Series, vol. 9, *John Benet's Chronicle for the years 1400-62*, ed. G. L. Harriss and M. A. Harriss, 177.

10. Monstrelet; *The Brut* (1908); Harley, 53; Oman; Kingsford (1913); Curry, S & I, 382.

11. Goodman, 139. The Ruisseauville chronicle states that the archers had their breeches hanging down – Curry, S & I, 125; S& H, 286, 329.

12. In his *History of Cheshire* (1882), 673–8, George Ormerod stated that Legh did indeed fight at Agincourt, but died in Paris in 1421 'of honourable wounds, probably received at the siege of Meaux'; and that his body was returned to Macclesfield for burial. No mention here of a mastiff, and Ormerod was not even certain that Legh was knighted at Agincourt. Fuller (1662) lists Sir Hugh Calvely and Sir Robert Knowles in his list of Cheshire worthies, but not Legh.

13. Boucicaut fought at Nicopolis, founded an order of chivalry and was governor of Genoa: Barber, *The Knight and Chivalry*, 144–5, 242.

14. Caxton, *The Book of the Ordre of Chyvalry*, cited by Keen, ELMA, 416.

15. ODNB (Helen Castor); Burke's *General Armory*; notes compiled for St Mary's Church Dennington, Suffolk by G. L. Harriss; Charles Boutell, *Historical and Popular* (London, 1864); Labarge, 71, citing Anthony Wagner, *Heralds of England*, 1967; Saul, 227.

16. *The Debate between the Heralds*, 113 para 193.

17. E.H.D. vol. V, 208; Curry, S & I, 40; Jones, 58. For the ballads, see Nicolas, 10–11 and App. XIX, 70, XX, 79.

18. ODNB.

19. www.pepysdiary.com/diary.

20. *Walpole's Correspondence*, vol. 18, 224; vol. 37, 200, 203; vol. 19, 327; vol. 28, 174.

21. Curry, S & I, 376.

22. Nicolas, Appendix, 24.

23. *The Times* digitalised archive, 27 August 1800; 13 July 1854; 26 October 1899; Curry, S & I, 391. The scare of 1863 was responsible for William Durrant Cooper's *Sussex Men at Agincourt*.

24. ODNB (Fortescue); *The Diaries of C. Fortescue*, ed., O. W. Hewett (John Murray); *John Iddon, Strawberry Hill & Horace Walpole* (Guidebook, 2013).

25. Hunter, *The History and Topography of the Parish of Sheffield* (3rd edition, London, 1875), 59 (n. 4).

26. Smith, 43.

27. See John Terraine, *The Smoke and the Fire* (Sidgwick and Jackson, London, 1980); Girouard, 284–5.

28. Smith, 35.

29. Sutherland and Watts, 109, 113.

30. Smith, 66. I am indebted to Emma Smith's excellent book in general.

Conclusion

1. On 23 January 2013 the Prime Minister David Cameron announced that there would be a commitment to an 'in–out' referendum on UK membership of the EU in the next Conservative party manifesto.

2. I owe much of this to a discussion with Anne Curry in May 2013.

Bibliography

Printed Primary Sources

Actes de la Chancellerie d'Henri VI Concernant La Normandie, Paul Le Cacheux, Rouen & Paris, 1907.

The Anglo-French Negotiations of 1439, C. T. Allmand, *Camden Miscellany*, vol. XXIV, 1972.

The Annals of Loch Cé, ed. W. M. Hennessy, Longman & Co, 1871.

Armorial of the Peace of Arras, ed., Steen Clemmenson, Copenhagen, 2006.

The Bagford Ballads, ed. J.W. Ebsworth, Stephen Austin and Sons, 1878.

Basin, Thomas, *Histoire de Charles VII*, 2 vols, Paris, 1933.

The Beauchamp Pageant, edited and introduced by Alexandra Sinclair, Richard III & Yorkist History Trust, 2003.

The Black Book of the Admiralty, ed. Sir Thomas Twiss, London, 1871.

The Book of the Ordre of Chyvalry (translated and printed by Caxton), ed. Alfred T. P. Byles, Early English Text Society, 1926.

The Brut, or The Chronicles of England, 2 vols., ed. F. W. D. Brie, Early English Text Society, 1906–8.

Calendar of Letters Books of the City of London, Letter-Book I (1400–22), ed. Reginald R. Sharpe, London, 1919.

Calendar of Patent Rolls, 3 Henry V, 1416.

Calendar of Plea & Memoranda Rolls of the City of London 1413–1437 and 1437–1457, ed. A. H. Thomas, Cambridge University Press, 1953, 1957.

Chappell, William, *The Ballad Literature and Popular Music of the Olden Time*, Chappell & Co., 1859.

Calmette, J., & G. Perinélle, *Louis XI et L'Angleterre (1461-1483)*, Éditions Auguste Picard, 1930.

Choix de Pièces Inédites Relatives au Règne de Charles VI, ed. L. Douët D'Arcq, Jules Renouard, 1864.

Chronique de Jean le Fèvre, Seigneur de St Rémy, ed. Francois Morand, La Société de l'Histoire de France, 1876.

Chronique du Mont-Saint-Michel (1343–1468), ed. Siméon Luce, 1879.

Chronique Normande de Pierre Cochon, ed. Charles de Robillard de Beaurepaire, Rouen, 1870.

Chronique du Religieux de St Denis, vol. 5, ed. L Bellaguet, Documents Inédits Sur L'Histoire de France, 1844.

Chroniques du Roi Charles VI, par Gilles le Bouvier called Berry Herald, ed. Corteault and Celier, Paris, 1979.

Collections des Documents Inédits sur L'Histoire de France, 1st series II, ed. M. Champollion-Figeac, Paris, 1847.

Commynes, Philippe, *Mémoires*, Librairie Generale Française, 2001.

Coke, John, *Le Débat Hes Hérauts d'Armes de France et d'AngleterreI*, followed by The Debate between the Heralds of England and France, Paris, 1877.

Elmham, Thomas, *Liber Metricus de Henrico Quinto* in *Memorials of Henry V*, ed. C. A. Cole, 1858.

Cornforth, M.C., *Rebels and Their Causes, Essays in Honour of A. L. Morton*, Lawrence and Wishart, 1978.

An English Chronicle 1377–1461 A New Edition, ed. William Marx, The Boydell Press, 2003.

Ellis, Henry, *Original Letters Illustrative of English History*, London, 1824.

English Historical Documents, 1485–1558, ed. C. H. Williams, Eyre and Spottiswoode, 1967.

Fauquembergue, *Journal de Clément de Fauquembergue, Greffier du Parlement de Paris, 1417–35*, 3 vols, Paris, 1909.

The First Life of Henry V, written in 1513 by an anonymous author commonly known as The Translator of Livius, ed. C. L. Kingsford, Oxford, 1911.

Fortescue, Sir John, *De Laudibus Legum Anglie*, Cambridge University Press, 1942.

———, *On the Laws and Governance of England*, Cambridge University Press, 1997.

Forty-Fourth Annual Report of the Deputy Keeper of the Public Records (London 1883) – containing the French Rolls for 1415.

Gesta Henrici Quinti, 'The Deeds of Henry V', translated and edited by Frank Taylor and John S. Roskell, The Clarendon Press, Oxford, 1975.

Hansen – *The Little Grey Horse –Henry V's Speech at Agincourt and the Battle Exhortation in Ancient Historiography*, Mogens Herman Hansen, Copenhagen Polis Centre, 1998 – www.dur.ac.uk.

Hardyng' Chronicle, ed. H. Ellis, London, 1812.

Horace Walpole's Correspondence with Sir Horace Mann, ed. W. S. Lewis and others, London University Press, 1960.

Jacob, E. F., *The Register of Henry Chichele*, Oxford University Press, 1945.

Jean Juvenal des Ursins, *Histoire de Charles VI* in *Nouvelle Collection des Mémoires pour server Á L'Histoire de France*, Paris, 1836.

Journal d'Un Bourgeois de Paris, Lettres Gothiques, Libre de Poche, 1990.

Journal de Nicolas de Baye, 1400–1417, Librairie Renouard, 1888.

(Le) Mistère du Siège d'Orléans, Collection des Documents Inedits sur l'Histoire de France, Paris, 1862.

Lelewel, Joachim (ed.), *Guillebert de Lannoy et Ses Voyages en 1413, 1414 et 1421*, Brussels, 1843.

Lewis, P. S., *Later Medieval France. The Polity*, New York, 1968.

Livio, Tito, *Vita Henrici Quinti*, ed. Thomas Hearne, Oxford, 1716.

Memorials of London and London Life,,1276–1419, ed. H. T. Riley, Longmans, Green and Co, 1868.

Monstrelet, *The Chronicles of Enguerrand de Monstrelet*, translated by Thomas Johnes, Esq., 2 vols., London, 1845.

Morosini, Antonio, *Chronique, Extraits Relatifs à L'Histoire de France (1396–1433)*, ed. G Lefèvre-Pontalis, Paris, 1899.

Morton, A. L., *A People's History of England*, Victor Gollancz Ltd, 1938.

Nouvelle Collection des Mémoires pour servir à L'Histoire de France, ed. Michaud & Poujoulat, vol. II, Paris, 1836.

The Norman Rolls (Rotuli Normanniae), vol. I, ed. T. D. Hardy, London, 1835.

The Parliament Rolls of Medieval England 1275–1504, ed. Chris Given-Wilson, The Boydell Press, 2005.

(Bishop) *Percy's Folio Manuscript, Ballads and Romances*, ed. John W. Hales and Frederick J. Furnival, London, 1867.

Pisan, Christine de, *The Book of Deeds of Arms and of Chivalry*, Pennsylvania State University Press, 1999.

Political Poems and Songs relating to English History, ed. Thomas Wright, vol. II, Longman, Green and Roberts, 1861.

Proceedings and Ordinances of the Privy Council of England, ed. Sir Harris Nicolas, 1834 [PPC], 4 Henry V (1417).

Pius II, *Commentaries*, ed. M. Meserve and M. Simonetta, I Tatti Renaissance Library, Harvard University Press, 2003.

Poquet de Haut-Jussé, B-A, *La France Gouvernée par Jean Sans-Peur*, Paris, 1959.

Pyne, Henry, *England and France in the Fifteenth Century (The Debate between the Heralds of France and England, presumed to have been written by Charles Duke of Orléans)*, Longmans, Green & Co, 1870.

Reliques of Ancient English Poetry, Bishop Thomas Percy, London, 1812.

Rymer's *Foedera*, London, 1740.

Rotuli Parliamentorum (The Rolls of Parliament), London, 1832.

Salisbury First General Entry Book 1387–1452, ed. David R. Carr, Wiltshire Record Society, vol. 54, 1998.

Scotichronicon by Walter Bower, vol. 8, Books XV and XVI, edited by D. E. R. Watt, Aberdeen University Press, 1987–98.

Stevenson, Reverend Joseph, *Letters and Papers Illustrative of the Wars of the English in France During the Reign of Henry VI King of England*, 3 vols., Longman, Green & Co, 1861–4, reproduced by Elibron Classics, 2007.

Strecche, *The Chronicle of John Strecche for the Reign of Henry V*, ed. Frank Taylor, *Bulletin of the John Rylands Library*, vol. 16, no. 1, 1932.

The Unconquered Knight, A Chronicle of the Deeds of Don Pero Niño, trans. and selected by Joan Evans, Kessinger Reprints, Harcourt, Brace & Co, 1928.

Usk, Adam, *The Chronicle of Adam of Usk 1377–1421*, ed. C. Given-Wilson, Clarendon Press, 1997.

Vegetius, *Epitome of Military Science*, Liverpool University Press, 1993.

Walsingham, Thomas, *St Albans Chronicle 1406–1420*, ed. V. H. Galbraith, 1937.

Walsingham, Thomas, *The Chronica Maiora of Thomas Walsingham 1376–1422*, trans. David Prest, intro. by James G. Clark, The Boydell Press, 2005.

Waurin, Jehan de, *Recueil des Croniques et Anciennes Istories de la Grant Bretagne à présent nommé Engleterre*, ed. William Hardy, Longman, London, 1864–79.

William Worcester, *The Boke of Noblesse*, ed. J. G. Nichols, The Roxburghe Club, 1860.

———, *Itineraries*, ed. John H. Harvey, Oxford, 1969.

Secondary Sources

Allmand, C. T., *Lancastrian Normandy*, Clarendon Press, 1983.

———, *The Hundred Years' War*, Cambridge University Press, 1989.

———— (ed.), *The Hundred Years War: England and France at War c.1300–c.1450*, Cambridge University Press, 1988.

————, *Henry V*, Yale, 1997.

Autrand, Françoise, *Charles VI*, Fayard, 1986.

Barber, Richard, *The Knight and Chivalry*, Boydell Press, 2000.

Barker, Juliet, *Agincourt, The King, The Campaign, The Battle*, Little, Brown, 2005.

————, *Conquest*, Little, Brown, 2009.

Barratt, John, *War for the Throne, The Battle of Shrewsbury 1403*, Pen & Sword, 2010.

Barron, Caroline M. (ed., with Clive Burgess), *Memory and Commemoration in Medieval England*, Shaun Tyas, 2010.

Bates, David and Curry, Anne, *England and Normandy in the Middle Ages*, The Hambledon Press, 1994.

Bate, Jonathan, *Soul of the Age, The Life, Mind and World of William Shakespeare*, Penguin Books, 2009.

Bayley, John, *The History and Antiquities of the Tower of London*, T. Cadell, 1821.

Bellamy, J. G., *The Law of Treason in England in the Later Middle Ages*, Wm. Gaunt & Sons, 1986.

Belleval, Rene de, *Azincourt*, Paris, 1865; Kessinger Publishing Legacy Reprints, c. 2010.

Bennett, Matthew, Jim Bradbury, Kelly Devries, Ian Dickie & Phyllis G Jestice, *Fighting Techniques of the Medieval World AD 500 – AD 1500*, Spellmount, 2005.

Bradbury, Jim, *The Medieval Archer*, The Boydell Press, 1985.

Bragg, Melvyn, *The Adventure of English*, Sceptre, 2003.

Breeze, Andrew, *Medieval Welsh Literature*, Four Courts Press, 1997.

Burke, Sir B., *The General Armory*, London, 1884.

Burne, Lt-Colonel Alfred H., *The Agincourt War*, Eyre & Spottiswoode, 1956.

Burrows, John, *A History of Histories*, Penguin, 2007.

Butterfield, Herbert, *The Whig Interpretation of History*, W. W. Norton, 1963, first published 1931.

Calmette, Joseph, *Les Grands Ducs de Bourgogne*, Éditions Albin Michel, 1949.

Champion, Pierre, *Vie de Charles d'Orléans* (1394–1465), Paris, 1911.

Churchill, Sir Winston, *A History of the English-Speaking Peoples, volume I The Birth of Britain*, Cassell, 1956.

Cooke, G. A., *Monmouth*, London, 1820.

Collins, Hugh E. L., *The Order of the Garter 1348-1461*, Clarendon Press, 2000.

Colvin, H. M. (ed.), *The History of the King's Works, volume I The Middle Ages*, HMSO, 1963.

Contamine, Philippe, *War in the Middle Ages*, translated by Michael Jones, Blackwell, 1992.

Corvisier, André, *Histoire militaire de la France vol 1 Des Origines a 1715*, Quadrige PUF, 1992 (relevant chapters by Contamine).

Cosgrove, A. (ed.), *A New History of Ireland, volume II Medieval Ireland*, Oxford University Press, 1987.

Coss, Peter, & Kevin Tyerman (eds), *Soldiers, Nobles and Gentlemen*, The Boydell Press, 2009.

Curry, Anne (ed.), *Agincourt 1415, Henry V, Sir Thomas Erpingham and the triumph of the English archers*, Tempus, 2000.

————, *The Battle of Agincourt, Sources and Interpretation*, The Boydell Press, 2000.

———, *Agincourt, A New History*, Tempus, 2005.

———, *Participants in the battle of Agincourt*, article in ODNB, September 2012.

———, & Michael Hughes, *Arms, Armies and Fortifications in the Hundred Years War*, The Boydell Press, 1994.

Dickinson, J. G., *The Congress of Arras 1435*, New York, 1972.

Dockray, Keith, & Fleming, Peter (eds), *People, places and perspectives: essays on later medieval & early Tudor England in honour of Ralph A. Griffiths*, Nonsuch, 2005.

Dockray, Keith, *Warrior King The Life of Henry V*, Tempus, 2007.

Earle, Peter, *The Life and Times of Henry V*, Weidenfeld and Nicolson, 1972, 1993.

Émond, André, *Constitution du Royaume-Uni: Des Origines À Nos Jours*, Montreal, 2009.

Fortescue, The Rt Hon J.W., *A History of the British Army* vol 1, The Naval & Military Press Ltd, 2004.

Fowler, Kenneth, *Plantagenet and Valois*, Elek Books Ltd, 1967.

Fox, Levi (ed.), *English Historical Scholarship in the Sixteenth and Seventeenth Centuries*, published for the Dugdale Society by the Oxford University Press, 1956.

Freeman, Mark, *St Albans*, Carnegie Publishing Ltd, 2008.

Gillingham, J., 'Richard I and the Science of War in the Middle Ages', in Strickland, Matthew, *Anglo-Norman Warfare*, The Boydell Press, 1992.

Fudge, Thomas A., *The Crusade against heretics in Bohemia, 1419–37*, Ashgate, 2002.

Girouard, Mark, *The Return to Camelot, Chivalry and the English Gentleman*, Yale, 1981.

Girtin, Tom, *The Mark of the Sword, A Narrative History of the Cutlers' Company*, Hutchinsom Benham, 1975.

Goodman, Anthony, *The Wars of the Roses*, Tempus, 2005.

Goodwin, T., *The History of the Reign of Henry the Fifth, King of England*, 1704.

Gransden, Antonia, *Historical Writing in England*, vol. ii, Routledge & Kegan Paul, 1982.

Green J. R., *A Short History of the English People*, 1874.

Green, V. H. H., *Bishop Reginald Pecock*, Cambridge University Press, 1945.

Griffiths, R. A., 'The Sense of Dynasty in the Reign of Henry VI', in Ross, Charles (ed.), *Patronage, Pedigree and Power in Later Medieval England*, Alan Sutton, 1979.

———, *The Reign of Henry* VI, Ernest Benn, 1981.

———, 'The island of England in the fifteenth century: perceptions of the peoples of the British Isles', *Journal of Medieval History* 29, 2003.

——— (ed.), *Gwent County History*, University of Wales, 2008.

Hall, Edward, *The Union of the Two Noble and Illustre [sic] Families of Lancaster & York*, London, 1548, 1808.

Hanotaux, G., *Histoire de la Nation Française*, Tome VII vol 1 by Col F. Reboul, Paris, 1925.

Hardy, Robert, *Longbow*, Sutton Publishing Ltd, 1976, 2006.

Harper-Bill, Christopher, *Medieval East Anglia*, The Boydell Press, 2005.

Harrison, Brian, *The Tower of London Prisoner Book*, The Royal Armouries, 2000.

Harriss, Gerald (ed.), *The Practice of Kingship*, Oxford University Press, 1985.

Harriss, Gerald, *Shaping the Nation England 1360–1461*, The New Oxford History of England, Oxford University Press, 2005.

Harvey, I. M. W., *Jack Cade's Rebellion of 1450*, Clarendon Press, 1991.

Hewitt, H. J., *The Black Prince's Expedition*, Manchester University Press, 1958.

Hollaender, A. E. J., & Kellaway, William (eds.), *Studies in London History*, Hodder and Stoughton, 1974.

Holmes, Richard, *Fatal Avenue*, Vintage, 2008.

Holt, J. C., *Robin Hood*, Thames and Hudson, 1989.

Hope, W. H. St., 'The Funeral Monument and Chantry Chapel of King Henry the Fifth', *Archaeologia*, vol 65, 1913–14.

Howard, Michael, *War in European History*, OPUS, 1976.

Hudson, Anne, *The Premature Reformation*, Clarendon Press, 1988.

Hutchison, Harold F., *King Henry V, A Biography*, Dorset Press, 1967.

Inwood, Stephen, *A History of London*, Macmillan, 2000.

Jacob, E. F., *The Fifteenth Century*, Oxford History of England, Oxford University Press, 1961.

Jones, Michael K., *Agincourt 1415*, Pen & Sword, 2005.

Jones, Terry, *Chaucer's Knight*, Methuen, 1994.

——, *Medieval Lives*, BBC Books, 2004.

Keen, Maurice, *The Outlaws of Medieval Legend*, Routledge and Kegan Paul, 1961, 1977, 1987.

——, *The Laws of War in the Late Middle Ages*, Routledge and Kegan Paul, 1965.

——, 'Chaucer's Knight, the English Aristocracy and the Crusade', in Scattergood, V. J, & J. W. Sherborne (eds.), *English Court Culture in the Late Middle Ages*, St Martin's Press, 1983.

——, *Chivalry*, Yale, 1984.

——, *English Society in the Later Middle Ages*, Penguin, 1990.

——, *Nobles, Knights and Men at Arms in the Middle Ages*, Hambledon Press, 1996.

—— (ed.), *Medieval Warfare, A History*, Oxford University Press, 1999.

——, *Origins of the English Gentleman*, Tempus, 2002.

——, *England in the Later Middle Ages*, 2nd edition, Routledge, 2003.

——, 'English Political History of the Later Middle Ages, 1272–c.1520', in Deyermond, Alan (ed.), *A Century of British Medieval Studies*, published for the British Academy by Oxford University Press, 2007.

Kekewich, Margaret L., *The Good King René of Anjou and Fifteenth Century Europe*, Palgrave Macmillan, 2008.

——, and Rose, Susan, *Britain, France and the Empire 1350–1500*, Palgrave Macmillan, 2005.

Kelsall, Jane, *Humphrey Duke of Gloucester, 1391–1447*, The Friends of Saint Albans Abbey, 2000.

Kendall, Paul Murray, *Louis XI: The Universal Spider*, Phoenix Press, 2001.

Kingsford, C. L., *Henry V, The Typical Medieval Hero*, 1901.

——, *English Historical Literature in the Fifteenth Century*, 1901.

——, *Prejudice and Promise in XVth Century England*, Clarendon Press, 1925.

Knowles, Dom David, *The Religious Orders in England, vol II The End of the Middle Ages*, Cambridge University Press, 1955.

Labarge, Margaret Wade, *Henry V: The Cautious Conqueror*, Stein and Day, 1976.

Lavisse, Ernest, *Histoire de la France vol IV*, Paris, 1902.

Leland, John, *The Itinerary*, ed. Lucy Toulmin Smith, George Bell and Sons, 1908.

Lewis, P. S., *Essays in Later Medieval French History*, The Hambledon Press, 1985.

Lloyd, Alan, *The Hundred Years War*, Book Club Associates, 1977.

Maurois, André, *An Illustrated History of France*, Paris, 1957; The Bodley Head, 1960.

McFarlane, K. B., *England in the Fifteenth Century*, The Hambledon Press, 1981.
——, *Lancastrian Kings & Lollard Knights*, Oxford University Press, 1972.
——, *The Nobility of Later Medieval England*, Oxford University Press, 1973.
McKisack, May, *Medieval History in the Tudor Age*, Clarendon Press, 1971.
Maltzahn, Nicholas von, *Milton's History of Britain, Republican Historiography in the English Revolution*, Clarendon Press, Oxford, 1991.
Matthew, D. J. A., *The Norman Monasteries and Their English Possessions*, Oxford University Press, 1962.
McEvedy, Colin, *The Penguin Atlas of Medieval History*, Penguin, 1961.
Meyrick, Samuel Rush, *Medieval Knights and Armour*, Dover Publications, 2007.
Michelet, Jules, *Histoire de France*, vols IV & V, Édition des Équateurs, 2008.
Mercer, Malcolm, *Henry V: The rebirth of chivary*, The National Archives, 2004.
Morgan, Philip, *The Naming of Battlefields in the Middle Ages*, in Dunn, Diana (ed.), *War and Society in Medieval and Early Modern Britain*, Liverpool University Press, 2000.
Mortimer, Ian, *The Fears of Henry IV*, Jonathan Cape, 2007.
Mowat, R. B., *Henry V*, Constable, 1919.
Newman, John, *Gwent/Monmouthshire*, in the series The Buildings of Wales, Penguin, 2000.
Nicolas, Sir Harris, *History of the Battle of Agincourt*, London, 1827.
Nightingale, Pamela, *A Medieval Mercantile Community, The Grocers' Company 1000–1485*, Yale, 1985.
Oman, Sir Charles, *A History of the Art of War in the Middle Ages, Volume Two 1278–1485*, Greenhill Books, 1991.
Owst, G. R., *Literature and Pulpit in Medieval England*, Cambridge University Press, 1933.
Oxford Dictionary of National Biography, Oxford University Press, 2004.
Paladilhe, Dominique, *La Bataille d'Azincourt*, Perrin, 2002.
Parker, Geoffrey (ed.), *The Cambridge History of Warfare*, Cambridge University Press, 2005.
Pernoud, R., *La Libération d'Orléans*, Gallimard, 1969.
Perroy, Edouard, *The Hundred Years War*, Eyre & Spottiswoode, 1965.
Philpotts, C., 'The French Plan of Battle during the Agincourt Campaign', *English Historical Review*, 1984.
Pollard, Tony (ed.), *Property and Politics, Essays in Later Medieval English History*, Alan Sutton, 1984.
Postan, M. M., *Medieval Trade and Finance*, Cambridge University Press, 1973.
——, *Essays on Medieval Agriculture and General Problems of the Medieval Economy*, Cambridge University Press, 1973.
Powell, Edward, *Kingship, Law and Society*, Clarendon Press, 1989.
Powicke, Sir Maurice, *England in the Thirteenth Century*, Oxford University Press, 1962.
Powicke, M. R., 'Lancastrian Captains' in Sandquist and Powicke (eds), *Essays in Medieval History presented to Bertie Wilkinson*, University of Toronto, 1969.
Pugh, T. B., *Henry V and the Southampton Plot*, Southampton Record Series, 1988.
Ramsay, Sir James, *Lancaster and York, A Century of English History 1399–1485*, Oxford, 1892.
Rapin de Thoyras, P., *History of England*, 1728–32.
Reid, Peter, *Medieval Warfare, The Rise and Fall of English Supremacy at Arms 1314–1485*, Robinson, 2008.

Robb, Graham, *The Discovery of France*, Picador, 2007.

Robert, Marilyn, *The Mowbray Legacy*, Queens-Haven Publications, 2004.

Rodger, N. A. M., *The Safeguard of the Sea, A Naval History of Britain*, vol. 1, Harper Collins, 1997.

Rogers, Clifford J., 'The Military Revolutions of the Hundred Years' War', *Journal of Military History*, vol. 57, 1993.

———, *War Cruel and Sharp*, The Boydell Press, 2000.

Rose, Susan (ed.), *The Navy of the Lancastrian Kings*, George Allen & Unwin for the Navy Records Society, 1982.

———, *Calais. An English Town in France 1347–1558*, The Boydell Press, 2008.

Ross, Charles, *Richard III*, Yale, 1981.

———, *Edward IV* , Yale, 1997.

Rowse, A.L. *Historians I have Known*, Duckworth, 1995.

Rundle, David, 'The Unoriginality of Tito Livio Frulovisi's Vita Henrici Quinti', *English Historical Review*, 2008.

Saccio, Peter, *Shakespeare's English Kings, History, Chronicle and Drama*, Oxford University Press, 1977.

Scattergood, V. J., & Sherorne, J. W. (eds), *English Court Culture in the Later Middle Ages*, New York, 1983.

Schama, Simon, *A History of Britain volume 1, At the Edge of the World*, BBC, 2000.

Seward, Desmond, *The Hundred Years War*, Constable, 1996.

———, *Henry V As Warlord*, Penguin, 1987.

Smith, Emma, *King Henry V*, Cambridge University Press, 2002.

Sot, Michel, Jean-Patrice Boudet & Anita Guerreau-Jalabert, *Le Moyen Âge: Histoire Culturelle de la France–* 1, Éditions du Seuil, 1997.

Spinka, Matthew, *The Letters of John Hus*, Manchester University Press, 1972.

Spufford, Peter, *Power and Profit: The Merchant in Medieval Europe*, Thames and Hudson, 2002.

Squibb, G. D., *The High Court of Chivalry*, Clarendon Press, 1959.

Steel, Anthony, *The Receipt of the Exchequer*, Cambridge University Press, 1954.

Strickland, Matthew, & Hardy, Robert, *The Great Warbow*, Sutton Publishing Ltd, 2005.

Stubbs, W., *Constitutional History of England*, vol. 3, 1878.

Sumption, Jonathan, *The Hundred Years War*, vols I, II, III, Faber & Faber, 1990, 1999, 2009.

Sutherland, John & Watts, Cedric, *Henry V, War Criminal?And Other Shakespeare Puzzles*, Oxford University Press, 2000.

Sutherland, Timothy, 'The Battle of Agincourt: An Alternative Location', *Journal of Conflict Archaeology*, Vol. 1, No. 1 (2005), 245–63.

———, 'Archaeological evidence of medieval conflict – case studies from Towton, Yorkshire, (England (1461) and Agincourt, Pas de Calais, France (1415)' in *Schlachtfeldarchäologie, Battlefield Archaeology*, Landesmuseum Für Vorgeschichte, 2009.

Sutton, Anne F., *The Mercery of London: Trade. Goods and People, 1130–1578*, Ashgate, 2005.

Taylor, Craig, 'English writings on chivalry and warfare during the Hundred Years War', in Coss, Peter, & Kevin Tyerman (eds.), *Soldiers, Nobles and Gentlemen*, The Boydell Press, 2009.

Thomson, J. A. F., *The Later Lollards*, Oxford, 1965.

Tout, T. F. *Chapters in Administrative History*, Manchester, 1928–37.

Vale, M. G. A., *English Aquitaine 1399–1453*, Oxford University Press, 1970.

———, *Charles VII*, University of California Press, 1974.

———, *The Ancient Enemy*, Continuum, 2007.

Vaughan, Richard, *Philip the Good*, Longmans, 1970.

———, *John the Fearless*, The Boydell Press, 2002.

Vincent, John, *An Intelligent Person's Guide to History*, Duckworth, 2006.

Wagner, Sir Anthony, *Heralds of England, A History of the Office and College of Arms*, HMSO, 1967.

Wakelin, Daniel, *Humanism, Reading & English Literature 1430–1530*, Oxford University Press, 2007.

Watts, John, *Henry VI and the Politics of Kingship*, Cambridge University Press, 1999.

Welsh, Frank, *The Battle for Christendom, The Council of Constance and the Struggle to Unite Against Islam*, Constable, 2008.

Williams, E. Carleton, *My Lord of Bedford*, Longmans, 1965.

Williams, Glanmor, *Recovery, Reorientation and Reformation, Wales c.1415–1642*, Clarendon Press, Oxford, 1987.

Wolffe, Bertram, *Henry VI*, Yale, 2001.

Wood, Michael (ed.), *The Great Turning Points in British History*, Constable & Robinson, 2009.

Woolf, D. R., *The Idea of History in Early Stuart England*, University of Toronto Press, 1990.

Woolf, Daniel, *The Social Circulation of the Past, English Historical Culture 1500–1730*, Oxford University Press, 2003.

Wright, C. J. (ed), *Sir Robert Cotton as Collector*, The British Library, 1997.

Wylie, J. H., *The Reign of Henry V, 1415–16*, Cambridge University Press, 1919.

Other Media
Radio
In Our Time, discussion on BBC Radio 4, 16 September 2004, with Anne Curry, Michael Jones, John Watts, chaired by Melvyn Bragg.

Film and Television
The Chronicle History of King Henry the Fifth with His Battell Fought at Agincourt in France, directed by Laurence Olivier, 1944.

Henry V, directed by Kenneth Branagh, 1989.

Chivalry and Betrayal: The Hundred Years' War, Dr Janina Ramirez (BBC 4, February 2013).

DVD – *Agincourt, Triumph of the Longbow*.

Facebook – *Agincourt Battlefield Archaeology Project*.

YouTube – there are several videos and clips, of varying quality.

Websites
www.archerylibrary.com
www.british battles.com
www.deremilitari.org
www.dur.ac.uk
www.historytoday.com

www.historyofparliamentonline.org/
www.icmacentre.ac.uk
www.medieval.mrugala.net/Guerre/Azincourt
www.militaryhistoryonline.com
www.nationalarchives.gov.uk
www.nltaylor.net
www.thepeerage.com
www.scortonarrow.com
www.wikipedia.org
www.fr.wikipedia.org

Index